Wright and DeLisi provide an invaluable primer in the much-neglected area of conservative criminology. They indict the dominant liberal paradigm for using its power to silence uncomfortable views and for using ideological purity, not science, to decide controversial issues. Whether readers find its claims irritating or illuminating, *Conservative Criminology* promises to provoke important debates and to force progressives, such as myself, to sharpen our thinking and compile more convincing evidence. It is a volume that should be read by all.

Francis T. Cullen, University of Cincinnati

Using reason and data Wright and DeLisi persuasively argue that criminology has been contaminated by an overwhelming commitment to leftist ideology. *Conservative Criminology* offers a refreshing and open discussion regarding the need for a diversity of thought in criminology that includes a conservative voice. A must read for all criminologists!

Michael G. Vaughn, Saint Louis University

Wright and DeLisi's *Conservative Criminology* presents an inconvenient truth that criminology has shut out an important way of looking at the world. As a liberal criminologist, I found it compelling, frustrating, and challenging, all at the same time! It's a must read for scholars and students alike.

Travis Pratt, University of Cincinnati Corrections Institute

CONSERVATIVE CRIMINOLOGY

Conservative Criminology serves as an important counterpoint to virtually every other academic text on crime. Hundreds of books have been written about crime and criminal justice policy from a variety of perspectives, including Marxist, liberal, progressive, feminist, radical, and postmodernist. To date, however, no book has been written outlining a conservative perspective on crime and criminal justice policy. Not a polemic against liberalism, *Conservative Criminology* nonetheless focuses on how liberal ideology affects the study of crime and criminals and the policies that criminologists advocate. Wright and DeLisi, both senior scholars, give a voice to a major political philosophy—a philosophy often demonized by academics—and to conservatives in the academic world. In the end, *Conservative Criminology* calls for an investment in intellectual diversity, a respect for varying political philosophies, and a renewed commitment to honesty in scholarship.

The authors encourage debate in the profession about the proper role of ideology in the academy and in public policies on crime and justice. *Conservative Criminology* is for the criminal justice professional and student. It serves as a stimulating supplement to courses in criminology and criminal justice, as well as a primary text for special issues or capstone courses. This book supports the reader in recognizing ideological biases, whatever they might be, and in considering their own convictions.

John Paul Wright is Professor of Criminal Justice in the School of Criminal Justice at the University of Cincinnati and a Distinguished Adjunct Research Professor at King Abdulaziz University, Jeddah, Saudi Arabia. Wright has authored or coauthored almost 200 scholarly works. His work primarily focuses on the connection between biological factors and criminal behavior, with an emphasis on how biological factors play out across the life course. Wright has published in a broad range of scientific and scholarly journals, including journals in the social and hard sciences. His work has been covered by the *New York Times*, *National Geographic*, and *National Public Radio*. It was his work in biosocial criminology that sensitized him to the fundamental role of political ideology in the social sciences generally and in criminology specifically.

Matt DeLisi is Professor and Coordinator of Criminal Justice Studies and Faculty Affiliate of the Center for the Study of Violence at Iowa State University. DeLisi's primary research interests include criminal careers/career criminals, self-control theory, corrections, psychopathy, and the molecular/behavioral genetics of antisocial behavior. DeLisi is a member of the American Association for the Advancement of Science, Academy of Criminal Justice Sciences, and Association for Psychological Science. DeLisi has published over 300 scholarly works and is Editor-in-Chief of the *Journal of Criminal Justice*.

CONSERVATIVE CRIMINOLOGY

A call to restore balance to the social sciences

John Paul Wright and Matt DeLisi

Routledge
Taylor & Francis Group

NEW YORK AND LONDON

First published 2016
by Routledge
711 Third Avenue, New York, NY 10017

and by Routledge
2 Park Square, Milton Park, Abingdon, Oxon OX14 4RN

Routledge is an imprint of the Taylor & Francis Group, an informa business

British Library Cataloguing in Publication Data
A catalogue record for this book is available from the British Library

Library of Congress Cataloging in Publication Data
A catalog record for this book has been requested

ISBN: 978-1-138-12513-1 (hbk)
ISBN: 978-0-323-35701-2 (pbk)
ISBN: 978-1-315-64771-5 (ebk)

Typeset in Bembo
by Taylor & Francis Books

(JPW): My father, Deputy Paul Wright, passed away while I was writing this book. His life was forever changed by an encounter with a violent criminal. Similarly, I would like to recognize those who work to protect our communities and those who have lost their lives in the process, those who intervene with at-risk children and who protect them from harm, those who help the alcoholic and drug addicted find peace and redemption, and those who do the thankless jobs to manage the plague that is criminal behavior.

Finally, I would like to thank my longtime friend and mentor, Francis T. Cullen. Frank is well known for his prolific scholarship, his depth and breadth of knowledge, and his imposing academic record. Over the years, Frank has guided me through some very tough times and has been a source of support, discipline, and encouragement. Frank is as liberal as I am conservative. Our academic and political differences have never interfered with our friendship—indeed, they have helped to solidify our mutual respect and admiration. Frank is the very best of liberal scholars and the very best of friends.

(MD): This book is dedicated to criminal justice practitioners whose daily sacrifice and labor is too easily impugned by too many in the media and in academia. The writings of James Q. Wilson, Travis Hirschi, Thomas Sowell, Heather MacDonald, Charles Murray, Steven Levitt, and John McWhorter were inspiring to me, especially while working on this book. Their work fuels my chutzpah, and I am appreciative. I also thank Dr. Rakesh Suri and Dr. Raul Espinosa—you guys are all heart.

CONTENTS

LIST OF ILLUSTRATIONS

Figures

Tables

ACKNOWLEDGEMENT

We owe a debt of gratitude to Mickey Braswell who believed in this project and who helped this book find a home. Mickey's sage advice and direction were instrumental in our thinking. Similarly, we are deeply thankful for the encouragement and guidance received from Pamela Chester at Routledge. Pamela was brave to take on a book like ours and has shown the highest dedication to scholarly principles.

Writing a book is an arduous process requiring the assistance of multiple people. We thank Annelise Pietenpol and Catherine Sacarrellos for their editorial and research contributions. We also wish to thank Mark Morgan, Michelle Coyne, Matt Logan, and Tony Walsh for their critiques and helpful comments.

We would also like to thank the reviewers of our book. We realized our book would put reviewers in a difficult position and that impartial reviews would be difficult. Nonetheless, through their criticisms we were forced to reconcile important points of argumentation. Their input was deeply valuable. We thank specifically Professor Travis Pratt and Professor Alex Holsinger for their balanced, direct, and candid assessments as well as other anonymous reviewers.

Finally, we would like to acknowledge how deeply our lives have been affected by our fellow scholars, our students, and our friends. It is difficult in this time and age to find friends who respect you enough to disagree with you. By this metric, we are men rich in relationships.

1

WHY CONSERVATIVE CRIMINOLOGY?

If you picked up this book and started turning through the pages or, while online, ventured across the book and opened it electronically, your interest was probably piqued by the title. There is something almost odd, out of place, even counterintuitive about a book with the title of "Conservative Criminology." If you have ever inspected the offering of books in a campus bookstore, chances are excellent that you will not find a single book written by a conservative, about conservative political thought, or even critical of academia. It is equally likely that if you are a college student you will read any number of books by feminists, communists, racialists, radicals, liberals, postmodernists, and political progressives. Classes in the humanities and in most of the social sciences will likely expose you to the broad array of leftist thinking and theorizing. To be fair, maybe a professor will require you to read something by a conservative author. Maybe. At most, however, you likely read what other scholars have to say about conservatives, their personalities, their faults, and their inevitably backwards ideas. You see, the reason this book seems so out of place is because, well, it is.

It is no secret that professors are typically politically liberal and that in many academic departments being politically liberal is almost a union requirement. Nor is it a secret that politically conservative professors are a rarity on college campuses. If you could round them all up they could probably fit easily into one small hotel. Okay, maybe one non-small hotel, but you get the point. Conservative professors just don't exist on many campuses and they are such a small minority in some academic fields that they are numerically insignificant. In the humanities, for example, liberals outnumber conservatives by 40:1 (Klein & Stern, 2003, 2005). The social sciences are not far behind. Depending on the academic field, the disparity can range from a low of 3:1 in economics to 20–40:1 in sociology and anthropology. In other programs, such as teacher education and social work, it is safe to say that conservatives are simply absent—their numbers so low as to not be measurable. Unfortunately, this disparity appears to be increasing (Jaschik, 2012; Rothman, Lichter & Nevitte, 2005).

The numerical disparity, however, tells only a small part of the story. While most conservative faculty report that they would happily re-enter academia and that they enjoy their careers (Woessner, 2012; Woessner, Kelly-Woessner & Rothman, 2011)—a fact their liberal colleagues happily report—conservative faculty also report high levels of job and professional discrimination—something their liberal colleagues typically deny (Inbar & Lammers, 2012; Yancey, 2011). Yet empirical studies from a variety of sources find statistical evidence that being branded "conservative" frequently results in loss of jobs, reduced professional status, and having your scholarly work impugned. Conservative faculty, you see, are not only numerically outnumbered, they are entirely powerless, are often marginalized, and frequently have to hide their beliefs out of fear (Graham, Nosek & Haidt, 2012; Haidt, 2012) Many conservative faculty elect to live a lie rather than to "come out" because the consequences can be so odious—even career threatening.

This is part of the reason our book is so unique. As politically conservative social scientists we are a true minority on campus and we are some of the only conservative faculty that have actually "come out" of the closet. While we don't lead protest marches demanding more conservatives to be hired, or work on political campaigns, or sponsor conservative support groups for those questioning their political identity, we don't shy away from confronting the stranglehold leftist political ideology has in the academy. As you might imagine, our views are sometimes very different from those expressed by powerful voices in the academy and, as you might imagine, many do not like what we have to say. You see, for all their talk about the importance of "diversity" and "tolerance" and even "free speech," many but not all leftist academics harbor deep resentments against conservatives (Altemeyer, 1981; Altemeyer, 2006; Block & Block, 2006; Graham et al., 2013). They see us as things to be studied and understood because we are so foreign to them, they stereotype us as anti-intellectual deadheads, and they accuse us of the worst imaginable sins (Block & Block, 2006; Carney, Jost, Gosling & Potter, 2008; Kugler, Jost & Noorbaloochi, 2014). We are racists, sexists, homophobic Neanderthals who wish only to impose our morality over others, they argue.

The hatred of conservatives on many campuses is so widespread that many faculty feel safe enough to write about their "hatred" of republicans—republicans is a code word for conservatives—as the head of the department of communications did at the University of Michigan (Douglas, 2014). They even feel safe enough to tell us that conservatives worship a God that is "a complete asshole," a "God of white supremacy and patriarchy." This professor of Africana Studies at Rutgers went on to say:

> Any time right-wing conservatives declare that they are trying to restore or reclaim something, we should all be very afraid. Usually, this means the country … is about to be treated with another round of time travel, to … the 1950s, wherein women, gays, and blacks knew their respective places.
>
> *(Cooper, 2015)*

These are just a few examples, but they highlight the degree to which many leftist academics hate—and we do mean *hate*—anything conservative. If you still don't believe us, consider the fact that reviewers of our book—fellow criminologists—warned us against publishing our work. Our careers and our reputations, they said, would be permanently marred. Maybe we could chalk this up to an over-reaction, but it fits with our overall experiences. Consider, too, the fact that other academic publishers—publishers who think nothing of producing books from radical feminists, communists, and liberal pundits—turned down publishing our book because our work was, as they said, "too controversial." We wish we were joking but we think it proves our point.

Academia is a strange and wonderful and eccentric place to work. Creative, thoughtful, and intelligent people surround us. We love the freedom an academic career offers, the opportunities it has presented to us, and the intellectual vibrancy we sometimes find. We have good friends in the academy and have had the privilege of teaching thousands of students. Yet for all the positive things that come along with working in academia, and there are many, there are some very real problems. These problems are deeply troubling, in part because they signal a shift in the academy away from the principles that have made the institution great: freedom of thought, freedom of speech, freedom of conscience, freedom of association, due process protections, and an understanding that government had to be restrained to protect these freedoms. These principles once defined classical liberalism, a political ideology we subscribe to, but now in many ways reflect a "conservative" worldview. Left unchecked we are afraid that the prevailing political ideology on campuses across the United States will continue to hamper science, that it will continue to isolate universities from mainstream society, and that students, faculty, and even citizens will be increasingly less free.

Indeed, the signs are ominous and growing. Recently, Professor Laura Kipnis, a highly regarded if not controversial feminist scholar found herself under investigation for not one but two Title IX complaints (Kipnis, 2015). Title IX was passed by Congress in 1972 in an effort to address legally matters of sexual discrimination on campus. In the years following, Title IX was used to create "gender equity" in athletics, largely by defunding men's sports teams and funding women's athletics. Over the decades, however, Title IX has been expanded to include sexual harassment and even sexual assault. Of course, what constitutes sexual harassment and even sexual assault has undergone revision—to the point where Title IX complaints are now being leveled against faculty for what they say in a classroom or, as in Professor Kipnis' case, for what they write.

The complaints against Kipnis were lodged by two graduate students, one of whom filed the complaint in the name of the broader university community, because Professor Kipnis wrote an article against what she perceived as the continued infantilizing of young women. Feminism, according to Kipnis, was about liberating the sexuality of women from legal and bureaucratic oversight. Kipnis objected to universities continually expanding their efforts to regulate the private lives of faculty and students—adults who may freely decide to see each outside of campus, who may decide to date, or who may even decide to marry. Kipnis' essays were immediately subject to criticism and protest, including female students carrying mattresses on their backs into her office complex and across campus. Her essays were what triggered the Title IX complaints and the subsequent investigation.

By law, all Title IX complaints have to be officially investigated. And to be fair, universities are now struggling to manage the legal requirements of Title IX against a backdrop of increased federal scrutiny by the Department of Education and the Department of Justice. Both agencies have threatened lawsuits against universities which do not take affirmative steps to end alleged sexual harassment and discrimination on campus and effectively prosecute allegations of sexual assault. The DOE and DOJ are clearly driven by political agendas— agendas that conflict with due process protections offered to alleged violators like Kipnis (Adams, 2011; LeTourneau, 2015).

While Professor Kipnis was eventually cleared of wrongdoing, the university hired an outside law firm to conduct the investigation. She was not initially told of the charges against her, had no right to legal counsel, and had no right to directly challenge those who made the allegation. These new procedures, which universities have embraced, are the direct result of the DOJ's efforts to make it easier to convict and punish individuals, almost always males, charged with sexual harassment or sexual assault (U.S. Department of Education, 2011). Kipnis, unfortunately, encountered the same Kafkaesque system (Bartholet et al., 2014; "Harvard law professors," 2014; Rudovsky et al., 2015; Save Our Sons, 2015).

The Kipnis debacle highlights the fact that in academia there is a huge cost to even the smallest disagreement. Similar to Kipnis, faculty may now find themselves investigated by law firms for comments made in class or for what they have published if students or other faculty take offense. Faculty who run afoul of liberal dogma may find their likeness plastered on the *New York Times* with a laundry list of professors denouncing them. They may have colleagues charge them with creating a "hostile work environment" or accuse them of bullying simply because they can and simply because the method effectively shuts down debate and silences critics. Indeed, now that the door has been opened, it takes no stretch of the imagination to see the ways in which the system can be abused. Disagree with affirmative action, for example, and you will be labeled as a racist and investigated. No questions asked. Teach about a controversial subject, such as sexual assault, and you can now be investigated. It is the ultimate betrayal of academic values.

The problems of liberal domination of the academy are not restricted to what professors say or cannot say but extend to the teaching of students. Liberal hegemony shapes what students are exposed to and, more importantly, what they are not exposed to. Many professors, for example, now simply refuse to cover material they fear will generate a complaint (Schlosser, 2015). Yet liberal hegemony goes well beyond the classroom. Entering freshmen, for example, are now routinely forced to undergo "diversity" training—training that is designed to make whites feel guilty and minorities feel aggrieved. Liberal hegemony also affects which students will receive scholarships and which ones will not. Almost daily universities discriminate against white students, male students, and especially Asian students not only in admission but also in awarding scholarships and stipends ("Harvard's Asian problem," 2014). And those restrictions now facing professors concerning what they say and what they write? Students, too, are now subject to draconian speech codes, often with the threat of arrest.

If you care about science, you should also care about liberal dogma on university campuses. Science, after all, has successfully supplied us with medicines, insights, technologies, and ideas that have alleviated the suffering of millions of people. You might think that the spread of postmodern gobbledygook throughout the humanities is unfortunate but not life threatening. After all, nobody dies because they used a gendered pronoun—at least not yet. Maybe you will even say that since science is peer reviewed it has built-in safeguards, that science is "self-correcting" so ideology will eventually give way and bad research will get weeded out. Right? Can we seriously claim that even science has been unduly influenced by liberal hegemony?

We are going to tell you something. Social science is not always self-correcting, nor is there any perfect filter against bad science being published. Science is a human enterprise so it is subject to all the standard human frailties. Rarely, individual scientists will fabricate their data and their findings. However, in one particularly glaring example, psychologist Diederik Stapel not only fabricated research results but made up entire experiments. His work was published in the top science journals in the world—including *Science*—and received extensive media coverage. Several of his more than 150 published studies, for example, found that whites were more likely to discriminate against blacks if their immediate environment was cluttered. Other studies showed that job applicants were favored if they had a deep, male voice. After being exposed as a scientific fraud, Professor Stapel was asked how he managed to pull off such an accomplishment—one that lasted for over a decade and passed the critical scrutiny of other scientists and editors. His answer was as simple as it was revealing: He simply told people what they wanted to hear (Bhattacharjee, 2013).

Clearly Professor Stapel is an anomaly and there is little reason to believe that professors are any more or less honest than anyone else. Fabricated data and experiments are an extreme examples of problems found in science. More often, however, scientists will distort their findings to increase the likelihood their work will get published. Distortion comes in many subtle and not so subtle forms: Distortion affects the subjects scholars choose to study, the way they measure important constructs, the variables they choose to not include in their study, how they analyze and report their findings, and the conclusions they draw. Distortion is far more common than outright deception in part because distortion can often be justified on scholarly grounds (Macfarlane & Cheng, 2008).

Let's look at this a bit more closely. Studies tell us that most social science findings cannot be replicated—strongly suggesting that the accumulation of various distortions affect published outcomes (Ceci, Peters & Plotkin, 1985; Fanelli, 2010; Franco, Malhotra & Simonovits, 2014; Goodstein & Brazis, 1970; Koehler, 1993; Peters & Ceci, 1982). Sometimes we can isolate this problem to the innumerable but honest distortions that occur along the research process. All scientists have to make decisions about how to conduct their studies and most do so in good faith. Much more troubling, however, is the reality that sometimes these distortions are influenced by a broader ideology that filters its way through the research process. Even more disturbing, however, is the likelihood that academics understand all too well that their work will be evaluated by scholars who will evaluate not only the scientific merits of their work but also its ideological direction. Scholars consequently make decisions along the research and writing pathway to address what they see as inevitable politically motivated criticisms.

As we will show, it is no longer uncommon for social science research to promote certain findings, advocate for specific policies, or affirm aspects of the liberal narrative. Indeed, social science research has become increasingly politically motivated, hiding its true intent behind the façade of objective empirical inquiry. In one study, for example, academics found that holding a gun triggered racist thoughts (O'Brien, Forrest, Lynott & Daly, 2013). Interesting, right? Yet later, in an interview about their findings, the authors stated that they couldn't come up with any other reason why anyone would want to own a gun. None. This study was published in a highly reputable journal and passed peer review but its flaws were almost immediately detected by outside readers. Yes, outside readers caught the fact that the study was inherently flawed, not the editors or the reviewers. We think the reason is fairly clear.

For those of you who place your faith in the power of science to be "self-correcting" or believe that peer review ensures only the best, most rigorous science gets published, we draw your attention to the comments of Richard Horton, editor of the esteemed medical journal, *The Lancet*. According to Horton (2000):

> We portray peer review to the public as a quasi-sacred process that helps to make science our most objective truth teller. But we know that the system of peer review is biased, unjust, unaccountable, incomplete, easily fixed, often insulting, usually ignorant, occasionally foolish, and frequently wrong.

If peer review is not sufficient to screen out biases in the medical sciences, it is likely entirely insufficient to screen out biases in the social sciences and humanities where standards are much more subjective. Alan Sokal, a self-described "unabashed old leftist," caused a firestorm when he published a paper titled "Transgressing the boundaries: Toward a transformative hermeneutics of quantum gravity" in the postmodern journal *Social Text*, itself published by Duke University. The paper, however, was completely nonsensical. Words and sentences were entirely made up yet Sokal was also careful to play to the political biases of the editors. After the paper was published, Sokal let everyone in on his deception. "The results of my little experiment demonstrate, at the very least," he wrote (Sokal, 1996: 45), "that some fashionable sectors of the American academic Left have been getting intellectually lazy. The editors of *Social Text* liked my article because they liked its conclusion: that 'the content and methodology of postmodern science provide powerful intellectual support for the progressive political project'." They apparently felt no need to analyze the quality of the evidence, the cogency of the arguments, or even the relevance of the arguments to the purported conclusion.

So much for the humanities. What about the social sciences? In one test of the peer review process, Mahoney (1977) asked 75 journal reviewers to assess a manuscript that described the same experiment. However, Mahoney changed the reported findings so that some reviewers would read the study showing positive findings, others would read the same study but showing null findings, while others would read the same study but showing negative findings. In short, Mahoney found very little inter-rater agreement about the merits of the study. One reviewer would gush about the study while another would be hypercritical. More importantly, however, Mahoney found that reviewers "were strongly biased against manuscripts which reported results contrary to their theoretical perspective." In short, when the results of the fictional experiment didn't confirm their pre-existing biases, many scholars voted to reject the paper for publication. Sound objective?

We need to recognize that ideology in the social sciences also causes many questions to go unasked and makes some findings more likely to get published than others. Important topics are not broached, sometimes for decades or even centuries, because scholars fear having their careers and reputations harmed. Indeed, our work in the gene–crime connection is a good example. The social sciences purged the study of biology–crime for almost a hundred years and then declared there was no evidence of a genetic or biological effect on criminal behavior. Well, there really wasn't because the topic had become so taboo that research in the area was effectively banned. Criminologists, most of whom were sociologists, did this because their political-moral worldview justified banning this line of research, not because they had adequate scientific justification. Even today we see calls for banning research published in the official journal of the American Society of Criminology (Burt & Simons, 2014). Do you care now?

There are thousands of ways for bias to not only creep into academic publishing but for it to define, direct, and control academic publishing. We are not just making up this stuff nor are we disgruntled underachievers. Between the two of us we have published hundreds of peer-reviewed articles, many book chapters, and dozens of books. We make "highly cited" lists and hold research positions at other universities. We have also reviewed an ungodly number of scholarly papers for publication. We serve on editorial boards, we review research grant proposals, we've held office in our national organizations, and Matt is a highly regarded editor of a criminal justice journal. We've testified before legislative bodies, advised criminal justice agencies, worked in the field, and have interacted with thousands of thugs, addicts, and convicts.

We have also published papers that have clearly violated the liberal ethos of academia. Our work, along with the work of our friends and colleagues, has examined the rather important role of genetic influences on human behavior, including criminal behavior (Beaver et al., 2013b; DeLisi et al., 2014), and various traits such as impulsivity and low self-control (DeLisi et al., 2010; Wright et al., 2012). Indeed, we and our colleagues have been instrumental in creating an arm of criminological study called "biosocial criminology." Biosocial criminologists, some of whom are politically liberal, look at the ways human evolution, human biology, human genetics, and environment work to produce differences between people in their proclivity to violate our laws and bring harm to people (Wright & Boisvert, 2009; Wright &

Cullen, 2012). As you might imagine, our work has generated some serious wrath—much of which has not been made public (Carrier & Walby, 2014). If this were not enough, we have also published papers on the biological foundation of race and on the rather unimportant racial connection to criminal justice processing (Beaver et al., 2013a). Unlike most scholars who publish "safe" studies, we have never shied away from tackling politically charged topics. The point of all of this is not to toot our own horns but to show to you, the reader, that we have extensive personal experience with the publishing process and with publishing on controversial topics. We are highly productive scholars who know the ins and outs of scholarly publishing and we know what goes on behind the scenes. When we say that social science has not only been affected by liberal biases but that a fair amount of what gets published is the product of those biases, you might want to at least think about the possibility and the consequences.

★★★

It is precisely because of our experiences that we chose to write this book, especially our experiences as scientists. So, what is this book about? Well, let's start with what this book is not about. First, and foremost, this book is not a defense of the Republican Party. The platform of the Republican Party does not interest us, nor does the idea of defending it interest us. We hold no allegiance to either party and disagree on a range of issues with Democrats and Republicans.

Second, this book is not a polemic against liberalism or progressivism. Both ideologies have their strengths and their weaknesses and they offer a unique understanding of crime and crime control that should not be ignored. Indeed, many of the leftist scholars we know are earnest people—people committed to making the world a better place. Some are friends and great scholars and some even agree with us on certain points and respectfully disagree with us on others. Our lives have definitely benefited from their humanity, their charity, and their scholarship. While we may disagree with some of their views, we nonetheless respect their views and take their views seriously. We even want to caution conservative readers, especially those unwilling to accept nuanced positions and who are strident in their political beliefs, not to reduce the humanity of leftist scholars to political talking points and we want to point out that some liberal faculty also suffer harm when they violate some aspect of accepted liberal dogma.

Maybe at this point it would helpful for us to deviate a bit and to define what we mean when we use the term "leftist," or "progressive," or "liberal," as our book makes use of these varied terms. We realize these are broad descriptive labels that overlook important differences between people on the political left and that sometimes these labels are used pejoratively. Unfortunately, impression in language necessarily translates into the use of such labels. Nonetheless, we are obviously invoking the classic "left–right" split in American politics. The modern left, for example, tends to want the expansion of government in areas they desire, while those on the right argue for "less government." People on the left tend to strongly support a minimum wage, a large welfare system, and a limited national defense. Those on the right, of course, are at odds with these views. While limited, it turns out that these self-identified political orientations are very important windows into the ideological world of an individual. They predict the types of people you will associate with, the type of career you will pursue, and even the type of person you will marry (Schweizer, 2008). More importantly, science now tells us that political ideology is almost intrinsic, part of our neurological makeup, and a solid and reliable proxy for values—values that are deeply, interpersonally, affectively, moral and morally understood (Englander, Haidt, & Morris, 2012; Graham et al., 2013; Haidt, 2007; Haidt & Kesebir, 2010). So when we use the term liberal, we are generally speaking not only of a person who falls to the left of the traditional political spectrum and who supports traditionally leftist causes, such as abortion and gun control, but also of one who holds a constellation of beliefs, values, and attitudes about relationships, justice, fairness, proportionality, equality, and tolerance.

Applied to academics, however, even this conception is too narrow. Similar to others, such as Gross and Levitt (1998), we recognize that some leftist scholars belong to the "academic left." The academic left overlaps entirely in their views about the nature of government and their support for certain policies but they differ in important ways from other liberals. The academic left includes a sometimes loose affiliation of scholars, mainly from the humanities and the social sciences, who share certain views about science, about the construction of knowledge, and about the purpose of the modern university. The academic left, write Gross and Levitt (1998: 5), are bound not by a "self-consistent doctrine" but by a shared belief that science should be used to advance liberal causes and that science is socially constructed and therefore can also be understood as another form of ideology. By extension, the academic left often sees science not as a mechanism to find the truth but as a tool to create the truth. Reduced further, science becomes an extension of a political viewpoint, an instrument to serve no higher purpose than to support the prevailing ideology. This is why the academic left will also attack fellow liberals if they are viewed as harming leftist causes.

Yet a crass utilitarian viewpoint of science masks the infinitely more important moral purpose of science advocated by the academic left. For science to be useful, for it to be valuable, for it to "true" it also has to confirm the moral precepts of the academic left. This is why very different scientific standards are applied to some studies. In our own work, for example, we once attempted to publish a study that examined whether teacher evaluations of students' behavior were racially biased (Beaver, Wright & DeLisi, 2011). To understand the importance of the topic, much educational policy and millions of tax dollars are spent on the unproven assumption that teachers—some of the most caring and most liberal people in the world—are either racist or so stupid that they don't realize their own racist beliefs. Our study found no evidence of such bias. Good news, right? Wrong. We sent the study to no less than a dozen education journals and were summarily dismissed from each. Reviewers and journal editors impugned our motives, cited tenants of "racial justice" ideology, and accused us of leading a right-wing assault on minority students. Some even accused us of wanting to overturn the Civil Rights laws.

The study is interesting, too, because another group of authors used the exact same data and measures and showed evidence of teacher bias. They did this by imputing, a fancy term for making up, data from thousands of missing cases. Same study, same data, different results. One study heralded as confirmatory evidence of teacher bias and thus used to justify a leftist ideology, the other relegated to a nondescript book chapter (Beaver et al., 2011; Downey & Pribesh, 2004). We include this anecdote because it represents how the academic left views science through a political-moral lens. It also demonstrates vividly how bias produces bodies of knowledge that eventually become sacrosanct. For the academic left, scientific findings fall under a broader political and moral umbrella. Not surprising, the academic left operates on the assumption, note Gross and Levitt (1998: 6), that their "moral authority … [is] sufficient to guarantee" the validity of their arguments. For the academic left, politics is morality and their morality trumps everything else.

Admittedly, many liberal scholars may only partially fit into this broad description and some may not fit at all. There are excellent liberal scholars in the social sciences and in the humanities. Even so, these faculty are often complicit in their tolerance for the excesses of the academic left. Again, turning to Gross and Levitt (1998: 35):

> the process has had the crucial goodwill of a kind of academic "silent majority," the great body of professors, who while they distance themselves from doctrinaire ideological formulations … somehow continue to believe vaguely that the left … remains (after all these decades) "the party of humanity," the locus of right thinking; and that it deserves to be nurtured and encouraged even if it goes overboard from time to time in the vehemence of its views.

Bad things happen when good people suspend their critical faculties and refuse to make reasonable judgments—really bad things. This is especially problematic on university campuses because one of the hallmarks of the American university system is that faculty share power with the administration. Universities are to be jointly managed with faculty given deference on all matters academic. When faculty refuse to question other faculty and administrators because they are either afraid to or because they are too accommodating, they allow all types of injustice to occur. The voices of reason, balance, and judiciousness do not just get drowned out by the fevered pitch of social justice advocates and others on the academic left—they are too often not even raised.

Having defined what we mean by "leftist," we turn again to what our book is about and what it is not about. Clearly, part of our intention is to expose and analyze the problems of liberal hegemony within the academy. Others have come before us who have made somewhat similar arguments (Gross & Levitt, 1998; Maranto, Redding, & Hess, 2009). For the most part these scholars were intent on measuring the disparity between liberal and conservative faculty across disciplines and some have explored how this might translate into an uneven education for students (Gross & Fosse, 2012; Gross & Levitt, 1998; Maranto, Redding & Hess, 2009). Our book, however, is also about gaining an appreciation for a politically conservative orientation—one that is nearly absent on campuses nationwide. Conservatism, properly understood, gives us insight into what is unique about American life, our history, and our political traditions. After all, conservatism is about "conserving" or retaining what we find valuable and useful in a society.

As a political ideology, conservatism emerged as a broader reaction against the deadly excesses of the French Revolution. It thus views with suspicion radical and unplanned change because history has taught us that radicalism has been responsible for some of the worst of humanities crimes. Conservatism also deeply fears concentrated power because power corrupts—always. Conservatism also focuses on individuals and the communities they create, on individual responsibility and accountability, and on the qualities that make for a moral and meaningful life. Conservatism has a history—a history unknown by most Americans and especially unknown by most liberals. And similar to liberals, conservatives, too, see the world through a political-moral lens. This lens is different, sometimes in degree and sometimes in kind, from the lens applied by liberals.

We will explore how liberal and conservative political-moral lenses shape views about important issues and how they shape views about each side. And since we are professional criminologists, we will also discuss the ways that conservatism has played a key role in protecting children and families from the destruction that is criminal behavior; how conservatism enumerates the various individual and institutional requirements necessary for the development of safe neighborhoods, safe schools, and safe cities. Moreover, we will discuss how conservative views on limited government are designed to encourage the flourishing of culture, aid in healthy individual development, and facilitate a "good society"—that is, a society guided by the rule of law and due process, committed to freedom and liberty, and where people care for one another not because of a government edict but out of genuine compassion.

On a more personal level, this book is also about taking a stand. For too long we have listened to, read about, and watched conservatism and conservative scholars being attacked, marginalized, and dismissed by leftist scholars. We have sat in any number of college meetings where faculty and administrators felt free to make egregious comments about conservatives. We have watched and listened as these same people—people who know no conservatives—twist conservatism into a code word for racism, sexism, homophobia, religious intolerance, or intellectual ignorance. The narrative, so prevalent on university campuses today, is that conservatism is a political ideology for the weak-minded, for the selfish, morally hypocritical, or just plain stupid individual. Our book takes a stand, declares an unpopular point of view, and challenges scholars to reaffirm the values that have made the American university system great.

Similarly, our book sounds a clarion call to all who will listen. The modern American university has been under constant attack since at least the 1960s. Attacks from conservative legislatures have proven ineffective but attacks from within the academy have not—and those people are almost entirely liberal. The greatest threat to the modern university and to science comes not from book-burning conservative dunderheads but from the blinding obedience to liberal dogma demanded by the academic left and wholly tolerated by the rest of the professoriate. This blinding obedience comes in a variety of forms and operates under a range of themes, from "social justice," to "diversity," to "equality," and even "fairness," but it can be reduced to a belief that the power of the university should be harnessed for liberal political causes and to justify liberal moral beliefs.

Under this ideological umbrella, individual conscience, liberty, freedom of speech, due process, and even science itself has to be controlled, shaped, and reformulated. It is what Herbert Marcuse (1965) called "repressive tolerance," a belief that reducing individual freedoms, such as free speech, is a necessary prerequisite to obtain broader liberal goals. The natural outgrowth of this ideological view is widely recognized today: universities no longer encourage unfettered debate, a diversity of views, or even a respect for law, order, or due process. They are no longer protectors of society's most celebrated values but are instead tinderboxes of balkanized interests unified by a common socio-political morality. This socio-political morality is pervasive and has, we believe, caused a decline in the legitimacy of science and in the legitimacy of the modern university—especially amongst conservatives.

References

Adams, J. C. (2011) *Injustice: Exposing the racial agenda of the Obama Justice Department.* Washington, DC: Regnery Publishing.

Altemeyer, B. (1981) *Right-wing authoritarianism.* Winnipeg, Canada: University of Manitoba Press.

Altemeyer, R. (2006) *The authoritarians.* Retrieved from http://members.shaw.ca/jeanaltemeyer/drbob/TheAuthoritarians.pdf.

Bartholet, E., et al. (2014) Rethink Harvard's sexual harassment policy. *The Boston Globe,* October 15. Retrieved from www.bostonglobe.com/opinion/2014/10/14/rethink-harvard-sexual-harassment-policy/HFDDiZN7nU2UwuUuWMnqbM/story.html.

Beaver, K. M., DeLisi, M., Wright, J. P., Boutwell, B. B., Barnes, J. C., & Vaughn, M. G. (2013a) No evidence of racial discrimination in criminal justice processing: Results from the national longitudinal study of adolescent health. *Personality and Individual Differences,* 55(1), 29–34.

Beaver, K. M., Wright, J. P., Boutwell, B. B., Barnes, J. C., DeLisi, M., & Vaughn, M. G. (2013b) Exploring the association between the 2-repeat allele of the MAOA gene promoter polymorphism and psychopathic personality traits, arrests, incarceration, and lifetime antisocial behavior. *Personality and Individual Differences*, 54(2), 164–168.

Beaver, K. M., Wright, J. P., & DeLisi, M. (2011) The racist teacher revisited: Race and social skills in a nationally representative sample of American children. In R. J. Newley (ed.), *Classrooms: Management, effectiveness and challenges*. Hauppauge, NY: Nova Science Publishers, pp. 115–132.

Bhattacharjee, Y. (2013) The mind of a con man. *The New York Times*, April 26. Retrieved from www.nytimes.com/2013/04/28/magazine/diederik-stapels-audacious-academic-fraud.html?pagewanted=all&_r=0.

Block, J., & Block, J. H. (2006) Nursery school personality and political orientation two decades later. *Journal of Research in Personality*, 40(5), 734–749.

Burt, C. H., & Simons, R. L. (2014) Pulling back the curtain on heritability studies: Biosocial criminology in the postgenomic era. *Criminology*, 52(2), 223–262.

Carney, D. R., Jost, J. T., Gosling, S. D., & Potter, J. (2008) The secret lives of liberals and conservatives: Personality profiles, interaction styles, and the things they leave behind. *Political Psychology*, 29(6), 807–840.

Carrier, N., & Walby, K. (2014) Ptolemizing Lombroso: The pseudo-revolution of biosocial criminology. *Journal of Theoretical and Philosophical Criminology*, 1(1), 1–45.

Ceci, S. J., Peters, D., & Plotkin, J. (1985) Human subjects review, personal values, and the regulation of social science research. *American Psychologist*, 40(9), 994–1002.

Cooper, B. (2015) The right's made-up God: How bigots invented a white supremacist Jesus. *Salon*, April 1. Retrieved from www.salon.com/2015/04/01/the_rights_made_up_god_how_bigots_invented_a_white_supremacist_jesus/.

DeLisi, M., Beaver, K. M., Vaughn, M. G., Trulson, C. R., Kosloski, A. E., Drury, A. J., & Wright, J. P. (2010) Personality, gender, and self-control theory revisited: Results from a sample of institutionalized juvenile delinquents. *Applied Psychology in Criminal Justice*, 6(1), 31–46.

DeLisi, M., Dansby, T., Peters, D. J., Vaughn, M. G., Shook, J. J., & Hochstetler, A. (2014) Fledgling psychopathic features and pathological delinquency: New evidence. *American Journal of Criminal Justice*, 39(3), 411–424.

Douglas, S. J. (2014) We can't all just get along. *In These Times*, December 15. Retrieved from http://inthesetimes.com/article/17426/we_cant_all_just_get_along.

Downey, D. B., & Pribesh, S. (2004) When race matters: Teachers' evaluations of students' classroom behavior. *Sociology of Education*, 77(4), 267–282.

Englander, Z. A., Haidt, J., Morris, & J. P. (2012) Neural basis of moral elevation demonstrated through inter-subject synchronization of cortical activity during free-viewing. *PLoS ONE*, 7(6).

Fanelli, D. (2010) "Positive" results increase down the hierarchy of the sciences. *PLoS ONE*, 5(4).

Franco, A., Malhotra, N., & Simonovits, G. (2014) Publication bias in the social sciences: Unlocking the file drawer. *Science*, 345(6203), 1502–1505.

Goodstein, L. D., & Brazis, K. L. (1970) Psychology of scientists: XXX. Credibility of psychologists: An empirical study. *Psychological Reports*, 27(3), 835–838.

Graham, J., Nosek, B. A., & Haidt, J. (2012) The moral stereotypes of liberals and conservatives: Exaggeration of differences across the political spectrum. *PLoS ONE*, 7(12).

Graham, J., Haidt, J., Koleva, S., Motyl, M., Iyer, R., Wojcik, S. P., & Ditto, P. H. (2013) Moral Foundations Theory: The pragmatic validity of moral pluralism. *Advances in Experimental Social Psychology*, 47, 55–130.

Gross, N., & Fosse, E. (2012) Why are professors liberal? *Theory and Society*, 41(2), 127–168.

Gross, P. R., & Levitt, N. (1998) *Higher superstition: The academic left and its quarrels with science*. Baltimore, MD: The Johns Hopkins University Press.

Haidt, J. (2007) The new synthesis in moral psychology. *Science*, 316(5827), 998–1002.

Haidt, J. (2012) *The righteous mind: Why good people are divided by politics and religion*. New York: Vintage Books.

Haidt, J., & Kesebir, S. (2010) Morality. In S. Fiske, D. Gilbert, & G. Lindzey (eds), *Handbook of Social Psychology*, 5th edition. Hoboken, NJ: Wiley, pp. 797–832.

Harvard Law professors object to sex harassment rules (2014) *Inside Higher Ed*, October 15. Retrieved from www.insidehighered.com/quicktakes/2014/10/15/harvard-law-professors-object-sex-harassment-rules.

Harvard's Asian problem: A lawsuit says racial preferences hurt high-achieving minorities (2014) *The Wall Street Journal*, November 21. Retrieved from www.wsj.com/articles/harvards-asian-problem-1416615041.

Horton, R. (2000) Genetically modified food: consternation, confusion, and crack-up. *The Medical Journal of Australia*, 172(4), 148–149.

Inbar, Y., & Lammers, J. (2012) Political diversity in social and personality psychology *Perspectives on Psychological Science*, 7(5), 496–503.

Jaschik, S. (2012) Moving further to the left. *Inside Higher Ed*, October 24. Retrieved from www.inside-highered.com/news/2012/10/24/survey-finds-professors-already-liberal-have-moved-further-left.

Kipnis, L. (2015) My Title IX inquisition. *The Chronicle Review*, May 29. Retrieved from http://chronicle.com/article/My-Title-IX-Inquisition/230489/.

Klein, D. B., & Stern, C. (2003) How politically diverse are the social sciences and humanities? Survey evidence from six fields. *Academic Questions*, 18(1), 1–20.

Klein, D. B., & Stern, C. (2005) Professors and their politics: The policy views of social scientists. *Critical Review*, 17(3/4), 257–303.

Koehler, J. J. (1993) The influence of prior beliefs on scientific judgments of evidence quality. *Organizational Behavior and Human Decision Processes*, 56(1), 28–55.

Kugler, M., Jost, J. T., & Noorbaloochi, S. (2014) Another look at moral foundations theory: Do authoritarianism and social dominance orientation explain liberal-conservative differences in "moral" institutions? *Social Justice Research*, 27(4), 413–431.

LeTourneau, N. (2015) Acting Director of the Civil Rights Division at DOJ: Vanita Gupta. *Washington Monthly*, May 24. Retrieved from www.washingtonmonthly.com/political-animal-a/2015_05/acting_director_of_the_civil_r055712.php.

Macfarlane, B., & Cheng, M. (2008) Communism, universalism and disinterestedness: Re-examining contemporary support among academics for Merton's scientific norms. *Journal of Academic Ethics*, 6(1), 67–78.

Mahoney, M. J. (1977) Publication prejudices: An experimental study of confirmatory bias in the peer review system. *Cognitive Therapy and Research*, 1(2), 161–175.

Maranto, R., Redding, R. E., & Hess, F. M. (eds) (2009) *The politically correct university: Problems, scope, and reforms*. Washington, DC: AEI Press.

Marcuse, H. (1965) Repressive tolerance. In R. P. Wolff, B. Moore, Jr, & H. Marcuse (eds), *A critique of pure tolerance*. Boston, MA: Beacon Press, pp. 95–137.

O'Brien, K., Forrest, W., Lynott, D., & Daly, M. (2013) Racism, gun ownership and gun control: Biased attitudes in US whites may influence policy decisions. *PLoS ONE*, 8(10).

Peters, D. P., & Ceci, S. J. (1982) Peer-review practices of psychological journals: The fate of published articles, submitted again. *Behavioral and Brain Sciences*, 5(2), 187–195.

Rothman, S., Lichter, S. R., & Nevitte, N. (2005) Politics and professional advancement among college faculty. *The Forum*, 3(1).

Rudovsky, D., et al. (2015) *Sexual assault complaints: Protecting complainants and the accused students at universities*, open letter from members of the Penn Law School faculty, February 18. Retrieved from http://media.philly.com/documents/OpenLetter.pdf.

Save Our Sons (2015) Due process rights. Retrieved from http://helpsaveoursons.com/category/due-process-rights/.

Schlosser, E. (2015) I'm a liberal professor, and my liberal students terrify me. *Vox*, June 3. Retrieved from www.vox.com/2015/6/3/8706323/college-professor-afraid.

Schweizer, P. (2008) *Makers and takers: Why conservatives work harder, feel happier, have closer families, take fewer drugs, give more generously, value honesty more, are less materialistic and envious, whine less and even hug their children more than liberals*. New York: Random House.

Sokal, A. D. (1996) Transgressing the boundaries: Towards a transformative hermeneutics of quantum gravity. *Social Text*, 46/47, 217–252.

U.S. Department of Education, Office for Civil Rights, Office of the Assistant Secretary (2011) Dear colleague letter, April 4. Retrieved from www2.ed.gov/about/offices/list/ocr/letters/colleague-201104.pdf.

Woessner, M. (2012) Rethinking the plight of conservatives in higher education. *Bulletin of the American Association of University Professors*, January/February. Retrieved from www.aaup.org/article/rethinking-plight-conservatives-higher-education#.VXC5KunbKUl.

Woessner, M., Kelly-Woessner. A., & Rothman, S. (2011) Five myths about liberal academia. *The Washington Post*, February 25. Retrieved from www.washingtonpost.com/wp-dyn/content/article/2011/02/25/AR2011022503169.html.

Wright, J. P., & Boisvert, D. (2009) What biosocial criminology offers criminology. *Criminal Justice and Behavior*, 36(11), 1228–1240.

Wright, J. P., & Cullen, F. T. (2012) The future of biosocial criminology: Beyond scholars' professional ideology. *Journal of Contemporary Criminal Justice*, 28(3), 237–253.

Wright, J. P., Schnupp, R., Beaver, K. M., DeLisi, M., & Vaughn, M. (2012) Genes, maternal negativity, and self-control: Evidence of a gene x environment interaction. *Youth Violence and Juvenile Justice*, 10(3), 245–260.

Yancey, G. (2011) *Compromising scholarship: Religious and political bias in American higher education*. Waco, TX: Baylor University Press.

2

THE TRIBAL MORAL COMMUNITY OF CRIMINOLOGY

At a meeting of the Society for Personality and Social Psychology (Haidt, 2011c), psychologist Jonathan Haidt asked members in the audience to show, by raised hands, how many considered themselves to be "liberal." Between 80 and 90 percent of the audience responded in the affirmative. He next asked how many considered themselves to be "moderate." About 20 hands were raised. "Libertarian," he asked? Exactly 12 hands went into the air. And finally, "conservative?" Only three people in an audience of over 1,000 social psychologists raised their hands. The ratio of liberal to conservative social psychologists, Haidt estimated, was 266:1. He went on to note that the ratio of 266:1 represented a "statistically impossible lack of diversity."

Haidt's talk was covered in a *New York Times* article that also made mention of the dominance of liberal ideology held by most professors in the United States. Taken together, Haidt's talk and the *New York Times* piece generated substantial debate, a debate long festering on the fringes of academia itself. How, the question goes, has a single political group come to dominate the majority of academic departments across the country? After all, polling data consistently show that the American population is center-right. About 40 percent of Americans identify themselves as "conservative" and another 40 percent identify themselves as "moderates." Only 20 percent classify themselves as "liberal."

Data on the political ideology of American professors is unambiguous. In every study published to date, a vast majority of faculty on American campuses report that they are highly liberal, with a large majority belonging to the Democratic Party (Duarte et al., 2014; Klein & Stern, 2009; Rothman & Lichter, 2009). In perhaps the most current and sophisticated study to date, Gross and Simmons (2007) analyzed self-report data from 1,471 professors across 927 institutions. Their study included faculty from community colleges through elite, Ivy League schools, and from a large variety of academic disciplines. When faculty were asked to report their political orientation (from very liberal to very conservative), over 62 percent of respondents classified themselves as some shade of "liberal." Only 19.7 percent classified themselves as some shade of "conservative." When Gross and Simmons broke down their data by the type of institution (community college through elite, Ph.D. school), they found that almost all of the faculty that reported a conservative orientation were clustered in community colleges or small, undergraduate schools. In traditional liberal arts schools and in major research universities, less than 4 percent of faculty identified themselves as having any conservative leanings.

When Gross and Simmons (2007) examined their data by academic discipline they found that self-described conservatives of any shade constituted a high of 24 percent in business schools, to a low of only 3.6 percent in humanities departments and 4.9 percent in social science programs. They also asked respondents to report their political party identification. In sociology, only 5 percent of faculty reported that they were registered Republican; in criminal justice that number was 19 percent. When asked who they voted for in the past presidential election, almost 88 percent of social scientists voted for John Kerry, as did over 83 percent of those in the humanities. Democrat to Republican ratios were computed to be 3:1 in economics, 18.9:1 in history, 18.8:1 in political science, and 19.5:1 in sociology.

Almost identical patterns have been found across a range of studies. Lipset (1972, 1982, 1994), Light (2003), and Klein and Stern (2003) have similarly found liberals and radicals form the clear majority of all academics. In a study of 1,678 scholars from a variety of disciplines, Klein and Stern (2003) found that Democrats outnumbered Republicans by 30:1 in anthropology, by 28:1 in sociology, by 13:1 in philosophy, by 9.5:1 in history, and by 3:1 in economics. The average Democrat to Republican ratio was 15.1:1.

It is unique in social science data to show such consistency in results. Indeed, the data are so clear on this issue that it is fair to say that it is a matter of fact that conservatives are virtually extinct on many university campuses and are extinct in the vast majority of academic departments. While the evidence of this gross disparity is consistent across time and disturbing in its potential consequences, the disparity is problematic only to the degree that political views of professors are imported into the classroom, woven into their scientific pursuits, or brought to bear in the administration of their department, college, or university. It is, after all, perfectly possible that professors keep their politics out of these domains.

But even here, the data paint a picture that is also disturbing. Klein and Stern, for example, also asked professors about their views on 18 policy issues, ranging from gun control, to immigration, to support for tariffs. Contrary to claims that political orientation is subservient to scientific objectivity, Klein and Stern (2005) found that support for specific policies was almost perfectly aligned with political orientation. Democrats uniformly supported gun control, government ownership of business, and minimum wage laws. Conservatives were less likely to support government intrusion into business and more likely to support government regulation of illegal drugs and prostitution. More importantly, Democratic professors in Klein and Stern's sample showed significantly less diversity in opinion compared to Republican professors. For Democratic professors, note Klein and Stern (2005: 271–272):

> The Democratic tent is relatively narrow. The academic social sciences are pretty much a one-party system. Were the Democratic tent broad, the one-party system might have intellectual diversity. But the data show almost no diversity of opinion among the Democratic professors when it comes to the regulatory, redistributive state: they like it.

Further analyses by Klein and Stern (2005) examined the predictors of whether a professor identified as a Democrat or Republican. Perhaps not surprisingly, having parents that voted Democratic or Republican increased (or reduced) the likelihood of Democratic affiliation. Beyond parental political orientation, however, support for traditionally liberal policies exerted only a small effect on the likelihood of voting Democratic, while working in academia, as opposed to a "think tank," exerted a larger effect. The strongest predictor of whether a professor identifies himself as a Democrat, however, was whether he or she was a sociologist or anthropologist. Note Klein and Stern (2005: 289): "there is something especially left-wing about the disciplines of anthropology and sociology."

That faculty political viewpoints can be almost perfectly predicted by which discipline they work in stands in stark contrast to the idea that faculty are strongly influenced by data or that they are as independently minded as they claim. Indeed, it is fair to say that the data show not only a remarkable lack of political diversity among university professors as measured by political party affiliation, but also a remarkable lack of diversity in public policy issues. This is even more problematic, however, than the lack of registered Republicans on campus because beliefs about public policy issues often rest on assumptions about the nature of human behavior, about the proper role of government in a free society, about what constitutes moral conduct, and about the inter-relationship between government and business. The uniformity in beliefs among faculty, especially faculty in social science departments, conveys more information about the views, biases, and thought patterns of faculty than the mere ratio of Democrats to Republicans reveals.

Available data reveal that conservatives are almost non-existent on many college campuses and that leftist beliefs have consolidated to form a near hegemonic worldview among faculty (especially in the social sciences). Sociologists call this "cultural hegemony," which refers to the beliefs, values, views, and mores that are created by the dominant culture and imposed on others to maintain compliance and uniformity (Gramsci, 1971). Cultural hegemony makes it more likely that individuals will at least tacitly agree with the views and political ideology of others whom they see as controlling rewards and incentives. University faculty are not unlike others who work in institutional settings where compliance with broader cultural beliefs is expected and rewarded, where individuals are selected into the institution based, in part, on their compliance with cultural expectations, and where departure from those beliefs is punished.

Conservative critics of academia regularly allege that liberal cultural hegemony works to exclude conservatives from hiring, from promotion, and from the rewards associated with an academic career. Recent data lend empirical support for these assertions. In a study of social psychologists, the same group Haidt gave his talk to, Inbar and Lammers (2012) found that 93 percent of respondents reported that they were liberal, compared to less than 4 percent who identified themselves as conservative. However, Inbar and Lammers also found that there was greater variation in beliefs when it came to foreign and economic policy. In foreign policy, 70 percent of respondents classified themselves as liberal, while in the economic policy domain, 74 percent classified themselves as liberal. While liberal viewpoints dominated each domain, Inbar and Lammers conclude that moderate and some traditionally conservative views are held by some social psychologists and that these views are often overlooked in discussions about the political leanings of university faculty.

However, even more revealing were the results of Inbar and Lammers' (2012) inquiry into the perceptions of discrimination against conservatives and the willingness of liberals to report they would discriminate against conservatives. We let Inbar and Lammers (2012: 21) speak to their findings:

> The more conservative respondents were, the more they experienced a hostile climate, were reluctant to express their views to colleagues, and feared that they might be the victims of discrimination based on their political views. These fears are quite realistic: a sizeable portion of our (liberal) respondents indicated at least some willingness to dis-criminate against conservatives professionally. One in six respondents admitted that she or he would be somewhat inclined to discriminate against conservatives in inviting them for symposiums or reviewing their work. One in four would discriminate in reviewing their grants. And more than one in three would discriminate against conservatives when

making hiring decisions. Thus, willingness to discriminate is not limited to small decisions. In fact, it is strongest when it comes to the most important decisions, such as grant proposals and hiring. *And the more liberal respondents were, the more willing they were to discriminate.*

(Emphasis added)

Inbar and Lammers' findings provide strong support for conservative critics who argue that faculty across American campuses are bound by a liberal cultural hegemony—a hegemony that in some programs has been cemented into a quasi-liberal religious orthodoxy. The results of Inbar and Lammer's study provide evidence that conservatives are likely discriminated against in hiring, in research reviews, in publication decisions, in tenure and promotion and that because of this discrimination, individuals—even liberal individuals—who hold anything close to a moderate or conservative view on some issue elect to keep their views to themselves. This is the power of cultural hegemony enforced by individuals who elevate liberal political beliefs above science, open discourse, and fairness.

Tribal Moral Communities

The debate that ensued after Haidt's talk fell along political lines. Conservatives, who have long argued that college campuses have been overtaken by liberal ideologues were quick to point out the various ways that conservatives were "locked out" of academia, including how they are discriminated against during the hiring process and how conservative students are pushed aside in favor of liberal students who share faculty beliefs. Yet, the reaction of many professors and liberals to Haidt's talk was one of disbelief and indignation. Psychologist John Jost, who has made a career of documenting the alleged shortcomings of conservatives, stated to the *New Yorker Magazine*, "Haidt fails to grapple meaningfully with the question of why nearly all of the best minds in science find liberal ideas to be closer to the mark with respect to evolution, human nature, mental health, close relationships, intergroup relations, ethics, social justice, conflict resolution, environmental sustainability, and so on" (Konnikova, 2014).

Megan McArdle, writing for *The Atlantic*, noted that her column on Haidt's talk received more comments than any prior article, and that "many, even most of them, were pretty angry." McArdle (2011) states that comments to her article on the "liberal slant in academia" could be reduced to seven coherent arguments:

- Smart people are almost always liberal.
- Curiosity and interest in ideas is a liberal trait.
- Conservatives are too rigid and authoritarian to maintain the open mind required of a professor.
- Education erases false conservative ideas and turns people into liberals.
- Conservatives don't want to be professors because they're more interested in something else (money, the military).
- Conservatives don't want to be professors because they're anti-intellectual.
- Conservatives hold false beliefs that make them ineligible to be professors.

McArdle also points out that bias can come in a variety of flavors, and that:

liberals, who are usually quick to assume that underrepresentation represents some form of discrimination—structural or personal—suddenly become fierce critics of the notion that numerical representation means anything. Moreover, they start generating explanations for the disparity that sound suspiciously like some old reactionary explaining that blacks don't really want to go into management because they're much happier without all the responsibility. Conservatives are too stupid to become academics; they aren't open to new ideas; they're too aggressive and hierarchical; they don't care about ideas, just money. In other words, it's not our fault that they're not worthy.

The reaction to Haidt's comments highlight what Haidt calls a "tribal moral community." A tribal moral community (TMC) is any group of individuals who share, if only implicitly, a set of "sacred values." These sacred values "bind and blind," according to Haidt. Sacred values define what can and cannot be studied and they define "acceptable" and "non-acceptable" answers to research questions. For the most part, sacred values constitute accepted wisdom within any academic discipline. They are not necessarily codified or written down, but they are understood and acknowledged by the majority of scholars in a field. They are informal social norms, instituted not (usually) through direct enforcement but subtly through intellectual pressure, conversation, and training.

Just what are these sacred values? Haidt (2012) argues that the left treats matters of race, class, intelligence, sex, and the connection between biology and behavior, what he terms "nativism," with an almost holy reverence. There is, according to Haidt, one narrative or script dictating how scholars communicate about these issues because the areas have been reified and laden with moral judgment. Discussions of minority groups, for example, have to be couched in the language of victimhood else they are thought to be racist or to invite racism. Any mention of sex differences that does not invoke the idea of patriarchy or feminism or that questions feminist perspectives is viewed as sexist. Similarly studies into human intelligence and the heritability of traits and behaviors are labeled "dangerous" because they allegedly provoke punitive state sanctions, justify eugenic policies, or justify a reduction in welfare spending.

Sacred values are not geared toward an acceptance and advancement of science or the scientific method. They do not establish boundaries against bad science, illogical thinking, or ideology—indeed, they almost guarantee bad science, illogical thinking, and ideological responses to research findings. By enshrining these subjects, leftist academics have effectively limited scientific discourse on these and other topics and they have imposed specific ideological boundaries around these topics that, in turn, shape research into these areas.

As an example, let's take the recent controversy about research into the effects "gay marriage" has on children. The American Sociological Association (2013, 2015), stated in their Amicus brief to the United States Supreme Court that "children fare just as well" when raised by homosexual parents. "The results of our review are clear," they stated, "There is no evidence that children with parents in stable same-sex or opposites-sex relationships differ in terms of well-being." Even the American Psychological Association stated, in 2004, that "there is no scientific evidence that parenting effectiveness is related to parental sexual orientation." "Not a single study," the APA committee stated, found any negative outcome (Patterson, 2005). These are rather strong pronouncements, especially considering the fact that child well-being was at stake, so one would assume that the science the APA and ASA drew on was rather strong methodologically. The matter, after all, was settled science.

That assumption would turn out to be wrong. While the studies cited by the ASA and APA generally did not find any differences between children raised in homosexual as opposed to heterosexual homes, the studies were at most suggestive. A more skeptical reading of the body of evidence at the time would have been less forgiving. Indeed, in a careful review of the 59 studies cited by the APA, Marks (2012) found that samples of homosexual parents contained in these studies were so small, often under 40 parents and children, that statistical tests were impossible. The samples of parents and their children were sometimes collected by researchers accessing their own networks of friends or collected by gay rights advocacy groups. In 26 of the 59 studies there were no comparison groups and those studies that did have comparison groups often used divorced heterosexual parents as their comparison. Homosexual parents in these samples, moreover, were typically highly intelligent, their relationships rather stable, and they were above average in education and economic status (see also Amato, 2012 and Eggebeen, 2012).

In 2012, a professor of sociology, Mark Regnerus, published the results of a large-scale study into the effects homosexual parenting had on child outcomes. Using data from the New Family Structures Study, the largest study on the subject ever done, Regnerus found that children raised by homosexual parents, mainly lesbian mothers, scored significantly worse on a large range of outcome variables. Needless to say, Regnerus' study set off a firestorm of criticism by gay rights groups and, more importantly, by scholars in and out of the area. Not one but two ethics complaints were filed against Regnerus, resulting in two university investigations. Both times he was exonerated. Even so, his email was searched, his records searched, his life was turned upside down, and his reputation sullied by scathing personal attacks from other scholars. Regnerus was accused of fabricating data, of being an incompetent scholar, of lying about his funding source—even the editor of the journal that published Regnerus' work was called on to step down. It was a scorched earth approach to academic disagreement.

Let's assume for the moment that Regnerus' findings were correct and that children in homosexual households encountered adjustment problems at rates higher than children from heterosexual households. Would this finding be any different to the pattern of findings from a very large number of studies that show that children raised in single-mother households do less well than children raised by two parents? Moreover, can we reasonably assume the ASA and the APA, who are on record supporting gay marriage, would suddenly alter their support if other large-scale studies confirmed Regnerus' results? We ask not only to show the inconsistency in standards applied to Regnerus but not to every other researcher in the area, but also because other large-scale studies have now also found that children raised in homosexual households do experience adjustment problems more often than children raised in traditional two-parent families (Sullins, 2015).

Sexual identity is an enshrined value for the left so, as the Regnerus episode shows us, every effort will be made to destroy the credibility of those who question the rather strong and clearly biased views of the APA and ASA. Moreover, when it comes to producing evidence that supports claims about sexual identity, staunch critics will suddenly turn into willing participants who suspend critical judgment. Recently, a paper was published in the journal *Science*—the top journal in the world—that allegedly showed a remarkable and sizeable effect of having homosexuals talk with individuals about their opposition to gay rights (LaCour & Green, 2014). In a 20-minute talk, the authors reported, individuals who initially stated their opposition to gay marriage would suddenly and dramatically, having finally been exposed to a homosexual, change their core beliefs. The conclusion from the experiment was clear: Exposure to homosexuals, even for very brief periods (20 minutes) is enough to affect public opinion and to reduce homophobia. Remarkable by any stretch of the word.

And totally fabricated. Hoping to expand on the results of the study, graduate students from Berkeley attempted to replicate and modify the experiment's results (Broockman, Kalla,

& Aronow, 2015). Unfortunately, when they looked a bit deeper, they found the data were cooked. They notified the second author of the paper, who investigated the issue. Professor Green found not only that the data were fabricated but that the company alleged to have collected the data had never heard of the project or of the first author, Michael LeCour, a graduate student at UCLA. Much to his credit, Professor Green issued an immediate retraction (McCook, 2015).

What went wrong? While the details have yet to be worked out and a full explanation from LeCour has yet to appear, we believe it fair to say that the LeCour and Green study appeared sophisticated, that it was written at a high level, that the analyses were advanced and that it appeared, at least on its face, as a major scientific breakthrough. However, the study also included signals, language, that clued in reviewers to the positive implications for the gay rights agenda and it cast those who opposed gay rights as ignorant bigots. More importantly, it offered results that reviewers and editors wanted to believe. In reality, the large effect sizes and remarkable results should have invited scrutiny. After all, it strains credulity to believe that individuals who see homosexuality as a sin would suddenly shift their views because they had a 20-minute conversation with one random homosexual. But this is what liberal bias and the merger of social advocacy with social science research produces: the uncritical acceptance of the impossible.

Readers should understand that we use the issue of gay rights to highlight how liberal sacred values and illiberal scholars operate. Both the APA and the ASA made strong, unqualified statements about an issue of critical importance. No caveats were offered, no careful language was employed, and in the case of the APA, no single study met the methodological standards proffered by the APA. When evidence did arise that contradicted these positions, the author was mercilessly attacked and prosecuted, and yet when evidence was produced allegedly showing almost entirely unbelievable results in support of gay rights, it was published in the top journal in the world. Neither of us are opposed to states extending marriage rights to homosexuals. What we are opposed to is the very clear and unscientific bias that has affected this enshrined area and that continues to affect other areas that liberals see as sacred.

The power of tribal moral communities to regulate thought and academic investigation emerges from the omnipotent threat that scholars who violate these values run a terrible risk. Like Regnerus, they may be subject to endless investigations and callous unprofessional attacks. They may have ethics charges leveled against them for the sin of conducting research, or they may face disciplinary banishment and the loss of reputation. Taken together, the omnipotent threat allows leftist academics an incredible amount of room to deny the existence of any disciplinary biases, and it gives them free rein to explain why so little intellectual diversity exists in their disciplines. They can claim, like the APA and ASA did, that liberal views are scientifically valid views, in part because no conservative views exist, because dissent is discouraged, and because contrary research brings repercussions. Hence, leftist academics often claim the mantle of science, but underneath the claim lies the very real reality that the freedom of thought necessary for objective science to occur has been hijacked. And while they claim that debate is fostered inside academia, that peer review is objective and weeds out bad science, events like the LeCour and Green paper seemingly call this conclusion into question.

We see the same forces at work in criminology. Issues related to capital punishment, to incarceration, and to gun control, for example, ooze political bias. To be certain, some scholars in these areas are ruthlessly objective. Spelman (2000, 2009) and Levitt's (1996) work on incarceration and Kleck's (2005) work on gun control stand out not only because of their level of scholarship but because they represent a degree of objectivity that is too infrequent. What many outside of the social sciences do not appreciate is that the disciplinary incentives are not aligned with publishing studies that are highly objective. Just the opposite. The incentives are aligned with telling other scholars what they want to hear. This is especially true when certain topics and policy issues are on the table. Scholars will jettison objectivity when the issue is one they support. They will not only jettison objectivity, they will make the facts suit their views. Even Haidt notes that a tribal moral community "will embrace science whenever it supports their sacred values," but that "they'll ditch it or distort it as soon as it threatens a sacred value."

How do scholars reject science when it suits them? Broadly speaking, it is an article of faith amongst liberals that they are scientific and that conservatives are "anti-science" and are thus irrational. The two most obvious examples are that some conservatives reject, in part, Darwinian evolution and that some conservatives also question the veracity of claims made about global warming. Indeed, we readily admit that some conservatives hold beliefs that are at odds with established science—including the rejection of evolution. The planet Earth, for example, is not 4,000 to 6,000 years old as some "young earth" creationists claim. Unfortunately, no amount of evidence will sway their views.

That said, the left is hardly immune from holding views that are not supported by science, they are not immune from accepting as scientific fact studies that are methodologically compromised, and they are not above abandoning science when the science may conflict with their strongly held views. For example, acceptance of Darwinian evolution—specifically the rejection of creationist views on the nature of man—is now *the* litmus test for one's alleged acceptance of science. Question the principles of evolution and you are immediately excommunicated. Even so, while many liberals love to "accept evolution" they are loath to accept the natural outcomes of evolutionary processes. Leftist academics, for example, have a long history of rejecting the idea that sex differences are the byproduct of evolutionary forces and that men and women are intrinsically different (Baumeister, 2010). They have gone to great lengths to deny the existence of biological race. Race, they have argued, is merely a "social construct" devoid of biology and unaffected by evolutionary forces (Graves, 2001). Of course, evolutionary theory would predict the existence of groups of people who vary on a range of traits and morphological characteristics that we would label as "race." Moreover, there is hard genetic and anthromorphological evidence showing race is not only a social construct but also a biological construct (Sesardic, 2010; Wade, 2015). Let's also not forget that for at least the last 60 to 100 years leftists advanced a "blank slate" view of human behavio by steadfastly denying the existence of evolutionarily crafted neural circuits in the brain and the important role of biology and genetics in human affairs. More recently, it has been people on the left who have shut down research on human intelligence, who have refused to inoculate their children because Jenny McCarthy said the vaccines caused autism, and who have pushed for bans on genetically modified food despite decades of experience showing GMOs have no impact on heath. Other studies show that people on the left are more likely to believe in the existence of aliens, more likely to believe in fortune telling, and more likely to believe in New Age religions. It is illuminating that those who now claim the mantle of science also reject science when it suits them. However, our point is not simply to highlight what may easily be passed off as liberal hypocrisy but to show that intelligent people on both sides of the political spectrum hold views that don't square with science (see also Berezow & Campbell, 2012). Science is sometimes hard to believe because it forces us to repress more natural beliefs and desires and because we have a natural tendency to engage in "motivated political reasoning"—that is, to seek out information that confirms our views, to discount evidence against our views, and to attack those who bring us the uncomfortable message (Lodge & Tabor, 2013). Accepting disconfirming evidence is a tall order for anyone, even scientists.

No social science is immune to the political context in which it operates. When science and ideology are merged, or become indistinguishable, the legitimacy of science suffers. When scholars become vocal advocates solely for liberal policies they invite scrutiny from other ideologues and they sacrifice the very foundation of legitimacy the university rests on. To be an open-minded, honest, objective scientist does not equate to support for abortion rights, affirmative action, banning individual possession of guns, or any other liberal position. In many ways, the lack of legitimacy faced by the social sciences, and by extension the university in modern American, can be traced to the ideological stranglehold that grips many disciplines.

The consequences, unfortunately, extend well beyond individual researchers. When politicians look at universities, they often see the advances in technology, the training of students, and the advancement of medicine produced by these institutions. But they also see large voting blocks, sources of financial support, and intellectual capital dedicated to the Democratic Party. This makes universities politically vulnerable. Research by Gauchat (2012), for example, found that trust in science has been relatively stable since 1974. One exception to that general trend, however, is that conservatives, who started the period scoring higher than any other group in their trust of science, ended the period scoring the lowest. This pattern was especially true for highly educated conservatives.

The reasons for this are likely complex and multifaceted but one reason not addressed by Gauchat may be that educated conservatives are more keenly aware of the role liberal orthodoxy now plays in science and how science has been used by liberal professors to justify any range of liberal policies. That said, the same may also be true of liberals. Research by Nisbet and Garrett (2015) is instructive. Nisbet and Garrett recruited 1,500 individuals and randomly assigned them to read about either science topics that were particularly partisan, such as climate change and hydraulic fracking, or non-partisan science topics, such as astronomy. Conservatives who read about climate change and evolution reported less trust in science. Liberals who read the same statements reported increased trust in science but, compared to other liberals and their reactions to scientifically neutral issues (astronomy or geology), reported significantly less trust in science. Nisbet and Garrett's study shows that trust in science is often dependent on whether scientific findings support political-moral positions. Liberals and conservatives can be quite biased in their assessments of what constitutes good science but then again, there are no conservatives on campuses.

Clearly, we agree with Haidt, and see the social sciences, including criminology, as having all the trappings of a tribal moral community. We see the influence of liberal political correctness and we see the inconsistent application of science in the pursuit of understanding crime and criminals. We also see the "sacred values" present in criminology and we have experienced first-hand what happens when these sacred values are violated. Moreover, we also are keenly aware of the domination of liberal ideology in criminology and how closely support for liberal ideology in general influences scholarly support for certain criminological theories and policies.

Tea Party Patriots, Occupy Movements and the Classroom

A professor of psychology at South Texas College compared the Tea Party to Nazis. "In 1931, which was really interesting, the Nazis—people were kind of tired of them.

They've been around since 1920, 11 years now. They've won seats—they're like the Tea Party! That's such a good example. Don't tell anybody I said that though. But in the sense of how they politically came to power, there's a good analogy there. That eventually people realized, 'Oh, these Nazis are a bunch of nuts,' 'These Tea Party people are a bunch of nuts.' I mean, the analogy really is a good analogy."

(Chumley, 2014)

Academics across the country have embraced the movement since it emerged in September, organizing classes, publishing reams of commentary and issuing calls to "occupy" not just Wall Street but also sociology, anthropology, history, philosophy or the entire "academic vampire squid" itself, as a poster for a session at the recent annual meeting of the International Studies Association put it.

"Everybody I know doing this is an activist of some sort," said Jeffrey Juris, an associate professor of anthropology at Northeastern University who is organizing strategy workshops for Occupy Boston while also studying it. "But Occupy is so open and broad based, it doesn't take much to consider yourself an activist."

(Schuessler, 2012)

Many critics of universities and university faculty argue that faculty use the classroom to indoctrinate students. We do not believe, nor does the research evidence support, the idea that the majority of university faculty attempt to politically indoctrinate students. Studies of students do not find this nor has our experience been that the majority of faculty are so unethical as to force students to accept their views. Moreover, students are often intelligent enough to know when a faculty member is substituting their views for science.

While it is true that the majority of faculty do not work to indoctrinate their students, there are other, more subtle ways to inject politics into the classroom. This occurs just below the surface and is sometimes difficult for the uninitiated to recognize. Faculty may shade discussions of certain topics, they may assign books that reflect a common liberal agenda, they may call on and reward students for providing certain types of answers over others, and they may emphasize certain research findings over others. At the subterranean level there are an infinite number of mechanisms faculty can use to tilt the presentation of materials in favor of liberal viewpoints and policies. And, we note, all of these ways are academically acceptable even if they are sometimes more or less obvious.

Thus, professors do not have to quote Marx or have students register for the Democratic Party to get the message across to their students that certain ideas are "right" and others are "wrong." To be charitable, we do not believe that most of those who engage in such practices are doing so malevolently. Instead, they do so because they believe the evidence supports their viewpoints. And this is the problem that is largely unrecognized—that most faculty do not indoctrinate their students but more frequently distort findings to support their views.

As we mentioned already, few topics highlight the intersection of professorial politics, political ideology, and academic research and teaching better than the academies reaction to two competing social movements: the Tea Party on the right and the Occupy Movement on the left (Nisbet, Cooper & Garrett, 2015; Parker & Barreto, 2013). As the quote from the professor in Texas shows, academics have not been kind to the Tea Party or to its members—linking them to the Nazi Reich and to racism. Recently, for example, a University of Washington political scientist equated Tea Party members with the Ku Klux Klan (Ryan, 2013). To quote the professor:

Tea Partiers are motivated both by conservative principles and racism … . Can we not say that the Tea Party is heavily involved in politics? Further, can we not also say that many Tea Partiers are not educated and accomplished? Finally, can we not also say that the Tea Party has an intolerant element? The answer to all three is yes. So, to answer your question, I recognize why some on the right are alarmed at the comparison, but they need to bear in mind that the comparison is *very* specific to the Klan of the 1920s: another national right-wing political movement, one with an educated, accomplished element that also has its share of intolerant people.

In a follow-on email to a website, the professor went on to show just how academic distortion functions. Asked how he would treat Tea Party students, he responded:

Generally, once I lay out the facts, supported by data and history, they can see there's another side to the Tea Party. Likewise, for students who aren't sympathetic to the Tea Party, once that part of the allure of the Tea Party is driven by a desire for small government, they come to a better understanding of the movement.

And here's the rub: The professor can claim to be scientific, to have fully investigated the Tea Party, to have applied the standards of scholarship to arrive at his conclusions. And he can make the honest claim that he is simply presenting evidence to his students. Again, to the uninitiated this may seem entirely reasonable, even noble. However, in the introduction of his book-length treatment of the Tea Party, he wrote:

Our argument is simple: We believe that people are driven to support the Tea Party from the anxiety they feel as they perceive the America they know, the country they love, slipping away, threatened by the rapidly changing face of what they believe is the "real" American: a heterosexual, Christian, middle-class, (mostly) male, white country.

(2013: 3)

The liberal bias is clearly obvious in the introduction and becomes all the more apparent as one reads through the rest of the book. Throughout the book, he and his coauthor pathologicalize conservatives, tarring them as racists who seek only to hold on to the privileges that come along with power and status. To be clear, we believe that he and his coauthor believe what they have written, but we also strongly suspect that the conclusions of the good professor were likely pre-ordained. In an environment where liberal political and moral values dominate, this is what passes as science.

Conversely, as the *New York Times* article noted, academics rushed to join and also "study" the Occupy Movement. They formed sit-ins, led protests, got arrested, produced pamphlets, strategized, created forums on campus, and created classes. The same cannot be said of their treatment of and participation in Tea Party demonstrations. Anecdotally, while we were able to locate multiple examples of pro-Occupy Movement classes being offered, we could not find any pro-Tea Party classes offered.

This is the distortion and it is far more common on university campuses than faculty who openly try to indoctrinate students—although that happens too. More importantly, the clearly partisan reaction of professors to these two social movements highlights one of the serious costs associated with having a one-party system on university campuses. When professors share political-moral values they easily fall into the trap of believing that their views are correct, right, and just and because they are isolated from competing views it is a short psychological walk to then view competing views not only as factually incorrect but also as immoral. Intellectual efforts to paint Tea Party members as racists sympathetic to the Klan or as morally equivalent to the Nazis make sense only when individuals share a political–moral ideology. They are reflections not of objective scholarship but of in-group/out-group dynamics that are cloaked in the veil of objective scholarship and teaching. Now ask yourself if you really believe that someone willing to link the Tea Party to Nazism or to the Klan can dispassionately dissect either the Tea Party or the Occupy Movement in a classroom full of college students? Similarly, ask yourself if the professor "studying" the Occupy Movement and who admits that "everyone I know" is an Occupy activist can objectively present to his students the problems with the ideology behind the Occupy Movement? Maybe, but in all likelihood, maybe not.

Motivated political reasoning affects all of us—especially those who have higher levels of education. Yes, research tells us that higher levels of education are associated with greater knowledge of science and with increased, not decreased, partisanship (Bolsen, Druckman & Cook, 2015; Kahan et al., 2012). This is true for the left and the right. As individuals climb the academic ladder they become more partisan—not less. The long filtering process of higher education, especially in the social sciences and even more so in the humanities, results in a large group of individuals who are better educated and even more politically partisan than the average person. Indeed, even Jonathan Haidt's massive contributions to science have not been well received by everyone. Scholars have taken particular aim at Haidt's work exploring the under-representation of conservative professors. One, Massimo Pigliucci accused Haidt of nothing short of professional misconduct. Writing in his blog, Pigliucci stated: "I suspect Haidt is either an incompetent psychologist (not likely) or is disingenuously saying the sort of things controversial enough to get him in the *New York Times* (more likely)" (Haidt, 2011a, 2011b). Similarly, in an interview in *The New Yorker*, Harvard psychologist Daniel Gilbert stated simply that "Liberals may be more interested in new ideas, more willing to work for peanuts, or just more intelligent." Echoing the sentiment that liberals are just brighter, Jost stated: "nearly all of the best minds in science find liberal ideas to be closer to the mark with respect to evolution, human nature, mental health, close relationships, intergroup relations, ethics, social justice, conflict resolution, environmental sustainability, and so on" (Konnikova, 2014).

Professors can recognize their own motivated political reasoning but it requires them to depart from the institutional and disciplinary incentives within their universities and their respective fields. It also requires them to take positions in direct conflict with the prevailing liberal dogma. A well-known Yale law professor was studying factors related to knowledge about science. At one point during his analysis he found that religious belief was largely unimportant when it came to science literacy. Many religious individuals were very scientific, he found, and many agnostics and atheists were not. But what really struck him was his analyses of how scientifically knowledgeable people were by their political identification. Professor Dan Kahan (2013) was startled to learn that members of the Tea Party were more scientifically literate than were liberals or even other run-of-the-mill conservatives! Embarrassingly, he quickly recognized that he, too, knew nobody in the Tea Party and that all of his information about Tea Party members came from other faculty and from liberal news sources, such as the Huffington Post.

Professor Kahan's experience vividly shows how the liberal bubble that most faculty live within functions to limit, to curtail, and to exclude their contact with conservatives. Because of this, they are free to create caricatures of conservatives and have their stereotypical reviews reinforced by their liberal peers. They are able to assume that all intelligent people believe as they do and they sincerely do not understand why anyone would embrace conservatism if not because they were racist, homophobic, or stupid. Their lack of contact with articulate conservative faculty, faculty who do not share their worldview, places severe constraints on their experiences, it limits their understanding of conservatives and conservatism and thus it distorts their understanding, their life experiences, and even their teaching and research.

Liberal Hegemony in Criminology

The study of crime and criminals is not an exact science. The people we study are not always truthful, the data we examine are not always valid or reliable, and the theories that guide our work are woefully inadequate. Criminologists, liberal and conservative, have to sometimes make sense of complex processes with data that are oftentimes not up to the task. Even so, as difficult as the study of crime and criminals can be, it is made even more difficult by the discipline's internal biases—biases that consistently favor the leftists' interpretations of the causes of crime and leftists' narratives about the criminal justice system.

We offer three pieces of evidence of the dominance of leftist political influence in the academic study of crime. First, it is striking that criminologists have produced no books that could be seen as supportive of anything bearing a conservative trademark. No book exists advocating for the use of incarceration, no book exists advocating for three-strikes laws or mandatory sentencing of certain classes of offenders, and no book exists advocating for the use of the death penalty. And unlike other disciplinary divisions, no book exists written from a conservative perspective—very different from the publishing record for a feminist perspective, a radical perspective, a postmodern perspective, or even a green perspective. None. This is not by chance nor is it because the evidence against "conservative" views is absent. Examining data from 85 U.S. cities, Ren, Zhao, and Lovrich (2008) found that crime rates declined when local governments shifted resources towards traditional conservative approaches, such as increased policing, and when cities invested in community development, a traditionally liberal response. "Effective crime control," they wrote, "should combine the merits of both the conservative and the liberal perspectives on crime."

The second piece of evidence comes from membership rolls of the academic divisions within the American Society of Criminology (ASC), the primary academic organization for criminologists. Data provided by the ASC show that the largest membership group in the ASC is the Division of Critical Criminology. "Critical Criminologists" are academic radicals, communists, and Marxists. They largely do not see themselves as empirically minded, objective analysts. Instead, they see themselves as social critics, and advocates for social and economic change, even anti-science. Their view is that scholars should effect radical change in society and should mobilize students in their efforts. In this vein, classrooms become instruments of open political indoctrination and political oppression. The university, moreover, is viewed not as an institution designed to pursue truth but as a political tool used to enforce specific views on "social justice." Where social scientists are constrained by data, where they have to temper their conclusions, and where they have to change their minds in the presence of new research findings, academic radicals are not and do not. That the Division of Critical Criminology is the largest division within the ASC speaks volumes about the leftist orientation of criminology.

- Division of Critical Criminology—684
- Division of Women in Crime—484
- Division of Corrections and Sentencing—462

- Division of International Criminology—367
- Division of People of Color in Criminology—281
- Division of Experimental Criminology—188

Finally, in Table 2.1 we present data from a survey of members of the American Society of Criminology (Cooper, Walsh, & Ellis, 2010). The purpose of the Cooper et al. (2010) study was to assess how political ideology influences the views criminologists have about the causes of crime. Cooper and his colleagues reported that 768 ASC members completed the survey. Of this, only 5 percent (n=40) self-identified as "conservative" and another 26 percent classified themselves as "moderate." Almost 60 percent classified themselves as "liberal," and almost 10 percent classified themselves as "radical." These estimates, however, contain individuals with master's and bachelor's degrees. When examining only those who reported holding a Ph.D., the number of self-identified "conservatives" fell to only 30, or about 4 percent of all Ph.D.-level criminologists. Again, almost 70 percent of all Ph.D.-level criminologists, the individuals who do the vast majority of research and teaching in criminology and criminal justice, reported being liberal to radical in their political beliefs. Only 26 percent reported holding "moderate" political beliefs.

TABLE 2.1 The political orientation of criminologists

	Political persuasion			
Primary training	Conservative	Moderate	Liberal	Radical
Criminal justice	47	115	131	17
Criminology	20	126	202	39
Psychology	5	12	46	5
Sociology	9	74	245	42
Race	Conservative	Moderate	Liberal	Radical
American Indian or Alaskan	1	4	3	1
Asian	1	13	18	0
Black or African American	1	21	24	3
Native Hawaiin or other Pacific Islander	0	0	1	0
White	78	294	589	94
Highest degree earned	Conservative	Moderate	Liberal	Radical
B.S./B.A.	4	24	25	3
Ed.D.	2	4	3	2
J.D.	6	8	10	3
M.D.	2	1	3	0
M.S./M.A.	38	120	185	33
Ph.D.	30	179	418	64

Note: Data graciously provided by Jon Cooper.

We can also see in Table 2.1 that only 2 percent of individuals trained in sociology considered themselves to be "conservative," a finding echoed in other studies (Klein & Stern, 2003, 2005). This compares to 7 percent of those trained in psychology, 5 percent of those trained in criminology, and 15 percent of those with primary training in criminal justice. Moreover, almost all self-described conservatives were white, and less than half hold a degree other than a Ph.D.

The dominance of liberal and radical scholars in the ranks of criminology wouldn't be so much of a problem if political orientation wasn't associated with the views criminologists hold about the causes of crime. Another interesting story to emerge from Cooper et al.'s analysis of ASC respondents was that support for specific theories and beliefs about the relevance of certain predictors was linearly correlated with political orientation. These patterns are clear, and we present them in graphical form in Figures 2.1, 2.2a, 2.2b, and 2.2c.

Respondents were asked to rank their level of support for the following causes of criminal behavior: a lack of empathy, impulsivity, poor parental supervision, and poor family functioning. In Figure 2.1 we show the graph of the relationship between political orientation and level of belief that these variables are causes of crime. As can be readily seen, the relationship is almost perfectly linear. Conservatives, the minority of all criminologists, rank all of these variables as more strongly related to crime than do any other group. Liberals and radicals, conversely, the dominant political orthodoxy, rank these variables as less important.

Examining Figure 2.2a, we see that the Cooper et al. data again reflect an almost perfect linear association between political orientation and belief that an unfair economic system, limited educational opportunities, and biased law enforcement are causes of crime. Conservatives rank these variables as significantly less important than do liberals or radicals. The same pattern is demonstrated in Figure 2.2b and Figure 2.2c. Beliefs about the importance of specific theories and certain criminogenic risk factors largely parallel political orientation. Unlike liberals and radicals, conservatives find little support for labeling theory or the idea that harsh punishments cause crime. They are also significantly more likely to believe that a lack of moral values or religious training is a cause of crime.

What we draw out from these patterns is that criminology, much like sociology, is dominated by a leftist political orientation. There are relatively few conservatives in criminology

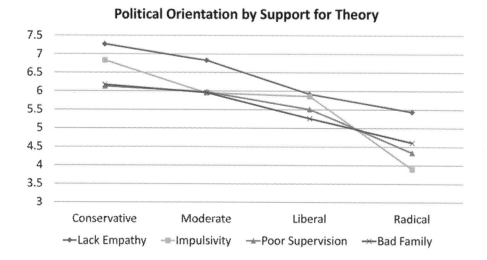

FIGURE 2.1 Causes of crime by political orientation

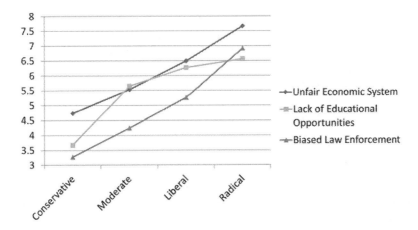

FIGURE 2.2A Political orientation of scholar and support for theory

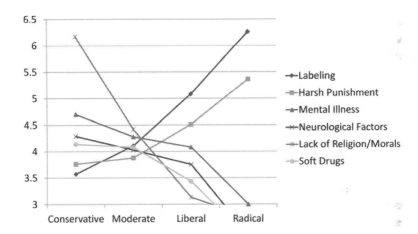

FIGURE 2.2B Political orientation of scholar and support for theory

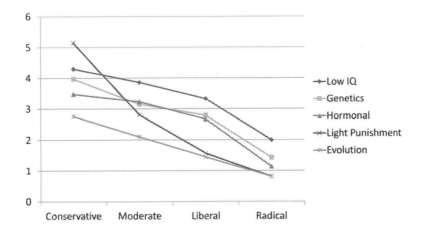

FIGURE 2.2C Political orientation of scholar and support for theory

and there are virtually no conservatives in criminology/criminal justice Ph.D.-granting programs. We can attribute part of this to the training that Ph.D.-level criminologists receive. Most criminologists, especially those at Ph.D.-granting institutions, have been trained as sociologists. Much of sociology is dominated by leftist, radical, and Marxist scholarship (Klein & Stern, 2005; Lipset, 1994), with over 80 percent of academic sociologists classifying themselves as liberal to radical in their political beliefs, and less than 2 percent classifying themselves as conservative (Sanderson & Ellis, 1992; Lord & Sanderson, 1999). Again, however, the problem is not so much that liberals and radicals make up the majority of sociologists but that political orientation predicts almost perfectly their choice of explanatory theories. Lord and Sanderson (1999: 65) argue that their survey of academic sociologists supports Irving Louis Horowitz's conclusions that sociology has become, to a large extent, "a series of demands for correct politics" (1993: 34), "a repository of discontent, a gathering of individuals who have special agendas, from gay and lesbian rights to liberation theology" (1993: 34). Similarly, sociology does not locate the causes of crime in individual traits or pathologies but in the broader social environment, however defined.

Other factors could explain why there are so few conservatives in academic criminology. Conservatives, for example, may find other lines of work more appealing, or they may perceive that the academic environment is hostile towards people who hold their political views. The fact remains, however, that the influence of liberal orthodoxy in the training and education of students is pervasive and extensive. About 70 percent of Ph.D.-level criminologists, the individuals who teach the majority of courses in criminal justice and criminology, the individuals who publish most of the research into crime, the individuals who mentor graduate students, and who guide dissertations and theses, are liberal to radical in their politics. We suspect that the number is even higher than the 70 percent reported by Cooper et al. (2010) because relatively few radicals, the largest division in the ASC, participated in the survey. If we extrapolate out by the proportion of members who belong to the Division of Critical Criminology, it may well be the case that 80 to 90 percent of academic criminologists are liberal to radical.

There is no doubt that some criminologists are empirically driven and take great pains to be objective. As in any large group, exceptions exist, but the exception does not invalidate the general rule. According to the Cooper data, objectivity in criminology may exist only when framed within a broader context of political-moral beliefs. This is particularly troubling given that support for specific theories of crime and belief in the potency of specific risk factors can be predicted almost perfectly by knowing the political orientation of the criminologist.

The Conservative Boogeyman

With no competing conservative voice or identifiable set of conservative ideas or theories, liberal criminologists have taken great liberties to create and perpetuate the myth of the "conservative criminologist" and "conservative" theories of crime. In turn, conservatism has been an easy target for academic criminologists, largely because they have been free to define what constitutes "conservatism" and to label those they disagree with as "conservative." Radical and liberal criminologists, such as Elliot Currie, Harry Allen, Jonathan Simon, Malcolm Feely, Nils Christie, Michael Tonry, and Jerome Miller frequently indict "conservatives" and "conservatism" in their critiques of the criminal justice system. Conservatives, it seems, have been responsible for just about every problem imaginable, whether they are exploiting rising crime rates and causing a moral panic (Simon, 2007), expanding the prison industrial complex (Tonry, 2012), or hunting down young black men for sport (Miller, 1997). Having effectively established that conservative criminologists and conservatism offer reactionary, racist, or overly punitive policies, liberal criminologists inevitably set about to promote "progressive" crime control agendas which, they claim, will lead to a more just, more humane society.

Yet somehow, liberal criminologists never define "conservatism" nor what it means to be "conservative." Moreover, they cannot point to the conservative criminologists that exercised so much power and influence that they convinced state legislatures and the federal government to enact harsh, punitive, and racists laws (Kania, 1988). The best they can do is point to the writings of James Q. Wilson (1985), John Dilulio (1992), and sometimes William Bennett (1996). These scholars have frequently been the target of liberal criminologists but none are or ever have been criminologists! They have never been trained in criminology, have never worked in a department of criminology, and have never viewed themselves as criminologists. Yet best-selling books on crime and on criminological theory label Wilson, Dilulio, and Bennett as "conservative criminologists" and several argue that their writings sponsored the rise of a new brand of conservative criminological thought which, in turn, was responsible for the growth in mass incarceration, greater use of the death penalty, harsher criminal sanctions, and other repressive crime control policies (Cullen & Agnew, 2006; Currie, 1985; Tonry, 1996). Award-winning books lambast conservatives for creating a moral panic during the 1990s just so they could expand the use of mass incarceration (Simon, 2007), while presidents of the major criminological organizations write prolifically about the "malign neglect" of minorities and prisoners—neglect caused by conservative policies that focused on brutalizing inmates in the name of deterrence (Tonry, 1996, 2012). Still others have been awarded these organizations' top honors for writing that the War on Crime was an openly racist conservative effort to control and eliminate black males (Miller, 1997).

The criminological animus towards conservatives was also illustrated when the then president of the American Society of Criminology awarded a black separatist named Zaki Baruti, a man who believes blacks should have their own state in what is now Montana, the President's Award for Distinguished Contributions to Justice. Mr. Baruti's contribution? When Mr. Baruti is not trying to establish a new black-only country in Central or South America, or in Africa, he specializes in indicting police officers as "Gestapo" agents, in suing police departments for various "racist" acts, and in presiding as president of the Universal African Peoples Organization—an overtly racist, Marxist organization.

The point of all of this is straightforward: the absence of any conservative voice in criminology has allowed liberal criminologists free rein in defining what constitutes conservatism, it has allowed them to lay blame for any number of criminal justice issues at the feet of conservatives, and it has allowed them to portray conservatives and conservatism in the worst possible light. Conversely, free from critique, they uniformly offer liberal policy prescriptions for dealing with crime and criminals. Moreover, their scholarly writings dominate the reading lists of undergraduate and graduate criminology and criminal justice students.

There is nothing ostensibly wrong with being liberal, holding liberal beliefs, or working for liberal causes, just as there is nothing ostensibly wrong with being conservative, holding conservative beliefs, or working for conservative causes. Part of the beauty of our current system is that it encourages competition in ideas, and it encourages people on both sides of the political spectrum to try to influence their communities and better the lives of citizens. Most people hold a balance of ideas, are politically centrist, and live their lives in a conservative fashion. They are pragmatic and seek a good life for themselves and their families. They abhor crime, especially violent crime, and they dislike the incivility and the lack of morality that plagues crime-ridden areas. More importantly, at least for our purposes, they do not always trust what social scientists have to say.

Certainly, social scientists, and especially criminologists, may hold legitimate views that counter widely held assumptions and beliefs. The knowledge produced by scholars is, to be certain, valuable, but it is also sometimes polluted by blind ideology and sometimes by biases that are subtle but potent. These biases, especially when they are grossly aligned with one political party and not another, call into question the legitimacy of criminological research and invite speculation about objectivity and scholarly independence. For criminological research to have an influence on policy, for it to be taken seriously, it has to have a degree of social legitimacy and trust extended to it. When academics uniformly align themselves with a liberal, progressive, or Marxist agenda, they send the message to politicians and lay people alike that their work is tinged with or dominated by political ideology.

Stated differently, would we trust any other large group of people who hold common political views? Would we trust the Republican Party to tell us the objective truth on social issues? Would we trust wholeheartedly the National Association for the Advancement of Colored People (NAACP) to tell us the unmitigated truth about race, and would we trust the AFL/CIO (big labor) to tell us the truth about the costs and consequences of union efforts? Of course not. Most people understand that members of the Republican Party, the NAACP, and the AFL/CIO share a common view of the world, that they lack ideological diversity, and that they push agendas consistent with their political worldviews. Scholars are supposed to be different. They are supposed to be ruthlessly empirically minded, committed to the scientific process, and to care little about the outcomes of their studies. If university faculty and, especially, criminologists wish to avoid being seen as yet another interest group, we believe they should welcome true, not faux, intellectual diversity, and we suggest that the current sacred values that place politically correct boundaries around controversial topics be removed. All views, no matter how uncivil, how politically repugnant, should be tested, analyzed, and open to debate. In it all, we should never lose sight that even science has limitations and that at the heart of the matter are fallible human beings who seek truth, understanding, and a good society.

References

Amato, P. R. (2012) The well-being of children with gay and lesbian parents. *Social Science Research*, 41(4), 771–774.

American Sociological Association (2013) ASA files amicus brief with U.S. Supreme Court in same-sex marriage cases. Retrieved from www.asanet.org/press/asa_files_amicus_brief_in_same-sex_marriage_cases.cfm.

American Sociological Association (2015) Amicus brief to the U.S. Supreme Court. Retrieved from www.asanet.org/documents/ASA/pdfs/ASA_March_2015_Supreme_Court_Marriage_Equality_Amicus_Brief.pdf.

Baumeister, R. F. (2010) *Is there anything good about men?: How cultures flourish by exploiting men*. New York: Oxford University Press.

Bennett, W. J., Dilulio, J. J., & Walters, J. P. (1996) *Body count: Moral poverty and how to win America's war against crime and drugs*. New York: Simon & Schuster.

Berezow, A., & Campbell, H. (2012) *Science left behind: Feel-good fallacies and the rise of the anti-scientific left*. New York: PublicAffairs.

Bolsen, T., Druckman, J. N., & Cook, F. L. (2015) Citizens', scientists', and policy advisors' beliefs about global warming. *The ANNALS of the American Academy of Political and Social Science*, 658(1), 271–295.

Broockman, D., Kalla, J., & Aronow, P. (2015) Irregularities in LaCour (2014). May 19. Retrieved from http://stanford.edu/~dbroock/broockman_kalla_aronow_lg_irregularities.pdf.

Chumley, C. K. (2014) Texas professor teaches students tea party akin to Nazi party. *The Washington Times*, December 9. Retrieved from www.washingtontimes.com/news/2014/dec/9/texas-professor-teaches-students-tea-party-akin-to/.

Cooper, J. A., Walsh, A., & Ellis, L. (2010) Is criminology moving toward a paradigm shift? Evidence from a survey of the American Society of Criminology. *Journal of Criminal Justice Education*, 21(3), 332–347.

Cullen, F. T., & Agnew, R. (2006) *Criminological theory past to present*, 3rd edition. Los Angeles, CA: Roxbury Publishing Company.

Currie, E. (1985) *Confronting crime: An American challenge*. New York: Pantheon Books.

Dilulio, J. J. (1992) *No escape: The future of American corrections*. Philadepia, PA: Basic Books.

Duarte, J. L., Crawford, J. T., Stern, C., Haidt, J., Jussim, L., & Tetlock, P. E. (2014) Political diversity will improve social psychological science. *Behavioral and Brain Sciences*, July, 1–54. Retrieved from https://journals.cambridge.org/images/fileUpload/documents/Duarte-Haidt_BBS-D-14-00108_preprint.pdf.

Eggebeen, D. J. (2012) What can we learn from studies of children rasied by gay or lesbian parents? *Social Science Research*, 41(4), 775–778.

Gauchat, G. (2012) Politicization of science in the public sphere: A study of public trust in the United States, 1974 to 2010. *American Sociological Review*, 77(2), 167–187.

Gramsci, A. (1971) *Selections from the prison notebooks of Antonio Gramsci*, ed. and trans. by Q. Hoare & G. Nowell-Smith. New York: International Publishers.

Graves, J. (2001) *The emperor's new clothes: Biological theories of race at the millennium*. New Brunswick, NJ: Rutgers University Press.

Gross, N., & Simmons, S. (2007) The social and political views of American professors. Working Paper, Department of Sociology, Harvard University.

Haidt, J. (2011a) Haidt requests apology from Pigliucci. *Your Morals Blog*, February 13. Retrieved from www.yourmorals.org/blog/2011/02/haidt-requests-apology-from-pigliucci/.

Haidt, J. (2011b) Discrimination hurts real people. *Your Morals Blog*, February 17. Retrieved from www.yourmorals.org/blog/2011/02/discrimination-hurts-real-people/.

Haidt, J. (2011c) The bright future of post-partisan social psychology. Talk given at the annual meeting of the Society for Personality and Social Psychology, San Antonio, TX. Retrieved from http://people.virginia.edu/~jdh6n/postpartisan.html.

Haidt, J. (2012) *The righteous mind: Why good people are divided by politics and religion*. New York: Vintage Books.

Horowitz, D. (1993) Democracy in divided societies. *Journal of Democracy*, 4(4), 18–38.

Horowitz, I. L. (1992) The decomposition of sociology. *Academic Questions*, 5(3), 32–40.

Inbar, Y., & Lammers, J. (2012) Political diversity in social and personality psychology. *Perspectives on Psychological Science*, 7, 496–503.

Kahan, D. (2013) Some data on education, religiosity, ideology, and science comprehension. *The Cultural Cognition Project at Yale Law School*, October 15. Retrieved from www.culturalcognition.net/blog/2013/10/15/some-data-on-education-religiosity-ideology-and-science-comp.html?lastPage=true&postSubmitted=true.

Kahan, D. M., Peters, E., Wittlin, M., Slovic, P., Ouellette, L. L., Braman, D., & Mandel, G. (2012) The polarizing impact of science literacy and numeracy on perceived climate change risks. *Nature Climate Change*, 2, 732–735.

Kania, R. E. (1988) Conservative ideology in criminology and criminal justice. *American Journal of Criminal Justice*, 8(1), 74–96.

Kleck, G. (2005) *Point blank: Guns and violence in America*. New Brunswick, NJ: Aldine Transaction.

Klein, D. B., & Stern, C. (2003) How politically diverse are the social sciences and humanities? Survey evidence from six fields. *Academic Questions*, 18(1), 40–52.

Klein, D. B., & Stern, C. (2005) Professors and their politics: The policy views of social scientists. *Critical Review*, 17(3/4), 257–303.

Klein, D. B., & Stern, C. (2009) By the numbers: The ideological profile of professors. In R. Maranto, R. E. Redding, & F. M. Hess (eds), *The politically correct university: Problems, scope, and reforms.* Washington, DC: AEI Press, pp. 15–37.

Konnikova, M. (2014) Is social psychology biased against Republicans? *The New Yorker*, October 30. Retrieved from www.newyorker.com/science/maria-konnikova/social-psychology-biased-Republicans.

LaCour, M. J., & Green, D. P. (2014) When contact changes minds: An experiment on transmission of support for gay equality. *Science*, 346(6215), 1366–1369.

Levitt, S. D. (1996) The effect of prison population size on crime rates: Evidence from prison over-crowding legislation. *Quarterly Journal of Economics*, 111(2), 319–352.

Light, P. C. (2003) *Fact sheet on the new true size of government.* New York: Brookings Institution.

Lipset, S. M. (1972) The politics of American sociologists. *American Journal of Sociology*, 78 (July), 67–104.

Lipset, S. M. (1982) The academic mind at the top: The political behavior and values of faculty elites. *Public Opinion Quarterly*, 46(2), 143–168.

Lipset, S. M. (1994) The state of American sociology. *Sociological Forum*, 9(2), 199–220.

Lodge, M., & Taber, C. S. (2013) *The rationalizing voter.* New York: Cambridge University Press.

Lord, J. T., & Sanderson, S. K. (1999) Current theoretical and political perspectives of western sociological theorists. *The American Sociologist*, 30(3), 42–66.

Marks, L. (2012) Same-sex parenting and children's outcomes: A closer examination of the American Psychological Association's brief on lesbian and gay parenting. *Social Science Research*, 41, 735–751.

McArdle, M. (2011) What does bias look like? *The Atlantic*, February 14. Retrieved from www.theatlantic.com/national/archive/2011/02/what-does-bias-look-like/71153/.

McCook, A. (2015) Science retracts troubled gay canvassing study against LaCour's objections. *Retraction Watch*, May 28. Retrieved from http://retractionwatch.com/2015/05/28/science-retracts-troubled-gay-canvassing-study-against-lacours-objections/.

Miller, J. (1997) *Beyond the bare numbers, search and destroy: African-American males in the criminal justice system.* New York: Cambridge University Press.

Nisbet, E. C., & Garrett, R. K. (2015) Biased interpretations of science? Liberals do it, too. *The Washington Post*, February 26. Retrieved from www.washingtonpost.com/blogs/monkey-cage/wp/2015/02/26/biased-interpretations-of-science-liberals-do-it-too/.

Nisbet, E. C., Cooper, K. E., & Garrett, R. K. (2015) The partisan brain: How dissonant science messages lead conservatives and liberals to (dis)trust science. *The ANNALS of the American Academy of Political and Social Science*, 658(1), 36–66.

Parker, C. S., & Barreto, M. A. (2013) *Change they can't believe in: The Tea Party and reactionary politics in America.* Princeton, NJ: Princeton University Press.

Patterson, C. J. (2005) Lesbian and gay parents and their children: Summary of research findings. *American Psychological Association: Lesbian and Gay Parenting.* Retrieved from www.apa.org/pi/lgbt/resources/parenting-full.pdf.

Regnerus, M. (2012) How different are the adult children of parents who have same-sex relationships? Findings from the New Family Structures Study. *Social Science Research*, 41(4), 752–770.

Ren, L., Zhao, J., & Lovrich, N. P. (2008) Liberal versus conservative public policies on crime: What was the comparative track record during the 1990s? *Journal of Criminal Justice*, 36(4), 316–325.

Rothman, S., & Lichter, S. R. (2009) The vanishing conservative: Is there a glass ceiling? In R. Maranto, R. E. Redding, & F. M. Hess (eds), *The politically correct university: Problems, scope, and reforms.* Washington, DC: AEI Press, pp. 60–76.

Ryan, J. (2013) Prof. Christopher Parker of the University of Washington takes questions on race, and the Tea Party. *Campus Reform*, December 5. Retrieved from www.campusreform.org/?ID=5289.

Sanderson, S. K., & Ellis, L. (1992) Theoretical and political perspectives of American sociologists in the 1990s. *The American Sociologist*, 23(2), 26–42.

Schuessler, J. (2012) Academia occupied by Occupy. *The New York Times*, April 30. Retrieved from www.nytimes.com/2012/05/01/books/academia-becomes-occupied-with-occupy-movement.html?_r=0.

Sesardic, N. (2010). Race: A social destruction of a biological concept. *Biology & Philosophy*, 25(2), 143–162.

Simon, J. (2007) *Governing through crime: How the war on crime transformed American democracy and created a culture of fear.* New York: Oxford University Press.

Spelman, W. (2000) What recent studies do (and don't) tell us about imprisonment and crime. *Crime and Justice*, 27, 419–494.

Spelman, W. (2009) Crime, cash, and limited options: Explaining the prison boom. *Criminology & Public Policy*, 8(1), 29–77.

Sullins, D. P. (2015) Emotional problems among children with same-sex parents: difference by definition. *British Journal of Education, Society and Behavioural Science*, 7(2), 99–120.

Tonry, M. (1996) *Sentencing matters*. New York: Oxford University Press.

Tonry, M. (2012) *Punishing race: A continuing American dilemma*. New York: Oxford University Press.

Wade, N. (2015) *A troublesome inheritance: Genes, race, and human history*. New York: Penguin Books.

Wilson, J. Q. (1985) The rediscovery of character: Private virtue and public policy. *The Public Interest*, 81, 3–16.

3

WHAT IS CONSERVATISM?

Power concedes nothing without a demand. It never did and it never will. Find out just what any people will quietly submit to and you have found out the exact measure of injustice and wrong which will be imposed upon them, and these will continue till they are resisted with either words or blows, or with both. The limits of tyrants are prescribed by the endurance of those whom they oppress.

Frederick Douglas

Conservatism emerged out of man's experiences with various forms of government, it emerged out of a process of trial and error that has occurred over thousands of years, and it emerged out of the recognition that government could help reduce human suffering, or conversely, that government could be the cause of human suffering. Conservatism reflects the accumulated knowledge of generations, a knowledge born from the experiences of men and women who suffered from the tyranny of emperors and kings and the excesses of revolution and who witnessed the physical and spiritual genocide that was tribalism, Nazism, Communism, and Marxism. That said, it is difficult to describe exactly what constitutes "conservatism." As Kirk (1954) aptly notes, conservatism is as much a state of mind as it is a political orientation. It is a philosophy about social change as much as it is a unifying political ideology. Nonetheless, we will endeavor to provide an adequate description and explanation of conservative doctrine.

Before we do, however, it is important to note that conservatism is not a monolithic, uniform ideology—that is, there are many strains of conservative thought and theory. There are conservatives who emphasize moral and religious ideals, frequently labeled Christian Conservatives or as Cultural Conservatives. What these conservatives share is a belief that American culture thrives, in part, because of the value it places on religious liberty, religious beliefs and what they see as uniquely American values that emanate largely from Christian ethics. There are Neo-Conservatives who believe that America should take an active role in promoting democracy across the globe, and there are Libertarians who emphasize the link between free markets, individual choices, and social freedoms. There are also what we call Classical Conservatives, whose beliefs mirror those of early classical liberals—the belief in law, individuality, personal responsibility, ordered liberty, and rights to private property. Far from being a uniform political ideology, or dogma, conservatism has many threads that form the core of what it means to be "conservative."

To the uninitiated, however, conservatism is defined solely by advocacy of certain policies, such as religious liberty, and resistance against other policies, such as gun control. Indeed, when liberals typically define conservatives, they usually do so in reference to public policy differences. This viewpoint, however, misses the depth of conservative political philosophy and entirely ignores what motivates conservatives to support certain policies. Why, after all, would some conservatives not favor a minimum wage, why would they want to restrict abortion, and what would motivate conservatives to desire a system of government that is limited in scope? Do conservatives, after all, hate the poor, as liberals in favor of the minimum wage often argue? Are conservatives waging a "war on women," as leftist rhetoric states? Or are there other, more principled motives at work? Below we examine the political-moral lens through which liberals and conservatives see the world. Again drawing heavily on the work of Haidt (2012), we outline the core cognitive-emotional differences in the "moral matrices" of individuals on the left and on the right. From there we then discuss the broader political philosophy of conservatism and the principles that inform conservative thinking.

The moral matrices of liberals and conservatives

The stale and largely inaccurate depictions of liberals and conservatives so prevalent in today's culture emphasize somewhat contrived stereotypes and work to emphasize in-group solidarity and out-group discrimination. Fortunately, modern science has much to tell us today about what motivates liberal and conservative viewpoints. Today, scholars understand that political views are not the product of joining a political party, nor are they the product of unbiased evaluations about public policies, nor are they produced by individuals evaluating rationally differing political philosophies. Instead, science now tells us that liberals and conservatives differ at a fundamental level and that these fundamental differences are linked to an innate evolved moral framework that is highly emotional and not entirely rational.

The connection between our morals and our politics is realized as a psychologically evolved political-moral framework that is rooted in the brain. This psychological framework serves as the lens through which individuals see, experience, and understand their social world. The lens affects us cognitively and, more importantly, emotionally. Indeed, what modern research tells us is that liberals and conservatives weigh evidence, evaluate events, support certain policies, and judge others based on emotionally charged moral sentiments. Far from being rational decisions, political-moral views and subjective evaluations are intensely emotional and because they are intensely emotional, they are not always rational.

No other scholar has done as much work to understand the motives of liberals and conservatives as Jonathan Haidt (2012). He and his team have interviewed hundreds of individuals and surveyed thousands of individuals through their website (www.yourmorals.org). Haidt's work has received substantial empirical and scholarly attention for at least two reasons: First, Haidt has addressed directly the problems associated with liberal bias in his own field, social psychology, and more broadly in the social sciences. He and his colleagues have produced dozens of empirical papers documenting the existence of bias and the various negative effects of this bias. Second, Haidt has empirically shown that the "moral minds" of liberals and conservatives are different—that is, liberals and conservatives intuitively see the world in ways that sometimes fundamentally differ. Finally, Haidt has been one of the few scholars to tackle these issues without disparaging people on the left, or as is more often the case, people on the right (Block & Block, 2006; Jost, 2006, 2008).

According to Haidt and his Moral Foundations Theory, the "righteous mind" is organized around six moral foundations:

- The "care/harm" foundation "makes us sensitive to signs of suffering and need; it makes us despise cruelty and want to care for those who are suffering (Haidt, 2012: 153). This foundation motivates us to protect children, the elderly, minority groups, animals, and the environment. It provides us with the emotional zeal to intervene in situations where we extend care to others even if doing so places our own lives at risk. This foundation also makes us more acutely aware of harm, things that may harm us, and the various manifestations of harm in a modern society.

- The fairness/cheating/reciprocity dimension reflects our desire to be treated fairly in exchange relationships and, more broadly, to see the rudimentary conditions of fairness applied equally to others. Fairness, however, is more about proportionality. It is about receiving what you have earned and about others getting what they deserve. Haidt calls this the karma foundation because it draws attention to whether exchange relationships are proportional, or conversely, whether they are seen as unfair.

- Liberty/oppression motivates people to define certain behaviors and policies as unfair infringements on their lives and their liberties. For Haidt, this dimension represents the right to be left alone and to live and work as one sees fit. However, once a behavior of policy is viewed through this moral lens as oppressive, individuals will often rise up in opposition to those engaging in the behavior or they will mobilize politically, socially, and even physically.

- Loyalty/betrayal represents our desire to be part of our in-group and to make certain that others understand that penalties for betrayal of the group will be met out. In-group loyalty causes people to extend trust and forgiveness to people within the group but it can also motivate people in the group to demonize and even subjugate people in the out-group.

- The authority/subversion dimension recognizes that humans live in social hierarchies and that these hierarchies help to keep social order and social stability. Respect for authority and respect for agents of authority, such as the police, allows for predictable and beneficial exchange relationships to emerge.

- Sanctity/degradation reflects our human capacity to attach meaning and social importance onto cultural symbols, such as the American flag, and on specified cultural behaviors, such as serving in the military. Sanctity creates the psychological motivations to protect symbols and behaviors against criticism and debasement.

Analyzing data from thousands of self-reported surveys, Haidt and his colleagues began to detect a discernable pattern associated with how liberals scored on measures of these "moral matrices" compared to how conservatives scored. For liberals, the dominant lens through which they see the world is the care/harm dimension, followed by the fairness dimension. The more liberal the survey respondent, the more likely they were to score high on these two dimensions and the lower they would score on the other dimensions. Conservatives, however, scored roughly equally on each dimension. What did this pattern mean in terms of the moral ideology of liberals and conservatives?

First, the more liberal the individual the more likely they are to view events, situations, and policies in terms of the care/harm dimension. This is why support for social welfare spending remains very high ("Partisan polarization surges," 2012) among liberals and why images of suffering, violence, and economic deprivation influence them to such an extent. Moreover, their belief in fairness is more global and applied broadly. If one sees criminal sanctions as inherently unfair and even as causing harm, then logically one would be intrinsically opposed to efforts to stiffen criminal penalties.

Second, Haidt's data clearly show that conservatives value each dimension, not just two dimensions, and they value these dimensions relatively equally. For conservatives, issues invoking a care/harm response are balanced against the other dimensions. Haidt notes that conservatives are especially prone to sacrilizing nation symbols, such as the flag, and desire a type of society where shared values form the glue to communities and to the nation. Haidt also notes that conservatives value loyalty more strongly than do liberals and value a respect for authority more than liberals do. To conservatives, loyalty and respect for authority always have to be balanced against notions of liberty, but for society to function well people have to be loyal to each other, to their families, to their employers and to their country. They also have to respect the social institutions created by a society even if they work to change those institutions. However, this respect will end if conservatives believe that individual or government action is oppressive or unfairly infringes on their liberty. For conservatives, liberty translates into freedom to live and work without undue government oversight.

We can think of any number of ways that Haidt's work is reflected in the academic malice against conservatives and how it affects social science. Recall that most academics are not just liberal but score on the far left end of the political spectrum. They are drawn from a rather distinct pool of people—people who place inordinate weight on care/harm and fairness. From their ideological-moral lens, their efforts to protect minorities, support affirmative action, reduce incarceration, promote public housing, and even control speech are justified based on their emphasis on care/harm. Because these are deeply emotional moral values, they do not fully understand why anyone else would not support these positions. The current hysteria surrounding the alleged "rape culture" on American campuses likely has its roots in views about care and harm, as did the historical denial of biology in social behavior.

Conservatives, according to Haidt, hold a strong advantage in dissecting policy issues and even in building neighborhoods and societies that are relatively fair and functional. Their weighing of varying moral dimensions brings an added complexity to understanding issues and behaviors that affect society. Societies, he notes, are not built on two moral dimensions but rather on how we understand and prioritize all moral dimensions. Take, for example, the matter of fairness. Liberals and conservatives are clearly concerned about fairness in society but they are concerned for different reasons and their concern extends to different groups. Liberals, for example, see the economic problems experienced by families as inherently unfair so they support policies aimed at addressing the harm generated from this unfairness, including harms allegedly connected to unfair economic systems, such as criminal behavior. For conservatives, however, matters of economic fairness are calibrated against other priorities, such as reciprocity, engaging in morally acceptable behavior, and adherence to prosocial cultural values. For conservatives, then, economic deprivation is causally linked to crime only when bad behavior caused both economic deprivation and crime. Discerning why people are poor thus takes on special priority with conservatives because it strikes the conservative moral matrix as unfair and potentially disastrous to reward bad behavior.

Academic reactions to the killing of Trayvon Martin by George Zimmerman, to the killing of Michael Brown by Officer Darren Wilson and the rioting that followed in Ferguson, MO, and to the Baltimore riots also highlight how different moral matrices interpret events. While there was variation in how individuals processed these events, liberals tended to support the narrative that racism was involved and that racism produced the conditions that led to the violence. It is simply remarkable that so many well-educated people so rapidly bought into what turned out to be a lie—i.e. that a white police officer executed an innocent black man in cold blood in a black neighborhood. Their singular focus on protecting minorities from harm, however, made this event not only seemingly possible but entirely likely and believable.

Conservatives were not insensitive to the possibility that an unjustified killing may have transpired across these three events. Their concern with harm was different to the concern echoed by liberals. For conservatives, police abuse and illegal behavior results in the loss of liberty and, as Haidt notes, liberty is a defining aspect of the conservative moral matrix. Police abuse is intolerable to the left and to the right but people on the right are much more likely to let the criminal justice system investigate and process these incidents because they also value our institutions of authority, such as the police, and at the same time they value reciprocity. If you attack a police officer, many conservatives would argue, serious bodily harm and even death may not only result but is likely entirely justifiable.

Lastly, the fueled rhetoric coming from the left, including our top political leaders, condemned the institution of policing as a bastion of bigotry and racism, even in Baltimore where the police department is mostly black. Police departments were accused of racial profiling, of aggressive policing, and of hammering blacks with arrests and fines simply because they were black. This was anathema to conservatives, not because conservatives are unconcerned about urban poor who also happen to be black but because they are well aware of how much crime occurs in these neighborhoods. Crime, conservatives would argue, that disproportionately harms black, urban poor. From the point of view of conservatives—who, remember, value respect for authority—the endless rhetorical and political attacks on the police could only result in more harm to those most in need of police. Predictably, the delegitimization of the police resulted in less policing and in a widespread and deadly uptick in violent crime across America. The price of this rhetoric has been paid for in blood.

Freedom and Liberty through Limited Government: Core Principles of Conservative Ideology

As a semi-organized political philosophy, conservatism can best be understood as a loosely coupled set of principles. These principles are sometimes unstated and sometimes compete for priority—even between conservatives. In turn, policies advocated by conservatives, usually but not always, flow from these core principles—a point that is often missing in broader social debates. So, what are these bedrock principles?

At its heart, conservatism is an attitude about social processes, social change, and social stability that is grounded in a set of beliefs, values, or principles. These principles establish the boundaries for what constitutes conservatism. First and foremost, the core principle of conservatism is that people should enjoy as much freedom, as much liberty, as is possible for social order to be maintained. Conservatives realize that freedom and liberty will be abused by some individuals and that occasions may arise where behaviors are so threatening to the social order that they must be curtailed to protect the rights of others. Criminal behaviors are often the types of behaviors that must be curtailed for social order to be maintained. Thus, we should recognize that conservatives actually value what has been termed "ordered liberty," or a belief that liberty should be maximized only to the point where it becomes obvious that certain liberties bring measurable harm to the social order.

Freedom and liberty from oppressive government are what conservatism holds dearest. Why? Under conservative political philosophy, individuals who are free to pursue their lives as they choose, free to speak and to debate ideas, free to protest when they believe they have been wronged, free to petition their government for grievances, free to associate with whom they desire, free to practice their religion, are individuals who will maximize their talents, who will be self-sufficient, and who will create a civil society. Through the exercise of free choice, choice unencumbered by political constraints or the mind-numbing political correctness that so characterizes our society today, people exercise their freedoms. In exercising their freedoms individuals will not only create a society that is just and civil, they will continue to foster an appreciation for the liberty and freedom other others.

An emphasis on individual liberty informs a conservative's belief about the proper role of government in a free society. To the conservative, the ultimate purpose of government is to ensure not only our national defense but also the protection of our individual freedoms and liberties. Protection of these liberties can be achieved in two ways: First, government can take active steps to protect our rights, or government action can be restrained to prevent it from infringing on our rights. For example, government has to protect your right to speak freely, to protest, and to question government officials. This is why all groups, regardless of their message, have to be given the opportunity to protest publicly. Government has to take active steps to accommodate individuals and groups so they can occupy the public square.

Second, and conversely, government can be restricted from taking steps that infringe our freedoms. This is clearly seen in our criminal justice system through the various due process protections offered to those accused of a crime. Government cannot simply accuse you of a crime, put on a sham trial, convict you and then strip you of your freedom. It has to follow certain rules—rules that sometimes severely limit its ability to prosecute and convict even obviously guilty individuals. Nonetheless, constitutional and legal restrictions placed on government and agents of government are rooted in a conservative belief that prioritizes individual liberty.

History is littered with examples where governments have curtailed the liberties of their citizens. Yet even in modern times, calls for restrictions to individual liberties remain. For example, various European governments have outlawed language they find offensive and the expression and publication of controversial ideas, and they have put people in jail for violating these laws. Countries like Canada, Britain, and France have severely curtailed the freedom of expression. Calls by government officials in the United States, mainly liberal government officials, have echoed European reform efforts. Often cloaked under the guise of "hate speech" laws or "harassment," governmental and even university officials have sought through a variety of means to limit what can be said in public and, as the examples we listed in the previous chapter highlight, to punish individuals for speech others may find offensive or hurtful. This is anathema to a conservative.

The power to control speech and thought is dangerous, has always been dangerous, and has always led to fairly awful social consequences. It doesn't matter if those who would control speech do it with the best of intentions, nor does it matter if it is accomplished through democratic action or through the narcissist actions of a petty dictator—the results are the same: a serious loss of freedom and a concomitant increase in the power of government over the lives of individuals.

Yet the impulse to control is powerful, and those who see government as an instrument to control others, even for their own good, are frequently tempted to exercise this power. Where the conservative emphasizes constraints placed on governmental power, liberals see the use of governmental power as a method to achieve a better society. Both sides are right, of course, depending on the argument, but for conservatives, many liberal actions to build a better society highlight the financial, personal, and cultural costs associated with governmental intervention. The Great Society programs enacted by President Roosevelt during the Great Depression, for example, sought to "get people back to work" and provide a "chicken in every pot." Yet the Great Society programs, economists tell us, delayed by seven years the country extricating itself from the Depression. Millions of people suffered longer than they might have done had the Great Society programs not been put in place (Cole & Ohanian,

2004). Moreover, many conservatives believe that the creation of a welfare culture, sponsored in part by Roosevelt's interventions and the ascendency of Progressivism in the 1960s, emerged and wreaked havoc on many families and their communities.

Restrictions on government action—what conservatives sometimes mean when they talk about "small government"—are also justified philosophically because in the equation of power, conservatism prioritizes the individual over the government and also the individual over whatever demographic group that individual may belong to. Conservatives, for example, place their faith in a belief that individuals will typically make good decisions about what is in their long-term best interest. Individuals know better about the circumstances of their lives, their motives, and their talents than do nameless bureaucrats. While some individuals will make uninformed or bad decisions, most will not. Even for those who make bad choices, however, the consequences that accrue through the unfolding of life are viewed as valuable teachers.

One byproduct of liberty is tragedy. You cannot have a society that values freedom and not have someone in that society abuse their freedom. Conservatives accept tragedy as an unfortunate byproduct of living in a free society, a society where the constraints on individual behavior and choice are limited. What, then, is an appropriate response when tragedy happens—that is, a response based on conservative principles of freedom, liberty, and limited government intrusion? These, of course, are questions people face every day. However, a conservative approach to tragedy values deliberative, judicial, and constrained responses to situations where tragedy may have occurred. Let's take, for instance, the issue of gun control.

Whenever a shooting occurs, especially if those harmed are famous or politicians, liberals rush to place more limitations on the sale, possession, and use of firearms. Some go as far as to push for absolute bans. In the 1990s, for example, the Clinton administration passed the "Assault Weapons Ban." The ban forbade the importation, sale, and distribution of weapons the government classified as assault weapons. The argument was straightforward: assault weapons kill too many people, are used in crime, and have no sporting value. Clinton famously quipped that you cannot hunt deer with an assault weapon.

Because liberals are strongly motivated by the suffering of others (Haidt, 2012), they tend to have highly visceral and emotional responses to tragedies. Indeed, many leftists view tragic events as unnecessary and controllable, and they frequently see tragedy as a political opportunity to restructure the country. If only, they typically argue, appropriate laws could be passed, tragic events wouldn't happen and people would be spared further grief and hardship. It is difficult to argue with the emotional sentiment to curb the afflictions people face, but sometimes the cure for the affliction comes with a series of costs—costs that may be worse than the supposed cure.

Applied to gun control, conservatives do not favor mentally ill people, people with violence in their past, or other high-risk individuals purchasing weapons. However, conservatism values elements of our uniquely American culture, and one element is the right of individuals to purchase and use firearms. It is a liberty that our Founding Fathers valued and a liberty that has helped to forge our national identity. Conservatives thus value the right to bear arms while recognizing that it will sometimes result in tragedy. A greater tragedy, however, would be if the apparatus of government power was used to overturn one of our prized rights. The typical conservative response to such events is to reaffirm the rights of free men, limit the ability of those who would expand government to accommodate their desire to suppress our rights, and hold accountable the individual(s) directly responsible for the tragedy. Tragedies always provide the impulse to expand government control. As Rham Emanuel, President Obama's chief of staff notoriously commented, "You never let a serious crisis go to waste.

And what I mean by that it's an opportunity to do things you think you could not do before." Such impulses are, again, anathema to conservatism.

Natural Law and Morality

Juxtaposed against an emphasis on freedom and individual liberty is the conservative belief in natural, moral limits to behavior. Undoubtedly, some will take umbrage at our characterization of conservatism—especially a conservatism that protects individual rights. They will, for example, point out that most conservatives oppose abortion—what they term a "woman's right to choose." To be certain, modern conceptions of conservative thought can be inconsistent, yet what they tend to share is a belief in an enduring moral order—an order that emanates from a power greater than ourselves. Some conservatives locate moral order in religious doctrine, while others see it as an inescapable force that governs, or should govern, human interactions. The "Golden Rule" illustrates well the conservative belief in an enduring moral order. It is against this backdrop, against a belief that some behaviors are so morally offensive that the state has the obligation to either heavily regulate the practice or to prohibit the behavior entirely, that ideological inconsistencies can appear. For a conservative, however, abortion represents a behavior that results in the death of another human being and thus is grounds for state intervention.

Perhaps this is a point that needs further explanation, if for no other reason than the fact that conservative belief in an enduring moral order has been under attack since at least the 1960s when human relativism and secularism found favor. While it is true that many conservatives locate morality in a divine presence—that is, in religious convictions about what constitutes "right" and "wrong" action—it is equally true that conservatives also argue that certain actions are morally wrong because of the harm they bring to others. Hence, secularist conservatives who have only weak ties to established religion also believe that wisdom about what constitutes moral and immoral action can be learned from our history. Take, for example, adultery. The three main world religions view adultery as a sin, or as an offense to God. Strong moral proscriptions accompany the act of adultery, including shaming, excommunication, and even death in some Islamist countries. But could there be another, less divine, reason why adultery was considered so socially harmful that it was elevated to the level of sin?

The answer, of course, is yes. In emerging civilizations, adultery created any number of social problems. Questions about paternity, for example, may have reduced the survival chances of offspring from adulterous relationships. Not certain if a child was actually his, a male may have simply abandoned both female and child. Moreover, male sexual jealousy undoubtedly caused serious social rifts in small communities—just as it does today (Daly, Wilson & Weghorst, 1982; Nisbet, 2010). These rifts would sometimes turn violent and result in murder, much like today. The point is, conservatives generally believe that morality, if not emanating from Divine Providence, certainly reflects the effective problem-solving of prior generations.

Conservatives also like to point out that men and women with principled convictions about justice, freedom, and respect will form a productive and moral society. When men and women, for example, believe that working is better than not working, when they believe that individual initiative is better than relying on the initiative of others, when they believe that self-control and sacrifice are better than hedonism, they will create the social conditions that will benefit the majority of people. To a conservative, then, a moral order, often, but not always, grounded in religious tradition, best serves the broad swathe of any society.

No other area of conservative doctrine has been subject to more venomous attack than the conservative belief in morality. Liberal attacks frequently portray conservative views of morality as dangerous, benefiting "old, white men," or socially repressive. They argue, sometimes very effectively, that morality unfairly infringes on individual choices and government action and that a focus on morality ignores social structures that produce inequality.

We do not deny that certain moral proscriptions have changed or that some moral proscriptions imposed a cost on some individuals and groups. While true, it does not logically follow that *all* moral proscriptions produced inequality or were unfair. Thus the wholesale attack on traditional moral values—values that have been proven to produce stable, orderly, and just societies—has been motivated by passion and the liberal desire to free individuals from any externally imposed constraint.

Conservatives generally think this is dangerous. When individuals are no longer constrained by considerations of what constitutes "good," "right," or "moral" action they are free not only to engage in harmful and personally destructive behavior but also to believe that their views are on a par with anyone else's. G. K. Chesterton summed this up nicely when he wrote, "When people stop believing in God, they won't believe in nothing—they will believe anything" (American Chesterton Society, 2014). And this is the seduction—the belief that there is no such thing as an ultimate moral authority or that morality is, in fact, immoral. It is the rejection of any moral, ethical system that allows or encourages behavior that is damaging to self or to others, and it is the rejection of morality that allows for a decay in culture, the rise of a narcissistic self-interest, and the exploitation of individuals (Bork, 2003). Moreover, when governmental power is used without regard to fundamental moral limitations and prescriptions, it is open to abuse. It is morality, our shared belief in "right" and "wrong," that binds us together, that allows us to trust that others will not hurt us, and that calls us to charity, understanding, and good will.

But doesn't recognition of a moral order automatically mean that conservatives violate their beliefs by having government enforce moral values? Let's be clear, no conservative we know is talking about forcing people to attend church. Instead, they see issues such as abortion and euthanasia as areas in need of control because they lead to tragic moral consequences. Honest people disagree about these issues but from a conservative point of view: these issues strike at the heart about what it means to live in a moral society. A moral society will stop and ask, "Is this right action?" The answer may be "yes," or "yes, but with conditions." But as Goldberg (2009) notes, a society that doesn't take the time to debate whether behaviors like abortion and euthanasia are moral or just, or under what conditions they are moral and just, is also a society that welcomes the potential of genocide. Liberals who reduce abortion to a mere "medical procedure," for instance, ignore the obvious moral ramifications of terminating life and they also ignore the science on human fetal development. Abortion and euthanasia are, at one level, medical procedures, but then again, under this line of reasoning, so too is capital punishment through lethal injection.

Suppose, for the sake of argument, research finds that crime is genetically caused and that we locate the genes for crime. Suppose, too, that research finds that parents have no influence on their child's behavior. What should we do with this knowledge, if anything? One obvious policy recommendation would be to mandate that fetuses be tested for the crime genes and automatically aborted if they are found to be the unlucky recipients of these genes. Would society be justified in imposing this measure on unwilling mothers and fathers? Moreover, if parents have no measured influence on their child's development, wouldn't it make sense to raise children in government-sponsored orphanages where they could all benefit equally from society's resources? It may surprise some to find that the United States, and much of Europe, engaged in these actions at the turn of the nineteenth century.

Known as the eugenics movement, various interest groups were successful in passing legislation that forced the sterilization of "unfit" women and that forced the removal of children from homes of low-functioning families. Also surprising to many is the fact that the eugenics movement was created by social progressives. We will discuss this movement in more detail later, but we note here that one of the reasons why liberals were successful in creating the eugenics movement was because they believed they could socially engineer a better society. If they could control the apparatus of human reproduction and socialization, they reasoned, they could reduce overall human suffering (Rafter, 1998). One of the morals of the eugenics story, no pun intended, is that just because we can engage in a behavior that may benefit society doesn't mean that we should engage in that behavior. Theoretically, we could today forcibly sterilize individual women—all that is needed is for laws to be passed outlining who, when, and how. We could also, again theoretically, forcibly remove illegal aliens from U.S. soil, re-impose slavery, and make it illegal for women to be educated and employed. It is shockingly easy to justify these actions based on some version of "social good," but that doesn't mean these actions are moral. In this sense it is our moral values that prevent us from engaging in this conduct and it is our moral values that are the building blocks for a civil society.

Human Fallibility, Stability, and Tradition

Trust in history as a teacher also serves as a fundamental guide to conservatives. Conservatives believe that social customs and conventions, what some call rituals, give people in a society meaning and shared identity. They allow people to coexist without violent conflict because they share beliefs and habits. Customs, like the rule of law, allow for the creation of precedence to guide future behavior. Precedence encourages inter-generational continuity, which the conservative values. Indeed, the point about conserving the best a society has to offer is meaningless unless what is conserved allows for stability in social order across time. Kirk (1954) relatedly notes that prescription and prudence should serve to temper impulses towards rapid social change. By this he means that modern humans should take seriously the wisdom passed down by prior generations and that we should value long-term continuity over rapid short-term change.

Conservatism recognizes that societies change and that sometimes change must occur if people are to enjoy freedom and liberty. What the conservative rejects is radicalized change, change for the sake of change, or change that limits the rights and freedoms of individuals. Writing in reaction to the French Revolution, Sir Edmund Burke, who many call the father of conservatism, made it clear that the excesses of revolution were to be avoided unless a country is at risk of falling into anarchy. Recall that the French Revolution, which ended (literally) the French monarchy, denigrated into blood lust that saw the execution of almost 40,000 people; another 10,000 to 20,000 died in jail. The Revolution also plunged the country into almost perpetual warfare, called the Napoleonic Wars, that cost millions of lives throughout Europe—in the Vendée revolt alone over 100,000 people died (Goldberg, 2009). Radical revolution led to the "Reign of Terror" that decimated much of Europe.

To Burke and other conservatives, planned changes to a society should be deliberative, thoughtful, and incremental lest they reduce or eliminate custom, convention, and precedence. Revolutions across the world, from the Communist Revolution in China to the Bolshevik Revolution in Russia, show us what can happen when women and men are swept away from convention and precedence by the emotional appeal of tyrants. Wars are started, families perish, people are enslaved, and great societies fall.

Human beings are social animals. We have a mix of complex appetites, yearnings, and desires. Left unchecked, these all too human characteristics can lead to dangerous, even fatal, results. This is part of the reason why many conservatives believe that man is naturally fallible, or imperfect. Our emotions are powerful and are not always offset by our ability to reason. As Rossiter (1955) notes, human reasoning independent of tradition is unreliable. But the conservative belief about the nature of man is even more fundamental: It is not just that we are imperfect, but that we are imperfectible. Human passions, biases, bigotries, and hatreds are interwoven into the human condition and nothing can permanently erase these harmful features. This assumption about the nature of man, an assumption well supported by endless historical examples of horrific human behavior, tempers conservative enthusiasm for efforts to socially engineer a good society. It also represents a major departing point between progressives and conservatives, as progressives assume that bad actions are the end result of bad social conditions. Herbert Croly, in *The Promise of American Life* (1909), epitomizes progressive thinking:

> Democracy must stand or fall on a platform of possible human perfectibility. If human nature cannot be improved by institutions, democracy is at best a more than usually safe form of political organization … . But if it is to work better as well as merely longer, it must have some leavening effect on human nature; and the sincere democrat is obliged to assume the power of the leaven.

For the conservative, bad actions are the natural product of hedonistic impulses, lack of character, or lack of self-control. This is why, too, laws are needed to govern human interactions, why contracts that spell out legal rights and duties are necessary, and it is why punishment for violating rules must exist. Humans free to pursue any course of action will, as history has taught us, sometimes wreak havoc.

Conservatism also recognizes natural differences that exist between individuals and groups of individuals. These differences not only characterize individuals and groups, they also predict why some are successful and some are not. Some individuals have outstanding athletic talents, others are musically inclined, while others are naturally more intelligent. Some people work hard, sacrifice for the future, and avoid engaging in immoral and/or illegal action. Since there are people at the top end of the distribution of human talents and abilities, there must be people at the bottom. While most readily agree that some individuals are better dancers, or better businessmen, or better teachers than others, we are today reluctant to draw attention to the fact that there are also individuals who refuse to work, who refuse to sacrifice, and who refuse to behave in ways that are productive. In this sense, conservatism respects individual differences and diversity, and it sees nothing wrong with the talents, efforts, and sacrifices of people being rewarded. Conversely, it sees as moral and just the withholding of social rewards and resources for those who refuse to play by the rules.

This is part of the reason that conservatism is uncomfortable with forced egalitarianism or the notion that "we are all the same." While politically popular, such notions fly in the face of reality. More importantly, forced "sameness" does not benefit society largely because it makes equivocal the life-long actions of moral and responsible individuals to those who have pursued courses of action that have been devastating to self or others. Conservatism thus prioritizes meritocracy over egalitarianism, largely because conservative doctrine places an emphasis on individual, and not collective, responsibility. Conservatism respects human difference, maintains that individuals who engage in proper and moral conduct should have access to the social and political resources of a society, and thus does not try to create situations or policies that force faux equality. Indeed, there are few things that conservatism rebels against more than forced equality. Forced equality is not consistent with freedom and liberty and invites the use of government power into the lives of individuals and businesses.

Conservatism also emphasizes voluntary community participation, as opposed to involuntary collectivism. Strong, functional communities are important to conservatives and liberals alike. Where the two differ is that conservatives believe that individuals should not be compelled through force or fear of force to join communities or organizations which they may disagree with. Just as conservatives would never argue that people should be forced to join the National Rifle Association (NRA), they also argue that individuals should not be forced to join labor unions, churches, or any other organization. This issue, however, is broader than emphasizing voluntary participation. Conservatives distrust many, but not all, collectivist notions because they substitute the power of government for the wisdom of the individual. This is why populist movements, socialism, and other political efforts to pigeonhole individual differences into egalitarian-based notions of "fairness" rile conservatives.

Along these lines, conservatism recognizes that a balance has to exist between the rights of individuals to be free to pursue the course of their own lives and the responsibilities individuals must shoulder for their conduct. Liberals tend to emphasize "rights-based" approaches, while de-emphasizing the social responsibilities of people. To be certain, liberals and conservatives in America value individual rights, but the focus on individual rights to the exclusion of individual responsibility has created a culture of entitlement, at least according to conservatives (Eberstadt, 2012; Lasch, 1991; Twenge & Campbell, 2009). The entitlement culture, readily visible on college campuses and in faculty ranks within universities, elevates human desires, expectations, and even greed without an equal awareness of the responsibilities owed. Research by psychologist Jean Twenge, for example, has readily documented the rise in narcissism amongst youth and young adults (Twenge & Campbell, 2009). Using data from the American Freshman Survey, she and her colleagues have found a steady increase in the number of youth who view their intellectual and work abilities as above average—although youth today also report spending significantly less time working and studying.

A conservative framework recognizes that individuals not only have rights guaranteed to them by law and by God but also have responsibilities that emerge as part of the social contract. During times of national emergency, for example, individuals old enough to join in armed conflict are expected to assist, for no other reason than the responsibilities of citizenship enjoin them to protect our way of life. During times of war and peace, individuals have a moral and legal responsibility to obey the law, and if they disagree with the law, they have an obligation to change it using our current institutions. Fathers and mothers, who enjoy unlimited rights to produce children, have a moral and legal obligation to provide for their offspring. And individuals on public welfare have obligations to the taxpayers who provide them with their sustenance. Our rights define the limits to what our government can do to us, but upholding our responsibilities defines our character.

Conservatism thus values tradition and social stability, it values ordered and deliberative change, it values an agreed-upon moral order, it values individual liberty and freedom over government control, it values rights and responsibilities, it values free markets and private property, and it values individual differences and true diversity. In contemporary language, conservatism champions limited governmental, individual liberty, and free and open markets.

Conservatism and Crime

So how does conservatism understand crime? First of all, conservatism values functional and safe communities, communities where people can form bonds, worship together, engage in exchange relationships, and pursue recreation. Conservatism also values communities where individuals, children, and families are safe from criminal victimization. Because of this, conservatism views crime primarily as a threat to social order. All social exchanges require order, or trust, to be functional. When trust and order erode or break down, people are less likely to engage in behaviors that make communities thrive. Without order, there can be no trust, and without trust, communities de-evolve. This is also why conservatives view criminal behavior as a threat to freedom and liberty. People cannot be free or pursue their lives on their own accord if they live in fear of being criminally victimized. They cannot engage in commerce, establish businesses, employ people, invest capital, or even present goods for sale when they are afraid of being victimized.

Second, crime is also viewed by conservatives as a deeply moral issue. Almost all world religions classify some behaviors, such as rape, child molestation, and murder, as sin. Conservatives and leftists fundamentally differ in this understanding. Conservatives tend to view people who commit rape, robbery, and premeditated homicide as immoral and worthy of condemnation. They see these actions as emanating from deep-seated and destructive character flaws. In the conservative mindset, there may be no daylight between the criminal behavior of the individual and their moral standing or worth. In short, a single act of child molestation or a single act of deliberate murder may be enough to qualify the individual as immoral.

Not so with leftists, who are often hesitant to morally condemn the behavior of individuals (white-collar offenders are, however, the exception). They tend to see grievous behaviors as somehow apart from the individual who committed the behavior, and they tend to want to highlight the "humanity" of individuals who have engaged in scurrilous and destructive conduct. A single act of child molestation or deliberate murder, the leftist would argue, must be balanced against all the other, possibly positive, behaviors the individual has engaged in.

Third, conservatism views criminal behavior through the same lens as it views any other behavior—that is, as the product of reasoned and deliberative choices made by individuals. Unfortunately, most criminologists confuse issues of "free will" with the underlying ability of all normally functioning humans to exercise choice. Free will reflects a philosophical paradigm that states, essentially, that human beings have an innate capacity to choose between any set of possible choices. Thomas Hobbes and David Hume, philosophers in the Western tradition, saw a connection between the idea of free will and that of moral accountability. Because behavior is the product of choice, and because behavior is under the control of the individual, it stands that some individuals will freely engage in immoral (criminal) behavior. Unlike leftists, conservatives do not argue that criminal behavior has to be wholly rational, nor do they argue that it has to be the product of an infallible hedonistic calculus for individual choices to still be relevant. Choice drives all human conduct. Why would criminal behavior be any different?

Much of criminology borders on a form of environmental determinism (Walsh, 2009). Consistent with a liberal or radical orthodoxy, the majority of criminological theories isolate the "causes" of crime in the environment, not within the individual. These causes are said to be "exogenous," or external to the actor. Because, the reasoning goes, factors outside the control of the individual propel them to engage in criminal behavior, free will and choice become mostly irrelevant. Indeed, criminologists, especially sociologically trained criminologists, continually try to locate the causes of crime in the environment. The "environment," however, is usually so broadly defined that it can mean just about anything. For example, it can be anything from someone's career (Hagan, 1989), to their family (Glueck et al., 1962), to their neighborhood (Ellen & Turner, 1997), or it can be even more broadly defined to mean "the economy" or "culture." The point is, most criminological theories either ignore the role of choice in crime causation, or they so qualify what constitutes choice that it becomes meaningless.

Fourth, conservatism argues that state intervention is warranted to achieve the simultaneous goals of public safety, social justice, and retribution. One of the critiques of conservatism is that it supports limited governmental intrusion into the lives of citizens, except as this intrusion relates to the criminal justice system. Indeed, our colleagues constantly tell us that support for public education, roads, parks, air traffic control, product safety, and other byproducts of our current system of governance offer ample evidence that the idea of limited government is misguided. This is, or course, a red herring. Limited government does not mean "no" government. And in the area of criminal justice, it is the government, and the government alone, that can and should exact justice.

Differences along these lines between leftists and conservatives are sometimes slight and on occasion glaring. Leftists and conservatives, for example, generally believe that retribution should be part of the philosophy of criminal justice. Crime, in a retributive sense, represents cheating, or the gaining of an unfair advantage over another. Retribution thus seeks to reduce the illegal gains or advantages enjoyed by the offender. Moreover, retribution also represents the moral enforcement of society's laws, customs, and mores. Although data are difficult to come by, it is likely safe to say that most political ideologies favor retribution as a guiding criminal justice philosophy, although there is also likely variance in this belief.

Public safety is another area where liberals and conservatives overlap in their support. Few leftists desire dangerous, predatory individuals to be free in society. Where the political orientations diverge is in what they see as predatory and dangerous. Liberals, for example, tend to argue that non-violent crime is less dangerous and less harmful than violent crime— unless, again, the crime is committed by a white-collar offender. Hence, they tend to view individual crimes like drug dealing, burglary, and auto-theft as less than dangerous, and by extension they view the people who commit these crimes as comparatively less dangerous. Conservatives, however, understand these behaviors as part of a broader context that includes not only the direct threat these crimes pose to individual victims but also the threat they pose to the normative functioning of families, neighborhoods, and communities. Conservatives also point out that a large volume of evidence shows that criminals commit a broad range of illegal and imprudent behaviors (Hirschi & Gottfredson, 1994). They may commit auto-theft one day, physically assault someone the next day, and commit forgery the day following. What they leave in their wake are individuals victimized by their actions, neighborhoods that are less safe for the people who live in them, and a loss of social trust and cohesion. Because of this, conservatives usually fall on the side of public safety. They do this not always because they see the individual as pathological, evil, or immoral, although they sometimes do, but also because they see the primary duty of government to be the maintenance of social order and the facilitation of functional communities.

Maintaining public order and safety is frequently criticized by liberals and by liberal criminologists so we will take a little extra time to explain what we mean. Liberals tend to see the maintenance of public order and prioritizing public safety as an act of state-sponsored oppression (Deutsch, 2005; Potter, 2015; Rev. Rebecca, n.d.). And in the United States they tend to tie the specter of racial animus to order maintenance ("Police violence," 2014; "The oppression," n.d.; Vysotsky, 2015). At one level, too vigorous an emphasis on public order and safety can result in oppression. Yet maintaining public order is much more than simply arresting criminals and it is far more important than liberals see or wish to admit.

We believe much of the liberal reluctance to prioritize social order and public safety exists because liberals are loath to admit that an antisocial culture exists in certain cities and neighborhoods. Crime, drug use and abuse, broken and dysfunctional families, and welfare dependency characterize many of these communities, and the culture that emanates from these communities provides the intellectual justifications for engaging in many forms of repugnant behavior. Men father numerous children and then abandon them, women are almost as violent as the men, and traditional values of education, hard work, self-sacrifice, and self-control are turned upside down. As any honest person will tell you, especially those who have seen at first hand the ravages of antisocial culture, antisocial culture is ugly and dehumanizing. However, admitting to the existence of an antisocial culture would violate one of liberalism's most valued creeds—that all cultures are the same and all have value. Doing so could also have practical political consequences, they argue, such as reducing public support for welfare programs, work programs, and other "investments" in these areas.

Lest the reader believe we are speaking only of inner-city America where many blacks are concentrated, the same cultural milieu has been observed in England. Theodore Dalrymple, the pen name of English psychiatrist Anthony Daniels, has written extensively about "life at the bottom" of English society. Drawing from his work inside English prisons and treating the medical needs of lower-class English citizens, Dalrymple (2010) notes that "English underclass life" can be characterized by "the easily inflamed ego, the quick loss of temper, the violence, the scattering of illegitimate children, the self-exculpation by use of impersonal language." Moreover, in lower-class English culture, similar to American lower-class culture, there exists "the complete absence of the idea that mental culture is a good in itself," and this "enables them to maintain the fiction that the society around them is grossly, even grotesquely, unjust, and that they themselves are the victims of this injustice." As a consequence, few aspire to improve themselves and even fewer believe that their behavior, values, and beliefs are responsible for disconnecting them from the processes that accumulate the personal and social capital necessary to live a more fulfilling life. Dalrymple's vivid descriptions of the violence, the unconstrained sexual behavior, and open rejection of authority prevalent amongst English underclass residents parallels ethnographic accounts of street crime and underclass life found in the United States (Anderson, 1999).

While attention is paid to the violence in these communities, little attention is paid to the culture that produces these various maladies. And when scholars or politicians point out the obvious ailments, the antisocial cultural beliefs, or the enormous financial costs associated with lower-class behavior, they are quickly castigated by protectors of cultural relativism—many of whom are themselves academics and criminologists. Yet it is "The combination of relativism and antipathy to traditional culture," according to Dalrymple (2010: 87):

> that has played a large part in creating the underclass, thus turning Britain from a class into a caste society. The poorest people were deprived both of a sense of cultural hierarchy and of the moral imperative to conform their conduct to any standard whatever. Henceforth what they had and what they did was as good as anything, because all cultures and all cultural artifacts are equal. Aspiration was therefore pointless: and thus they have been as immobilized in their poverty—material, mental, and spiritual—as completely as the damned in Dante's Inferno.

While some may accuse Dalrymple of hyperbole, we believe his criticism highlights the real problems that occur when an antisocial subculture is allowed to flourish. No, it is not just the violence we are discussing but the "material, mental, and spiritual" destruction that accompany any cultural beliefs that prioritize and glamorize intellectual ignorance, that elevates immoral conduct into a status system, that emphasizes taking advantage of others, and that views hard work, prudence, frugality, chastity, and individual responsibility as the province of idiots. Focusing on social order is thus not merely a repressive act of state domination, as many liberal criminologists argue, but a process that works to undermine the powerful culture messages that accompany the widespread acceptance of lower-class culture. In punishing those who violate laws, in shaming those who engage in immoral and reckless behavior, and in criticizing the destructive nature of antisocial and irresponsible behavior conservatives seek to prevent individuals from falling into the cultural trap described by Dalrymple. By depriving lower-class culture of the energy that sustains it, people will be better able to live up to their full human potential.

Finally, conservatives are often accused of advocating solely for harsh, punitive sanctions (Simon, 2007; Tonry, 2012). First, let's understand that when liberals and conservatives speak of "harsh" punishment they are concertedly speaking about incarceration. Harshness, moreover, is commonly defined as the length, in time, of incarceration. A term of five years, the reasoning goes, is harsher that a term of four years or of three years. This is the extent of harshness both groups are referring to, generally. Notice, however, that the range of possible punitive sanctions in the Western world is very limited. Western societies have outlawed torture, beating, caning, stoning, and the general infliction of physical pain. Instead, they have uniformly adopted the idea that the loss of freedom is itself punishing, and that the longer the loss of freedom, the more punishing the sentence. In this vein, liberals forget that imprisonment actually reflects substantial restraints placed on government, restraints accepted by conservatism as valid and necessary. At the same time, it is not entirely clear whether persistent offenders view incarceration as all that personally difficult, or even as very punishing.

Second, conservatives also favor intervention efforts with at-risk families, and they favor efforts to try to salvage the lives of young delinquents. They also favor efforts to reintegrate ex-offenders back into society, for no other reason than their belief that personal redemption is a transformative process that brings emotional and spiritual healing. Indeed, it has been those in faith-based movements, churches, and other religious institutions that have volunteered most frequently to work with inmates, mentor at-risk youth, and help to transform the destructive thinking and behavior of individuals captured by alcohol and drug addiction. Criminologist and evangelical Christian, Bryon Johnson, in his book *More God, Less Crime*, documented the influence of religion on motivating individuals to help with youth and criminals (2011). His book not only exposed the discrimination experienced by scholars who are religious but also examined the hundreds of studies that reveal an inverse relationship between religious belief and criminal behavior. Johnson carefully documented how conservatives such as Charles Colson, motivated by a desire to help inmates reformulate their lives, mentored parolees, men and women on probation, and youth. Thus, far from advocating only punitive responses and far from being hypocritical, conservatism differs mainly in degree rather than kind from a liberal understanding of criminal justice.

Conservatism is not rigid dogma—many blends of conservative thought fall under the umbrella of "conservatism." However, these blends of conservatism tend to share three main ingredients: First, conservatives of all stripes believe that culture matters. American culture—those beliefs, values, and morals that we share—uplifts more people when it places value on individual responsibility, when it values work and self-reliance over dependency, self-control over unadulterated hedonism, and moral action above immoral behavior. Cultural traditions, moreover, are at the heart of a "Good Society." In America, the traditions of free expression, the free practice of religion, private ownership of property, and private possession of firearms are fused to American ideals of freedom and individual liberty. Yet conservatives also warn against an American culture that is too "individualistic," too focused on rights and on materialistic goals. For conservatives, American culture is about individual rights and individual responsibilities. Businesses have an ethical responsibility, for example, to pay their employees a fair wage and to treat them with dignity. Employees have an ethical responsibility to show up to work on time and to be productive during business hours. More narrowly, parents have financial and personal responsibilities for their children and children have a responsibility to behave for their parents. Individuals, moreover, enshrined with their rights, also have an ethical responsibility to obey our laws, work to improve their material, economic, and spiritual condition, and help those in need. The point is, conservative views on American culture emphasize the union of rights and responsibilities because this union produces a society that is moral, just, compassionate, and interdependent.

Second, conservatives also share a belief that government should be as small as possible, as efficient as possible, and as effective as possible. While conservatives disagree about where to establish the boundaries of what distinguishes large from small government, most view government as necessary but also a source of potential evil. Government first serves to protect us from foreign enemies and to protect American interests abroad. Because of this, a strong national defense is necessary. How strong and how large is debatable. Also, conservatives believe that individuals should be as free from government oversight and regulation as possible. They should be free to travel from state to state, to own property, and to worship without interference. In this sense, conservatives believe that government should protect the rights of its citizens—all citizens, including the unborn. Finally, conservatives believe that it is the role of government to ensure public order and social stability by working to reduce crime, by penalizing those who violate American laws, and by protecting citizens from the ravages of unconstrained human behavior. Beyond these priorities, conservatives disagree about the proper role of government.

Finally, conservatives have a strong belief in tradition. To be a "conservative" is to desire the conservation of what makes America great—and yes, conservatives do believe that America is a great nation. What has made America great is, in part, the willingness to maintain certain traditions. The practice of celebrating Thanksgiving and Christmas, for example, helps Americans think about the blessings in their lives and provides a mechanism by which individuals can show care, compassion, and concern for others. These traditions, deeply rooted in Christianity, add to our culture and emphasize specific moral beliefs. Yet these are not the only traditions. The reliance on law to settle disputes and the value placed on marriage and child rearing are Western traditions worthy of preservation. Even so, conservatives are not opposed to changing, or even abandoning, some traditions. How a society changes, however, is a matter of dispute for conservatives. Change, conservatives argue, should be slow, deliberate, and gradual most of the time. It should be planned and not brought about by the inconsistent emotional passions of the day.

As we hope we have made clear, conservatism is not dogma. It has no set body of established rules, regulations, or even permanent beliefs. It is, instead, a way of viewing society and change and a way of viewing government and the relationship between an individual and government.

References

American Chesterton Society (2014) *When a man ceases to worship God*. Retrieved from www.chesterton. org/ceases-to-worship/.

Anderson, E. (1999) *Code of the street: Decency, violence, and the moral life of the inner city*. New York: W.W. Norton & Company.

Block, J., & Block, J. H. (2006) Nursery school personality and political orientation two decades later. *Journal of Research in Personality*, 40(5), 734–749.

Bork, R. H. (2003) *Slouching towards Gomorrah: Modern liberalism and American decline*. New York: Harper Perennial.

Cole, H. L., & Ohanian, L. E. (2004) New Deal policies and the persistence of the Great Depression: A general equilibrium analysis. *Journal of Political Economy*, 112(4), 779–816.

Croly, H. (1909) *The promise of American life*. Boston, MA: Northeastern University Press.

Dalrymple, T. (2010) *Life at the bottom: The worldview that makes the underclass*. Chicago, IL: Ivan R. Dee.

Daly, D., Wilson, M., & Weghorst, S. J. (1982) Male sexual jealousy. *Ethology and Sociobiology*, 3(1), 11–27.

Deutsch, M. (2005) Maintaining oppression. *Beyond Intractability*, March. Retrieved from www. beyondintractability.org/essay/maintaining-oppression.

Eberstadt, N. (2012) *A nation of takers: America's entitlement epidemic*. Conshohocken, PA: Templeton Press.

Ellen, I. G., & Turner, M. A. (1997) Does neighborhood matter? Assessing recent evidence. *Housing Policy Debate*, 8(4), 833–866.

Glueck, S., Glueck, E. T., & Kneznek, R. (1962) *Family environment and delinquency*. London: Routledge & Kegan Paul.

Goldberg, J. (2009) *Liberal fascism: The secret history of the American left, from Mussolini to the politics of change*. New York: Broadway Books.

Hagan, J. (1989) *Structural criminology*. New Brunswick, NJ: Rutgers University Press.

Haidt, J. (2012) *The righteous mind: Why good people are divided by politics and religion*. New York: Vintage Books.

Hirschi, T., & Gottfredson, M. R. (1994) The generality of deviance. In T. Hirschi & M. R. Gottfredson (eds), *The generality of deviance*. New Brunswick, NJ: Transaction Publishers, pp. 1–22.

Johnson, B. (2011) *More God, less crime: Why faith matters and how it can matter more*. West Coshohocken, PA: Templeton Press.

Jost, J. T. (2006) The end of the end of ideology. *American Psychologist*, 61(7), 651–670.

Jost, J. T., Nosek, B. A., & Gosling, S. D. (2008) Ideology: Its resurgence in social, personality, and political psychology. *Perspectives on Psychological Science*, 3(2), 126–136.

Kirk, R. (1954) Conservatism, liberalism, and fraternity. Speech given at the national meeting of the Chi Omega sorority, June. Reprinted with same title (1956) *Eleusis of Chi Omega*, 58, 121–130.

Lasch, C. (1991) *The culture of narcissism: American life in an age of diminishing expectations*. New York: W.W. Norton & Company, Inc.

Nisbet, R. (2010) *The quest for community: A study in the ethics for order and freedom*. Wilmington, DE: Intercollegiate Studies Institute.

Partisan polarization surges in Bush, Obama years: Trends in American values: 1987–2010 (2012) Pew Research Center, June 4. Retrieved from www.people-press.org/2012/06/04/partisan-polarization-surges-in-bush-obama-years/.

Police violence: Only tip of iceberg of racial oppression system (2014) *RT*, December 24. Retrieved from http://rt.com/op-edge/217403-police-shooting-brutality-racism-usa/.

Potter, G. (2015) Police violence, capital and neoliberalism. *Uprooting Criminology: A Reasoned Plot*, January 15. Retrieved from http://uprootingcriminology.org/essays/police-violence-capital-neoliberalism/.

Rafter, N. H. (1998) *Creating born criminals*. Champaign, IL: University of Illinois Press.

Rev. Rebecca (n.d.) *The US government's oppression of the poor, homeless, and orphaned*. Retrieved from www.franciscan-anglican.com/Homelessness.htm.

Rossiter, C. (1955) *Conservatism in America*. New York: Alfred A. Knopf.

Simon, J. (2007) *Governing through crime: How the war on crime transformed American democracy and created a culture of fear*. New York: Oxford University Press.

The oppression of black people, the crimes of this system and the revolution we need (n.d.) *Revolution*. Retrieved from http://revcom.us/a/144/BNQ-en.html.

Tonry, M. (2012) *Punishing race: A continuing American dilemma.* New York: Oxford University Press.

Twenge, J. M., & Campbell, W. K. (2009) *The narcissism epidemic: Living in the age of entitlement.* New York: Free Press.

Vysotsky, S. (2015) Baltimore beyond the riot. *Uprooting criminology: A reasoned plot,* April 29. Retrieved from http://uprootingcriminology.org/blogs/baltimore-beyond-the-riot/.

Walsh, A. (2009) *Biology and criminology: The biosocial synthesis.* New York: Routledge.

4

LIBERALS SLAYING DRAGONS

Liberals, in general, and liberal criminologists especially, love to slay dragons (Voegeli, 2012). The reference to "slaying dragons" comes from the legend of St. George. Quoting from Minogue's *The Liberal Mind* (1963: 11):

> The story of liberalism, as liberals tell it, is rather like the legend of St. George and the dragon. After many centuries of hopelessness and superstition, St. George, in the guise of Rationality, appeared in the world somewhere about the sixteenth century. The first dragons upon whom he turned his lance were those of despotic kingship and religious intolerance. These battles won, he rested a time, until such questions as slavery, or prison conditions, or the state of the poor, began to command his attention. During the nineteenth century, his lance was never still, prodding this way and that against the inert scaliness of privilege, vested interest, or patrician insolence. But, unlike St. George, he did not know when to retire. The more he succeeded, the more he became bewitched with the thought of a world free of dragons, and the less capable he became of ever returning to private life. He *needed* his dragons. He could only live by fighting for causes—the people, the poor, the exploited, the colonially oppressed, the underprivileged and the underdeveloped. As an ageing warrior, he grew breathless in his pursuit of smaller and smaller dragons—for the big dragons were now harder to come by.

At one time there were dragons to slay in the criminal justice system. Prison conditions were deplorable, the system was used to oppress certain groups, and some in law enforcement behaved as tyrants. Reforms have by and large reconciled long-standing injustices and helped to professionalize agents and institutions in the criminal justice system. We recognize that some liberal challenges to the administration of justice have, on occasion, resulted in more fairness and more justice. This, we believe, is good news. The bad news is that some of the reforms liberal criminologists have advanced have also harmed communities, made families less safe, and reduced the potency of the criminal justice system to deliver justice.

Today there are few dragons left, and those that may exist seem to be little more than innocuous lizards. The liberal impulse to exact change, however, cares little if it is a dragon or a lizard that has to be slayed because in absolute terms both equate to unnecessary human suffering. Liberal reformers have always sought to change how justice is administered in the

United States, for no other reason than leftist criminologists see the criminal justice system as an institution that creates pain and suffering. Limiting suffering, according to Minogue (1963), has been at the heart of twentieth-century liberal reform efforts. Focusing on "suffering" has a practical, political purpose because it "convert(s) politics into a crudely conceived moral battleground. On one side we find oppressors, and on the other, a class of victims."

In this sense, liberal criminologists have traditionally viewed criminals as victims and offenders as having "suffered" from one form of privation or another (Alexander, 2010; Goffman, 2014). The real reason they commit crime, according to liberal doctrine, is because they have suffered socially, economically, or personally. They are, in modern parlance, "disadvantaged." This idea forms the crux of much theorizing about the causes of crime. Strain theory and its variants locate the causes of crime in the physical, psychological, or cultural processes that bring some type of pain, suffering, or discomfort to the individual (Wacquant, 2009). Community theorists, too, argue that economic deprivation, poverty, low income, or low socioeconomic status (SES) cause crime because they bring suffering to individuals through no fault of their own (Wilson, 1987). Indeed, the idea that individuals offend only because they have faced some type of adversity is so ingrained in the criminological mindset that it is simply accepted as fact:

> Few groups in American society have been defended more diligently by sociologists against allegations of difference than ordinary delinquents. From the beginning, the thrust of sociological theory has been to deny the relevance of individual differences to an explanation of delinquency, and the thrust of sociological criticism has been to discount research findings apparently to the contrary. "Devastating" reviews of the research literature typically meet with uncritical acceptance and even applause, and new theories and "new criminologies" are constructed in a research vacuum, a vacuum that may itself claim research support.
>
> *(Hirschi & Hindelang, 1977: 571–572)*

If criminals are the victims of some sort of suffering, then it follows that any institution within society, or society itself, can be the source of suffering. Family and parents, schools, neighborhoods, and places of employment are all suspect in their potential contribution to misbehavior. At a broader level, leftists, critical criminologists and feminists point to often contrived versions of American society (Currie, 1985), capitalism, patriarchy, and masculinities as their favorite explanations for individual criminal behavior (Messerschmidt, 1986). While it is reasonable to investigate the empirical connections between these institutions and crime, we point out the connection between these "explanations" of crime and the liberal belief that individuals must face some type of difficulty, some form of deprivation, some form of discrimination in order to make the decision to commit crime.

Oppression is a favorite code word for academics. It hints at the outright oppression blacks faced during slavery and under "Jim Crow," but it also reflects another favorite theme of leftist criminologists—that is, that the criminal justice system functions to unfairly oppress individuals, to limit their chances for a successful life, and to distract policy makers from the sins of society. "Once the emotional disposition to see politics in this way is established," notes Minogue (1963: 15), "then we find people groping around trying to make the evidence fit." In criminology, "making the evidence fit" can be seen in a variety of areas, from sentencing studies to studies on racial disparity, the death penalty, racial profiling, gun control, and police discretion.

The Liberal Academic Attack on the Criminal Justice System

Criminologists and liberal reformers have been unrelenting in their attacks on "the criminal justice system." We place the term in quotes to highlight the fact that liberals and conservatives tend to speak about a singular, uniform system of criminal justice. In actuality, "the criminal justice system" is made up of thousands of local, municipal, state, and federal systems that are interconnected. The criminal justice system in Terre Haute, Indiana and Indianapolis, Indiana, while similar are also unique. While they follow many of the same rules and laws, the problems they face are unique, the populations they serve are unique, and the cultures within the institutions that compose their respective systems are unique. This makes it extremely difficult to speak of a uniform criminal justice system and it encourages gross exaggerations. It is common, for example, for people to argue that the criminal justice system is racist, or sexist, or unfair, or biased, or heavy-handed, or too easy on criminals. Yet there is no singular criminal justice system. This fact gets lost in the rhetoric of criminal justice policy but is critical to understanding the administration of justice and the way in which reforms are played out across thousands of local jurisdictions.

The decentralization of criminal justice is a hallmark of the United States. Our forefathers understood that the power of the state was exercised through the criminal justice system, so in an effort to reduce the power of the state reformers kept the administration of justice primarily at the local level. This is incredibly inefficient and it invites a wide range of variation in the administration of justice. Yet it is also a uniquely American mechanism, and for all the costs associated with inefficiency, it has worked. We have avoided the consolidation of power in the hands of justice officials and have kept the justice system subservient to local concerns and issues. The decentralization of criminal justice highlights a core conservative belief in local control and the rights of communities to control their fates. Local communities are much closer to the problems they need addressed than bureaucrats in state capitals or in Washington, DC.

Local control of criminal justice is, we believe, at the heart of much liberal animus. Local police, corrections, and social service agencies can vary tremendously in their pool of talent, management and supervision, and resources. Because of this, liberals often view local agencies as less professional, less responsive to broader social movements, and more open to the vagaries of personality and institutionalized biases. In some instances this is undoubtedly true, but in many instances it is not. Many local agencies are extremely professional, work closely with the community to address crime problems, and are responsive to research findings. Nonetheless, local control makes overall control very difficult. And this, as Shakespeare would say, is "the rub." Liberal criminologists speak of "the criminal justice system" not because they are unaware of the decentralized nature of the administration of justice but because the rhetorical value of criticizing "the system" is far more potent and far less personal than criticizing individual members of the Indianapolis police department. It also allows for critics of "the system" to speak in gross generalities, call for more federal control of the administration of justice, and use the courts at the state and federal level to impose specific rules and standards for the operation of local criminal justice systems. For liberals, the administration of justice is not about the control of crime but about the control of the criminal justice system in ways they favor.

It seems, at least to us, that much of what criminologists do is criticize the criminal justice system. Rarely do they take positive steps to assist or provide empirical guidance to those who work in the system, if for no other reason than many equate assisting the administration of justice as being complicit in the oppression of already victimized individuals. Indeed, entire academic careers have been spent attacking the criminal justice system, the police, prisons, and legislative bodies while blanket condemnations of criminal justice practices, often without solid or even convincing empirical evidence, have been officially recognized and rewarded by academic societies (the American Society of Criminology and the Academy of Criminal Justice Sciences).

Delegitimize the Criminal Justice System

Research can lead to discovery or it can be used to push an ideological agenda. The two, however, are not mutually exclusive. The problem, of course, is that it is often difficult to tell whether research is honest and objective or whether it is driven by or tainted by ideological biases. What concerns us most is that the overarching goal of the left is to delegitimize the entirety of the criminal justice system and that they often use research as a tool to achieve that aim. In these situations, many leftist scholars make no pretense of being objective but instead craft and mold data to support their ideological views. In other instances, overt ideological bias is hidden in the cryptic language used by researchers. Examples are abundant: Police actions are placed under a microscope, not with an eye towards analyzing any given situation but with an eye towards labeling all police behavior as racist, violent, or oppressive. Prosecutorial decision making is analyzed to find any pattern that could be used as evidence of prosecutorial bias. Criminal sentences are examined for any possibility, no matter how remote, that minority groups are discriminated against. Criminological research is often used, unfortunately, as a political instrument—an instrument that pushes a specific liberal agenda to delegitimize "the system."

The consequences of a lack of legitimacy are serious. Any criminal justice system, local, state, or federal, depends on legitimacy. Police must be seen as legitimate actors, as must judges and probation officers, or else they will simply be ignored or viewed with open disdain. For the most part the majority of Americans extend a fair amount of legitimacy to criminal justice system actors. People, for example, largely respect the police and show them an appropriate degree of deference (Engel & Swartz, 2012). Unfortunately, the continual liberal assault on the criminal justice system provides all the intellectual fodder needed for some individuals to rationalize away their own misbehavior. Criminals, for example, are notorious for "blaming the system" for their behavior and for pointing out the flaws in the system as a way to deflect responsibility for their own flaws (Samenow, 2004; Walters, 2006). We are not suggesting that criminals go to the library to read criminological journals. What we are suggesting is that they do pay particular attention to messages that support their antisocial worldview.

Yet the attack on the criminal justice system would not hold much weight if it was only criminals listening to the message. Unfortunately, an entire industry of liberal advocacy groups, liberal funding agencies, liberal lawyers, and liberal community organizers exists that feeds off of these messages. These groups uncritically latch on to criminological "evidence" to support their ideological position, vie for legitimacy, receive state and federal grants, alter legislation, or litigate what they deem unfair practices. While some of these groups are more, and less, focused on science, they all share a common belief that the criminal justice system acts in an arbitrary, capricious, if not entirely discriminatory fashion. Organizations, such as the Ford Foundation, the MacArthur Foundation, the Urban Institute, the ACLU, the Annie E. Casey foundation, and the Edna McConnell Clark foundation, to name only a few, have spent billions of dollars funding liberal criminal justice causes, funding "research" that advanced their views, and litigating when they couldn't effect change. While these organizations are well within their rights to fund projects they deem necessary and in line with their political beliefs, we believe it noteworthy that many criminologists and social scientists feed these organizations through their research, receive funding from these organizations, or belong to these organizations. They are, as Heather MacDonald (2000) noted, the "foot soldiers" of progressive organizations.

Delegitimize Punishment and Incarceration

Perhaps no other area of criminal justice has received as much academic attention as incarceration. The rapid increase in incarceration rates during the 1990s was nothing short of stunning, but so too was the volume and quality of violence that also shot up during this time (Snyder, 2011). All data point to the fact that almost every form of violence increased rapidly from the mid to late 1980s—generating intense concern from both liberals and conservatives. The answer to the escalating violence was straightforward: Increase the likelihood of going to prison. And with all due speed, states across the country poured money into their correctional agencies.

While the effectiveness of punishment and incarceration is questionable, the use of incarceration as a response to serious or prolonged criminal behavior is not. And while it is true that state prison systems expanded considerably from the 1990s through to about 2000, it is also true that the expansion did reduce the crime rate and thus also reduced the number of victims of crime (Levitt, 2004; Spelman, 2009). It also saved the lives of an untold number of criminal offenders—offenders who often die as a result of their criminal behavior or due to drug and alcohol addiction, or because they engage in very risky behaviors. Yet the response of criminologists was almost uniformly critical of the expansion of the correctional system—including the development of community corrections, new programs to deal with and manage offenders in the community, the development of super-max prisons, increased probation supervision, and, of course, application of the death penalty (Austin et al., 2000; Ross, 2007; Tonry, 2004).

The dirty secret of the criminal justice system is that there exists an unlimited number of people who should be incarcerated but are not. There are tens of thousands of individuals walking the streets of America who have committed serious crimes, who have lengthy histories of engaging in crime, and who pose a threat to the safety of their communities. These individuals are often on some form of court supervision, namely probation, but because they have managed to plea bargain their cases(s) or because they have had their charges reduced they are only rarely subject to the actual penalty of incarceration. Over two-thirds of individuals under correctional supervision are on supervision in the community (Gramlich, 2009; Moore, 2009) and a majority of these offenders will recidivate or will qualify to have their probation revoked due to a "technical violation"—that is, not following the rules of their probation.

Restrict Discretion

Discretion is a core element in the fair application of justice, in part because it allows room for officials to weigh criminal intent and the unique aspects of the criminal event. Discretion, however, requires that trust be placed in criminal justice officials, and since leftist criminologists place no trust in criminal justice officials, they have supported broad-based efforts to curtail discretion. This is now why police are legally compelled to make arrests for certain types of events, even when no obvious criminal intent was involved. Mandatory arrest policies have been implemented in a wide range of favored liberal causes, including drunk driving, white-collar crime, and domestic violence (Sherman & Berk, 1984; Sherman, Schmidt, & Rogan, 1992). Simultaneously, however, leftist criminologists have been loath to advocate for mandatory arrest in other areas, such as child molestation, prostitution, or illicit drug use and distribution. In restricting discretion within the system, leftists have also established the conditions where injustice is now more likely to occur. Mandatory decisions to arrest certain offenders, the empowering of local prosecutors, and the restricting of the authority of the judiciary have allowed the arrest, prosecution, and punishment of individuals, including adolescents, for "crimes" where there was no criminal intent.

The ultimate lack of discretion now occurs not in the criminal justice system but in our local schools. In reaction to the dreadful events of Columbine, schools across the country enacted "zero tolerance" policies. Zero tolerance, similar to mandatory arrest policies, takes away all discretion entrusted to men and women in positions of responsibility. It elevates policy above reason and ultimately punishes the innocent as much as the guilty. Mandatory arrest policies, similar to zero tolerance policies, achieve the dual liberal goals of absolute control and absolute "equality" in the application of law. That innocent children are suspended or expelled from school or are charged in juvenile court for violation of zero tolerance policies appears to be an acceptable consequence to achieve broader liberal goals. That men and women have been arrested and charged with crimes under conditions where arrest may not have been necessary or appropriate is casually overlooked.

Expand and Federalize the Criminal Law

States used to be referred to as laboratories of social experimentation, where social policies could be implemented, tested, and if found ineffective, discarded. This view has shifted, in part because of liberal efforts to influence national social policy and conservative efforts to respond to crime. Liberals have found greater success in affecting policy by expanding federal law and criminal procedure than by affecting change in independent states. Conservatives have also sought to expand the role and influence of federal law, albeit for different reasons. Both, in our minds, are misguided.

At America's founding, there were three federal crimes: treason, counterfeiting, and piracy. Today, there are over 4,500 federal laws governing everything from the importation of seafood to taxes, gun sales, financial transactions, and terrorism (Baker & Bennett, 2004; Walsh, 2010). There are tens of thousands more regulatory statutes governing business activity, environmental impact, job discrimination, drug testing, and food safety. The growth in federal criminal law has been unparalleled in the last 30 years, while growth in administrative law has reached record levels. The reason for this, we believe, is simple: Win in Congress or win in the federal courts and you will be able to impose your will across the United States—that is, there is no need to address the peculiarities of each state.

Efficiency alone, however, does not fully explain the massive expansion of federal power. While the federal government and the federal courts wield tremendous power, they also wield tremendous leverage. Where the brute exercise of power has proven difficult politically, the exercise of financial leverage has not. Bureaucratic heads of agencies now routinely couple compliance of federal directives, laws, or initiatives to the receipt of tax dollars. During the Carter era, for example, states were leveraged to alter their highway speed limits to 55 mph or face the loss of federal highway funds. This tactic has proven successful and has been used to compel changes in everything from drunk driving laws to child support enforcement practices, more recently forcing the Catholic Church to provide birth control and abortionist drugs in their insurance policies. In the end, however, the federal government has grown even more powerful, influential, and capable of depriving liberty.

Restrict the Rights of Honest Citizens

Liberals love regulations for things they don't like, but deplore regulations for things they do like. Mayor Bloomberg in New York, for example, imposed a set of highly invasive restrictions on individuals and businesses that can accurately be described as totalitarian and a hint of things to come. Bloomberg, with the backing of his liberal supporters, banned the "Big Gulp," a 32-ounce soda, because he deemed the Big Gulp a health hazard. Banning the Big Gulp was only the tip of the iceberg: Mayor Bloomberg and his group of righteous reformers also banned the use of trans-fat in restaurants, placed limits on how much salt can be used in a prepared meal, openly denied the constitutional rights of gun owners and those who wish to own a gun, and they passed ordinances that required hospitals to essentially force new mothers to breastfeed their infants. Hospitals, they said, now have to provide a documented medical reason why they provided a new mom with formula for their baby and must now keep baby formula in a locked cabinet.

Yes, in some places in the United States the government can now tell you what you can eat and drink and how much of a food product you can purchase. While obesity is clearly a problem in the United States, there are likely better responses than doing away with Happy Meals. This type of unrestricted use of governmental power is precisely the type our Founding Fathers warned us about and exactly the type that is so favorable to liberals. Responding to a court order that overturned Bloomberg's soda ban, he responded: "I do think there are certain times we should infringe on your freedom" (Chumley, 2013).

In terms of criminal justice, the most frequent assault on the rights of free people is the unending desire of liberals to eliminate, not just control, the ability of citizens to possess and carry weapons. Indeed, the entire history of gun control in the United States has been one where liberals and progressives have conjured new and unique ways to deprive citizens of their Second Amendment rights—rights recently affirmed by the Supreme Court in the *District of Columbia v. Heller* decision—and where liberal academics conjure new analyses and lines of argumentation in favor of gun control (Kleck, 1991; Lott, 2003).

Let us first examine why depriving individuals of their right to own and carry a weapon would be so appealing to liberals and liberal academics. Before we do, however, it is important to note that not all liberals favor gun control. Indeed, classical liberals have gone to some length to explain to progressives and other liberals why the Second Amendment should be protected (Baum, 2013; Whitney, 2012). First, liberals tend to emphasize the harm associated with guns—that is, the dramatic killing of large numbers of people by someone mentally ill or the accidental death of a young child. They point to these incidents as unnecessary—again, an emphasis on "harm" noted by Haidt (2012). Second, they point out that guns are often stolen by criminals during burglaries, that the presence of a gun can make a simple assault a murder, and that much violent crime is facilitated by weapons usage.

Yet in our view the most important reason why liberals and liberal academics favor banning individuals from owning or carrying weapons is that they equate gun ownership with conservatism—that is, they see it as part of a broader constellation of conservative principles that must be defeated. President Obama's now infamous comments about residents in small town American "bitterly clinging to their guns and to their religion" because of economic isolation was widely reported, but his follow-on comments about these same people showing "antipathy to people who aren't like them" or holding an "anti-immigrant sentiment" revealed how deeply liberals view gun owners as ignorant, flawed, racist, religious loons. To liberals, owning a gun or being part of a gun culture simply means you are conservative and stupid. It really is that simple.

We digress momentarily to highlight the degree to which academics hold anti-gun and anti-gun owner views. In a comprehensive survey and examination of political views across a variety of academic disciplines, Yancey (2011) found that job candidates for professor positions would be better served by lying about or concealing the fact that they hold religious views, are a member of the NRA (National Rifle Association), or are a hunter/outdoorsman. Yancey's advocacy for dishonesty was rooted in empirical data. Professors across a broad swathe of disciplines reported that if they knew a candidate held strong religious views, was an outdoorsman, or was a member of the NRA it would hurt the candidate's chances of being hired. Indeed, academics rated belonging to the NRA as on a par with being an evangelical or a fundamentalist in terms of negative bias. We believe this pattern of equating gun ownership with religious identification is at the heart of the academic bias against gun owners and it is exactly the type of rhetoric employed by President Obama behind closed doors to his liberal supporters. Interestingly, academics across disciplines uniformly reported that if they knew a job candidate was a Democrat or belonged to the ACLU that it would help their chances of being hired.

The problem with gun control, however, is that it simply does not work. Don't take our word for it. This was the conclusion of the National Research Council (2004) panel that looked into the effectiveness of gun control, the conclusion of Gary Kleck, a well-known criminologist at Florida State University (1991), and the conclusion of a lifetime of work by John Lott (Lott, 2003, 2010). Thousands and thousands of laws have had virtually no impact on gun crimes and some of the most violent cities in the United States have the most onerous gun controls (Kleck, 1991). Moreover, despite a dramatic increase in the number of individuals licensed to carry a concealed weapon, despite a massive increase in private ownership of guns associated with President Obama's election and gun control efforts, and despite gun manufacturers producing and selling record volumes of weapons, the rate of fatal violence associated with gun use has declined substantially since 1990. In 1993, for example, deaths from firearm homicides equaled 7 per 100,000; in 2010 that number had dropped to just 3.6 per 100,000. Victimization rates for non-fatal crime involving firearms also dropped from a high of 725.3 in 1993 to just 181.5 in 2011. Lastly, non-fatal violent crime dropped from 7,979 per 100,000 to 2,254.2 per 100,000 in 2011 (Pew Research Center, 2013).

Chicago has suffered from unbelievable violence over the past decade—with more individuals shot and killed than soldiers in the Afghanistan and Iraqi wars. The violence in Chicago has been so bad that some community leaders have requested that the National Guard be used to take over certain neighborhoods. Yet the irony in all of this is that innocent men and women who live in the neighborhoods where violence is the worst were not allowed to legally possess or carry weapons to defend themselves and their families. They were held hostage by the blind ideological loyalty Chicago powerbrokers hold to anti-gun interests. To be clear: Innocent people died because the city of Chicago prevented them from protecting themselves. Perhaps it is not surprising that the *Heller* decision, where the Supreme Court reaffirmed the individual right to possess a weapon, originated in Chicago.

We find it interesting that leftists generally support expanding a range of "rights" for certain people. They support "gay marriage" as a right, they support abortion-on-demand as a right, and they support providing taxpayer-funded birth control to young girls, but when it comes to firearms—the only right actually enumerated in the Constitution—they appear willing to go to any length to deny or infringe that right. Indeed, they have tried virtually every mechanism in their arsenal to control the manufacturing, sale, distribution, and ownership of firearms and ammunition. They have tried to impose costly taxes on firearms and their manufacture, impose heavy insurance burdens on owners, and hold gun makers responsible for crimes committed by criminals; they have restricted how many guns a person may purchase within a 24-hour period, they have tried to ban "Saturday Night Specials," they have banned (only to have the ban overturned) "assault weapons," they have restricted ammunition sales and the size of magazines that hold ammunition. We can think of no other American tradition and Constitutional right that has been attacked by liberals with such vigor. Yet their efforts are not supported by science, nor are they supported by American citizens—many of whom enjoy the "gun culture" and who live responsibly with guns (National Research Council, 2004; Pew Research Center, 2013).

Broader Liberal Attacks on United States Society

The United States is selfish

The answer to almost every liberal issue is to spend more tax money, and if the tax base is not sufficient, to raise taxes on certain people. To many liberals, Americans simply do not pay enough in taxes—or at least they do not pay enough to fund the programs liberals like to implement. And to many liberals, America remains a selfish and individualistic country because, they argue, we do not spend enough on social welfare programs.

This theme runs through much of sociology and is embedded in discussions of most major sociological theories of crime—especially those theories that focus on poverty or on communities as causes of crime. Yet under liberal administrations, and even some conservative administrations, welfare spending broadly defined has increased precipitously. According to data from the Department of Commerce, in 2012 4.3 million Americans were on welfare, almost 47 million were on "food stamps," another 5.6 million were on unemployment insurance. Interestingly, Commerce Department data show that individuals can make $1,000 per month and still qualify for welfare benefits and that in 40 states "welfare" payments and benefits exceed the value of an $8/hour job. In seven states welfare pays more than a $12/hour job, and in nine states welfare payments exceed the average salary of a school teacher (www.statisticbrain.com/welfare-statistics). The financial cost of welfare payments is staggering. The 14 percent of Americans receiving SNAP (food stamps) alone cost $71.8 billion per year, while general welfare payments cost another $131.9 billion. These numbers do not include the costs of Medicaid.

Yet these numbers also hide another source of major welfare support: disability insurance. Because Congress has liberalized who qualifies for disability, a larger and larger number of people are now eligible for disability payments. Not only has Congress liberalized who qualifies for disability payments, they have broadened the types of "injuries" and conditions people can use to apply for disability. For example, workers can file for disability because they are an alcoholic or drug addict. Not surprisingly, by 2011 almost 14 million people were on the disability roll—up over 53 percent from a decade ago. To be certain, part of this increase is the result of an aging and growing population, but even when those factors are considered the number of people on disability is staggering. Moreover, the financial cost of disability payments exceeds the combined payments for food stamps and welfare (http://apps. npr.org/unfit-for-work).

We are not arguing that some individuals do not need or do not appreciate receiving a disability payment. But because disability is a federal program, states now hire outside investigators to locate individuals on state welfare rolls to see if they qualify for the federal disability program. Moreover, the checks and balances available in other parts of government simply do not exist in the disability system. This may be why in the 1960s, when disability insurance became available, the leading cause of "disability" was heart disease and stroke but by 2011 the leading cause was undefined back pain followed by mental illness (http://apps.npr.org/unfit-for-work).

The expansion of the welfare state knows no boundaries. Obamacare, for example represents the single largest government expansion into the private lives of individuals ever and despite the rhetoric of providing "free health care to everyone," every indication is that health care costs will escalate and coverage will be reduced. Many people will lose benefits or will see their benefits taxed at a rate exceeding 40 percent! And all of this was done without a single Republican vote or a single Republican amendment being accepted. Yet other forms of welfare spending also exist that are often overlooked. Today, for example, low-income individuals can participate in a program called Lifeline, which helps to pay their phone bill and provides them cell phone service. The program has exploded and now costs taxpayers $2.2 billion per year (Meyers, 2013). We also spend about $9 billion per year on "Head Start"—a program that provides day care and educational support for low-income children (Burke & Muhlhausen, 2013; U.S. Department of Health and Human Services, 2015). Unfortunately, randomized studies find that Head Start simply does not work—that is, children who attend Head Start are no better or worse for their experience (Westat, 2010). And none of this discussion touches on the almost endless number of programs sponsored by the federal government designed to help low-income, sick, or struggling individuals and families.

But the "welfare state" is not simply composed of programs. It is an idea that government should do for individuals what individuals choose not to do for themselves. It is a cultural belief that government should have the power and force necessary to direct and dictate how people behave, how they spend their time, what they put into their bodies, how they spend their money, the types of jobs they are eligible for, and the ideas they are exposed to and can believe in, and the idea that government—not the individual or the family—is wiser and better situated to know what is best for the average American. Simply put, the "welfare state" is an idea that the individual matters least, the government most, and that the government should take whatever steps it deems necessary to "care" for its citizens.

Liberal criminologists' suggestions for crime control

Academic criminology is almost entirely antithetical to a conservative approach to understanding crime and administering justice. For an illustration, we focus on the November 2007 special issue of the journal *Criminology & Public Policy*, an official journal of the American Society of Criminology. This special issue contained 27 invited policy proposals from dozens of criminologists, and offers clear insight into how academic criminologists see the world of crime. Although it is just one issue, it is consistent with our professional experience of interacting with criminologists at conferences and engaging in the peer review process with them during the course of submitting research articles for journal publication. The special issue touched on a wide range of issues in criminal justice policy, and the discussion here covers a similar range of policies, from low-level policies such as truancy enforcement to the highest level policy, capital punishment.

★★★

Acker (2007) suggests that states should place an immediate moratorium on executions due to a variety of shortcomings that the sanction allegedly suffers from. These include costs, the possibility of executing an innocent person, fears of racial discrimination, concerns about the adequacy of counsel for indigent defendants, and other laments. Academic criminologists are almost unilaterally opposed to the death penalty (the American Society of Criminology published an official organization position against capital punishment) in part because they are wedded to arguments they can orchestrate to make the sanction look bad. For example, one of the most popular current criticisms of the death penalty is that it is too expensive to administer and states should look to cut it during the troubled economic times of the Great Recession. This seems pragmatic. However, almost all of the costs associated with capital cases center on appeals, which are convoluted legal attempts to forestall the final execution of the sentence. Yet jurisdictions automatically appeal death sentences immediately after securing them. In this way, the state plays the role of both prosecutor and defense to ensure that the conviction is veracious. The subsequent costs associated with appeals are created by capital defenses (whose job is of course to prevent their client being executed) and appellate judges who allow the appeals to continue for years onto decades.

Academic criminologists often avoid retributive arguments for the death penalty, not because they disagree with them or are afraid to debate them but because retributive arguments are themselves cast as inappropriate to use in death penalty discourse. To illustrate, Acker (2007: 645) argues:

> Research can help answer questions about the utility and application of the death penalty. In contrast, the retributive value of capital punishment involves normative judgments that may be largely immune to research findings … . Just as evidence about the empirical aspects of capital punishment may differ among jurisdictions, so may conclusions about the weight that should be afforded retributive considerations.

It is a clever ploy that criminologists use to discuss the death penalty. Arguments about deterrence, for instance, are empirical and thus sensible, logical, and smart. In contrast, retribution is immune to research findings. It is emotional, reactionary, and stupid.

But retribution is one of the most righteous concepts in law and justice. It is on a par with equality and fairness. Conservatives love retribution, especially in the context of capital punishment. Heinous criminals violate basic rules that are inviolable. For their violation, they must pay with their life. That their execution also denotes some deterrent value is immaterial.

★★★

An opportunity structure that is importantly related to antisocial behavior is unstructured, unsupervised time. This is particularly salient for juveniles. The most dangerous time of day for them, for example, is the hour or so of time that transpires between the end of the school day and the end of their parents' work day. It is during this period that neither adult teachers nor adult parents are present to monitor the behavior of children. As a result, it is ripe for delinquency and victimization. The same logic drives curfew ordinances which proscribe children and adolescents from being on the streets between the hours of approximately 10 p.m. to 6 a.m. The logic is simple: children and adolescents should be sleeping during these hours to prepare for attending school the next day.

Yet, in this issue, Adams (2007) suggests that criminal justice systems should abolish juvenile curfews. His concern is that the policies are inefficient, inconsistently enforced and thus potentially discriminatory, and involve a "counterproductive escalation of sanctions." On the latter point, Adams cites the Associated Press which published an article suggesting that confinement facilities in Texas include about 15 percent of youths who are low-level misdemeanor offenders, such as curfew violators. According to the news media, chronic curfew violations are leading to commitment to confinement facilities. That is unlikely. What is more likely is that juvenile delinquents with multiple curfew violations also have dozens of other delinquent offenses for which they are adjudicated.

A larger conservative idea is that children and adolescents should not be congregating in the streets during the wee hours of the night. Virtually any criminological theory and common sense suggests it is a bad idea. Moreover, given that so many antisocial acts are committed during these hours, curfew ordinances provide a legal justification for contacting youth who are likely engaging in antisocial behaviors, or planning to. Finally, there is ample conservatism in Benjamin Franklin's famous quotation, "Early to bed, early to rise, makes a man healthy, wealthy, and wise." Curfews make that happen.

★★★

A timeless conservative idea is that the interests of crime victims and public safety always take precedence over the interests of the criminal defendant and presumably due process. To conservatives, crime control trumps due process and it should be the criminal justice system, not the criminal's justice system. A unifying theme of the *Criminology & Public Policy* special issue takes an almost diametric view: the criminal justice system, not criminals, is the object of condemnation. As such, policy recommendations seek to address the putative shortcomings or outright abuses of the criminal justice system. There are several examples of this approach. Alpert (2007) recommends to police departments that they "eliminate race as the only reason for police–citizen encounters." There are many unspoken assumptions about this policy proposal. First, it assumes that race is and has been the only reason for police–citizen encounters. This was precisely the hypothesis of the criminal justice community and American society generally during the turbulent 1960s. The large-scale observational studies of that area, research by scholars such as Albert Reiss, Donald Black, James Q. Wilson, and others, did report evidence that suspect race was used by police to inform their decision making. But they did not report widespread evidence of racial bias. Moreover, these early policing studies found overwhelmingly that the police respond to criminal acts that were observed by victims, witnesses, the perpetrator, and sometimes all of these parties. This point is critical. The police respond or react to criminal behavior that has occurred and has been observed; they do not create or proactively manufacture criminal defendants who have particular demographic characteristics. The sloppy notion that the police zealously target blacks and Hispanics is at odds with the empirical reality of crime and the ways that police responses are mobilized.

The handwringing that surrounds the use of race in policing is also partly based on the mythological idea that racial and ethnic groups in the United States have comparable involvement in criminal behavior. Such a claim is rejected by every source of data available to criminologists. In an editorial that summarized recent policing research, DeLisi (2011) found significant race differences in, for example, the use of disrespect toward police, use of suspicious behavior toward police, holding of negative attitudes about police, perceptions that police act improperly, and perceptions that police behave improperly during traffic stops. All of these outcome variables disadvantaged blacks. In addition, another study found a significant association between racial identity among blacks and perceptions about police discrimination. Youth with low racial identity perceived low police discrimination. Youth with strong/high racial identity perceived that police discrimination was pervasive. Thus, any discussion of race and policing is largely spurious because of the multifaceted and significant race differences that exist not only for offending and victimization but also interaction with law enforcement personnel. Criminologists know this but minimize the magnitude of race differences in crime even though these differences are what most explain race differences in criminal justice system statuses.

The obviously specious way that criminologists treat race generally, and specifically in the case of arguing that police only stop individuals because of their race, can be best understood by considering a far less controversial demographic characteristic: sex. For a host of biological, psychological, and sociological reasons, males engage in a higher number and more severe forms of antisocial behavior than females. It is the reason why males are overrepresented in arrest data, in judicial data, in correctional data, and in virtually all criminological datasets. In the world of forensic psychology and psychiatry where the dependent variables of interest are murder, rape, sexual homicide, serial homicide, and related behaviors, there are usually zero females in datasets. Based on the incontrovertible evidence that males are at higher risk for antisocial conduct than females, would it make any sense to ignore sex differences in crime, or worse yet, pretend they do not exist? Yet, academic criminology and the justice system does just this with race and has devised an entire cottage industry (Disproportionate Minority Contact) to address this policy problem.

★★★

One of the most alarming experiences the authors recall as criminal justice practitioners was the observation of criminal lifestyles in all their depravity. Too many criminal offenders, specifically those who are addicted to various substances, lead an almost Neolithic existence in which shelter, food, water, exercise, family, school, and work are ignored in favor of fulfilling their addiction. The lifestyle of the average street offender is horrifyingly dysfunctional, unhealthy, and immoral. This means that many criminal offenders choose sensation-seeking over the most basic responsibilities of conventional society. They do not eat. They do not have a roof over their head. They abandon their spouse and children. This is a very gritty existence.

Nevertheless, of all of the behaviors that criminologists could focus on in terms of helping offenders reintegrate into society, it is not these basic responsibilities. It is voting. There is large variation across states; however, the basic logic of lifetime voting bans and felon disenfranchisement policies is to prevent felons from voting because of their legal status. In some places, the bans are permanent. In other states, the voting proscriptions expire once the offender has successfully completed his sentence. There are also various mechanisms that states require for felons to re-earn the right to vote. However, Bushway and Sweeten (2007) suggest that we "abolish lifetime bans for ex-felons." Crutchfield (2007) indicates that states should "abandon felon disenfranchisement policies." The logic is that voting bans and disenfranchisement is mean-spirited and contributes to a sense of hopelessness and fatalism among offenders that complicates their desistance from crime.

But where is the evidence that criminal offenders, particularly convicted felons, especially persons who choose the depraved criminal subsistent lifestyle described above, vote in the first place? The motivation for the question is that a large proportion even of prosocial, conventional people do not take the time to vote. According to data produced by Nonprofit VOTE (2013), the leading source of non-partisan resources to help non-profit organizations integrate voter engagement into their services, voter turnout is dismal. In terms of the 2010 election, just 60 percent of those earning $75,000 or more voted and just 40 percent of those earning below $50,000 voted. In terms of educational attainment, 61 percent of those with college or more voted, 35 percent of those with high school or less voted. For residential mobility, 62 percent of those who had lived at their residence for five years or longer voted; for those who had lived at their current residence for less than one year, voter turnout was 28 percent. For age, 51 percent of those over the age of 30 voted (or about half did not). Among those aged 18 to 29, 24 percent voted (or, more than three out of four did not). For race, 49 percent of whites, 44 percent of blacks, and 31 percent of Hispanics voted in the 2010 elections. Put another way, 51 percent of whites, 56 percent of blacks, and 69 percent of Hispanics did not.

In other words, people who have a domicile, who work, who pay bills, who invest in their families, who abstain from substance use, and, most importantly, who abstain from committing crime often do not vote. As one moves down the socioeconomic ladder, the likelihood of voting becomes less likely. The Nonprofit VOTE resource did not have access to data on the voter turnout among the criminal population. Anecdotal evidence suggests the voter turnout among offenders is approximately 0 percent. The authors have interviewed thousands of offenders in a variety of employment and research contexts. Although neither is an expert on voting, we have garnered insights about the civic engagement of criminals. It is mostly non-existent. Most offenders routinely do not vote, many have never voted. Most offenders also do not have a valid driver's license or state identification (many have their license revoked for criminal traffic violations). Most offenders do not insure their vehicles. Most offenders do not even have a library card. In other words, serious criminal offenders do not vote irrespective of the voting prohibitions that are applied to them. Yet leftists assert that voting bans are the proverbial straw that broke the camel's back in terms of determining in an offender's mind whether to desist from crime, or to keep violating the law.

★★★

Not all of the policy recommendations were just pie-in-the-sky academic notions of how governments should improve their justice systems: some of the recommendations have actually occurred. For instance, Fagan (2007) suggested that states "end natural life sentences for juveniles." In 2012, the Supreme Court held that life sentences without the possibility of parole for juveniles convicted of murder constituted cruel and unusual punishment and thus violated the Eighth Amendment. This decision came on the heels of another landmark decision where the Supreme Court invalidated life sentences without parole for juveniles convicted of non-homicide offenses, such as kidnapping and rape. And these decisions arrived seven years after juveniles were categorically exempt from capital punishment in the *Roper* decision.

Ironically, a major reason why the Supreme Court and the American zeitgeist generally has relaxed its punishment views on adolescents is the influence of neuroscientific research that demonstrates the limitations that youth display in decision making relative to adults. This is ironic because criminology has been almost exclusively sociological in its orientation. But it will latch onto neuroscience findings to vitiate criminal punishment. In other words, no matter how vicious the murder, abduction, rape, armed robbery, or child molestation a juvenile commits, he will not be punished in a way that is commensurate with the severity of the criminal conduct. It would be cruel and unusual to do so.

There should be no illusions about the criminal extremity of youths who had been sentenced to life imprisonment without parole. A variety of transfer mechanisms are used to waive juvenile delinquents to adult criminal court, including options where the discretion resides with the judge or the prosecutor. The most common waiver technique is a legislative waiver where the seriousness of the conduct, such as a Class A felony, requires prosecution in criminal court. This legal language is describing youth who perpetrate murder, rape, and kidnapping. These are the youths being spared life imprisonment.

We suspect that one reason why juvenile justice has relaxed so much in recent years is that American society continues to experience historically low levels of crime and violence after the proliferation of crime from the 1960s to about the middle 1990s. Large cities, most famously New York, experience a fraction of the murders and serious youth violence that characterized earlier eras. Despite the changes in youth violence over the past two decades and despite the landmark liberal decisions by the Supreme Court regarding the punishment of juveniles, the tenor of criminologists about juvenile justice has not changed. There are hundreds—perhaps thousands—of studies whose literature reviews contain phrases like "get tough," "new penology," "tough on crime," "conservative views on crime," "Republican crime control," "punitive turn" and the like in describing the prosecution and punishment of juveniles. Perhaps their constant haranguing worked in that it cultivated the notion that the most violent young offenders are not eligible for true punishment.

★★★

We would be unwise and foolish to argue that some liberal reforms of the criminal justice system did not produce a net social good. Some have. Nor would we be wise to argue that some large-scale social interventions have not helped some people. They have. Nor would we necessarily disagree that certain liberal critiques of American society are entirely without merit. They are not. Indeed, we readily and without hesitation believe that some liberal policies have professionalized the criminal justice system, that some individuals benefit from Section 8, Head Start, "Obamacare," and the litany of social welfare services advocated by liberals, and that American society and American capitalism are not without problems. We agree.

Even so, what is the standard by which we judge a reform to be effective, an intervention to be worthwhile, or a critique valid? The truth is, there is no objective standard. Instead, what is called for is a reasonable evaluation of the evidence and an awareness, no, an appreciation, that even our best efforts, best intentions, and best reforms and interventions will generate sometimes unforeseeable negative consequences. In some instances, reforms will produce negative results that are entirely foreseeable.

So it is with many liberal reform efforts and many liberal interventions. The fact that some reforms produce positive results does not negate the fact that other reforms produce negative results. The fact that some individuals are helped by large-scale interventions does not mean that many others haven't been harmed. A full and complete account of any intervention is difficult but necessary if we are to learn their full range and impact.

But this is not what happens. Instead, once political gains have been made and reforms passed or large-scale interventions put into law, their advocates dig in and defend them with vigor. Even if evidence emerges that the reforms had deleterious consequences or the costs of the interventions outstripped their benefits, liberals will fight tooth and nail to protect their efforts. Head Start is a perfect example. In an effort to reduce the apparent intelligence and educational gaps between blacks and whites, liberal reformers advocated for and implemented this large-scale program for very young children from low-income families. Today this program costs $9,000,000,000 a year. Sophisticated experiments—the results of which were shelved and not made available by the Obama administration—show the program does not work. The $9 billion program is now widely recognized as a very expensive babysitting service. That money could be better spent, spent more efficiently, and spent in ways that do produce measurable results.

Other reforms, too, have had deleterious effects. After an onslaught of lawsuits by various liberal interest groups, police departments were legally forced to hire on the basis of race and sex. Liberal advocates argued that the benefits of having more minorities in police departments would benefit the community. However, research by Lott (2000) found that when police departments were forced to hire more minorities they responded by dropping admission standards for everyone. The end result, Lott found, was that a 1 percent increase in the number of black officers was associated with a 4 percent increase in property crime rates and a 5 percent increase in the violent crime rate. These same lawsuits forced police departments to drop cognitive testing for police recruits and have ultimately caused some police departments to go so far as to to hire individuals with felony convictions. Because of these reforms, today you can be a police officer even if you can barely read or write and have several felony convictions. While likely not the rule, the mere fact that these conditions are even in the realm of the possible demonstrate how liberal reforms have sometimes caused real and direct harm.

The number of books published by liberal scholars arguing for reform and leveling criticism against our institutions, our legal processes, and American society would fill libraries. The number of books by conservative professors calling into question these assertions or examining the impact of liberal reforms or interventions couldn't fill a bookshelf. What this translates into is a very large and very important gap in our knowledge of what works and what doesn't work in managing our institutions and intervening in the lives of individuals. Without a reasonable dissenting voice, without individuals who would challenge many of the liberal claims, the continued thrust towards change of any type continues unabated. We learn nothing from our efforts, our successes, or our failures. Moreover, when certain programs and certain reform efforts become identified as "liberal" it is not at all uncommon to see liberal academics come out of the woodwork to protect these reforms and interventions—even if evidence of their ineffectiveness emerges.

To be certain, some liberal reforms have caused harm. They have eroded social trust, they have pitted groups against each other, and they have meant that untold sums have been spent on ineffective programs. Reforms that have helped serious felons avoid captivity have brought harm to innocent people. Reforms that have restricted the ability of people to own and to carry weapons have resulted in the death and victimization of innocent people. Reforms that have made it more difficult for police to make arrests and have delegitimized police operations and practices have brought harm to people. The "stop and frisk" policies of the New York Police Department are estimated to have saved some 15,000 predominately black lives. Reformers ended that practice. Reforms to have domestic violence suspects automatically arrested and prosecuted have caused harm not only to the men arrested but also to their families—the families they often go back home to. And today, the reforms we see on college campuses to address sexual harassment and sexual assault has done harm to the accused and to the legitimacy of the institution.

The cost of liberal reforms is rarely paid for by those demanding the reforms. Unfortunately, the serious uptick in violent crime across our major cities we are currently experiencing can be traced directly back to the efforts of liberals to delegitimize the criminal justice system. Even the Department of Justice, especially the Civil Rights Division, has contributed to the cacophony of liberal attacks against the police. In return, just as we witnessed in

Cincinnati, OH, after the riots of 2001, police have made the conscious and very rational decision to pull back and not make arrests. Afraid they will be crucified by the DOJ, by liberal activists, and by liberal politicians, police have simply retrenched. And just as we saw in Cincinnati after the riots, when the police stop policing, violent crime escalates dramatically. Again, the price of liberal reform is often not paid by those demanding that reform.

Public policy is messy business and crime policy can be very messy. Lives often hang in the balance. Neighborhoods rise and fall because of crime policies. Justice is sometimes denied and even subverted by crime policies. Given the gravity of crime policy we believe it prudent that public policy in this area be driven not by agenda politics and good intentions but by the best science possible. Even then, we should take very seriously the likelihood that our best intentions, our best information, and our best predictions will likely be wrong and will likely operate in ways that were not fully appreciated beforehand. We believe that when conservatives and liberals work together, make incremental changes, and take time to evaluate their efforts that effective public policy will gradually emerge. Until then, we will be held hostage to good intentions and bad results.

References

Acker, J. R. (2007) Impose an immediate moratorium on executions. *Criminology & Public Policy*, 6(4), 641–650.

Adams, K. (2007) Abolish juvenile curfews. *Criminology & Public Policy*, 6(4), 663–669.

Alexander, M. (2010) *The new Jim Crow: Mass incarceration in the age of colorblindness*. New York: New Press.

Alpert, G. P. (2007) Eliminate race as the only reason for police–citizen encounters. *Criminology & Public Policy*, 6(4), 671–678.

Austin, J., Bruce, M. A., Carroll, L., McCall, P. L., & Richards, S. C. (2000) *The use of incarceration in the United States* (national policy white paper). American Society of Criminology. Retrieved from www.ssc.wisc.edu/~oliver/RACIAL/Reports/ascincarcerationdraft.pdf.

Baker, J. S., & Bennett, D. E. (2004) Explosive growth of federal crime legislation, October 1. Retrieved from *The Federalist Society for Law & Public Policy Studies Website*: www.fed-soc.org/publications/detail/explosive-growth-of-federal-crime-legislation.

Baum, D. (2013) *Gun guys: A road trip*. New York: Knopf.

Burke, L., & Muhlhausen, D. B. (2013) Head Start impact evaluation report finally released (Issue Brief no. 3823). Retrieved from *The Heritage Foundation Website*: www.heritage.org/research/reports/2013/01/head-start-impact-evaluation-report-finally-released.

Bushway, S. D., & Sweeten, G. (2007) Abolish lifetime bans for ex-felons. *Criminology & Public Policy*, 6(4), 697–706.

Chumley, C. K. (2013) NYC Mayor Bloomberg: Government has right to "infringe on your freedom". *Washington Times*, March 25. Retrieved from www.washingtontimes.com/news/2013/mar/25/nyc-mayor-bloomberg-government-has-right-infringe-/.

Crutchfield, R. D. (2007) Abandon felon disenfranchisement policies. *Criminology & Public Policy*, 6(4), 707–715.

Currie, E. (1985) *Confronting crime: An American challenge*. New York: Pantheon Books.

DeLisi, M. (2011) Where is the evidence for racial profiling? *Journal of Criminal Justice*, 39(6), 461–462.

Engel, R. S., & Swarz, K. (2012) Race, crime, and policing. In M. Tonry (ed.), *Oxford handbook of ethnicity, crime, and immigration*. New York: Oxford University Press.

Fagan, J. (2007) End natural life sentences for juveniles. *Criminology & Public Policy*, 6(4), 735–746.

Goffman, A. (2014) *On the run: Fugitive life in an American city*. Chicago, IL: University of Chicago Press.

Gramlich, J. (2009) Study finds disparity in corrections spending. Pew Charitable Trusts, March 2. Retrieved from www.pewtrusts.org/en/research-and-analysis/blogs/stateline/2009/03/02/study-finds-disparity-in-corrections-spending.

Haidt, J. (2012) *The righteous mind: Why good people are divided by politics and religion*. New York: Vintage Books.

Hirschi, T., & Hindelang, M. J. (1977) Intelligence and delinquency: A revisionist review. *American Sociological Review*, 42(4), 571–587.

Kleck, G. (1991) *Point blank: Guns and violence in America*. Hawthorne, NY: Aldine de Gruyter.

Levitt, S. D. (2004) Understanding why crime fell in the 1990s: Four factors that explain the decline and six that do not. *Journal of Economic Perspectives*, 18(1), 163–190.

Lott, J. R. (2000) Does a helping hand put others at risk? Affirmative action, police departments, and crime. *Economic Inquiry*, 38(2), 239–277.

Lott, J. R. (2003) *The bias against guns: Why almost everything you've heard about gun control is wrong*. Washington, DC: Regnery Publishing.

Lott, J. R. (2010) *More guns, less crime: Understanding crime and gun control laws*, 3rd edition. Chicago, IL: The University of Chicago Press.

MacDonald, H. (2000) *The burden of bad ideas: How modern intellectuals misshape our society*. Chicago, IL: Ivan R. Dee.

Messerschmidt, J. W. (1986) *Capitalism, patriarchy, and crime: Toward a socialist feminist criminology*. Totowa, NJ: Rowman & Littlefield.

Meyers, J. (2013) "Obama phone" facts still a hang-up in Washington. *Politico*, April 24. Retrieved from www.politico.com/story/2013/04/obama-phone-facts-still-a-hang-up-in-washington-90606.html.

Minogue, K. (1963) *The liberal mind*. Indianapolis, IN: Liberty Fund.

Moore, S. (2009) Prison spending outpaces all but Medicaid. *The New York Times*, March 2. Retrieved from ww.nytimes.com/2009/03/03/us/03prison.html?_r=0.

National Research Council (2004) In C. F. Wellford, J. V. Pepper, & C. V. Petrie (eds), *Firearms and violence: A critical view*. Washington, DC: The National Academies Press.

Nonprofit VOTE (2013) *America goes to the polls: Voter participation gaps in the 2012 election*. Report by G. Pillsbury and J. Johannesen. Retrieved from www.nonprofitvote.org/documents/2013/09/america-goes-to-the-polls-2012-voter-participation-gaps-in-the-2012-presidential-election.pdf.

Pew Research Center (2013) Gun homicides down 49 percent since 1993 peak; Public unaware. Pew Charitable Trust. Retrieved from www.pewsocialtrends.org/2013/05/07/gun-homicide-rate-down-49-since-1993-peak-public-unaware/.

Ross, J. I. (2007) Supermax prisons. *Society*, 44(3), 60–64. Retrieved from www.convictcriminology.org/pdf/jiross/SupermaxPrisons.pdf.

Samenow, S. (2004) *Inside the criminal mind*, rev. edition. New York: Crown Publishers.

Sherman, L., & Berk, R. (1984) The specific deterrent effects of arrest for domestic violence. *American Sociological Review*, 49(2), 261–272.

Sherman, L. W., Schmidt, J. D., & Rogan, D. P. (1992) *Policing domestic violence: Experiments and dilemmas*. New York: Free Press.

Snyder, H. N. (2011) *Arrest in the United States, 1980–2009*. U.S. Department of Justice, Office of Justice Programs, and Bureau of Justice Statistics (NCJ 234319). Retrieved from www.bjs.gov/content/pub/pdf/aus8009.pdf.

Spelman, W. (2009) Crime, cash, and limited options: Explaining the prison boom. *Criminology & Public Policy*, 8(1), 29–77.

Tonry, M. H. (2004) *Thinking about crime: Sense and sensibility in American penal culture*. New York: Oxford University Press.

U.S. Department of Health and Human Services, Office of Planning, Research & Evaluation (2015) *Head Start impact study and follow-up, 2000–2015*. Retrieved from www.acf.hhs.gov/programs/opre/research/project/head-start-impact-study-and-follow-up.

Voegeli, W. (2012) *Never enough: America's limitless welfare state*. New York: Encounter Books.

Wacquant, L. (2009) *Punishing the poor: The neoliberal government of social insecurity*. Durham, NC: Duke University Press.

Walsh, B. W. (2010) The criminal intent report: Congress must justify new criminalization (no. 2933), June 9. Retrieved from *The Heritage Foundation Website*: www.heritage.org/research/reports/2010/06/the-criminal-intent-report-congress-must-justify-new-criminalization.

Walters, G. D. (2006) *The psychological inventory of criminal thinking styles (PICTS) professional manual.* Allentown, PA: Center for Lifestyle Studies.

Westat (2010) *Head Start impact study: Final report.* Retrieved from www.acf.hhs.gov/sites/default/files/opre/executive_summary_final.pdf.

Whitney, C. R. (2012) *Living with guns: A liberal's case for the Second Amendment.* New York: Public Affairs.

Wilson, W. J. (1987) *The truly disadvantaged: The inner city, the underclass, and public policy.* Chicago, IL: University of Chicago Press.

Yancey, G. (2011) *Compromising scholarship: Religious and political bias in American higher education.* Waco, TX: Baylor University Press.

5

PUBLIC HOUSING AND THE FAMILY COURT

Abstract sentimentality ends in real brutality.
Russell Kirk, The Conservative Mind: From Burke to Eliot *(1953)*

Human folly comes in all shapes and sizes. Those who imagine they are wiser than others may well be the most dangerous.
Kenneth Minogue, The Servile Mind: How Democracy Erodes Moral Life *(2010)*

J.A. Schumpeter said that the first thing a man will do for his ideals is lie. It is not necessary to lie, however, in order to deceive, when filtering will accomplish the same purpose. This can take the form of reporting selective and atypical samples, suppressing some facts altogether, or filtering out the inconvenient meanings or connotations of words.
Thomas Sowell, Intellectuals and Society *(2010)*

This chapter deviates somewhat from the others. In this chapter we examine closely two areas where liberal domination of the argument has led to harm and where liberal social scientists have been complicit in promoting an agenda rather than objective research. We point out these areas as examples of where politics and research have not clashed but joined and where the results of that union have had damaging consequences for individuals, families, and entire communities. Again, the point to be taken from these examples is not that all government intervention is wrong-headed and harmful but that many social scientists, including many criminologists, cannot be counted on to offer unbiased appraisals of specific policies.

Housing Policy and Crime: An Example of Failed Liberal Planning and the Misunderstanding of Human Pathology

Perhaps no other issue highlights the failure of liberal social engineering, if not outright liberal arrogance, than public housing. For decades, public housing was synonymous with crime, gangs, drug abuse and distribution, and all forms of social pathology. Infamous public housing projects, such as Cabrini Green in Chicago, spoke volumes about the failure of federal efforts to provide the poor with safe and adequate housing (Popkin et al., 2000; Whitaker, 2000). The notorious Chicago Housing Projects were so dangerous, so infested by gangs, and so violent that police officers frequently refused to enter the complex.

The diagnosis of a social problem is frequently made through an ideological lens (Hunt, 2009). In this sense, liberals were quick to argue that the problems of concentrated violence and depravity were caused not by the pathologies that accompany many, though not all, residents of public housing, but instead were caused by the failure of government to provide adequate services, by the design of high-rise public housing complexes, by racism, and by the concentration of poverty (Goetz, 2013; Hunt, 2009). This diagnosis, eerily similar to many sociological criminologists' arguments, allowed public housing to become a rallying cry for a new form of public housing, one that would desegregate public housing and decentralize social pathology. High-rise public housing apartments were torn down, new town homes were constructed, "mixed-income" neighborhoods were developed, and a new "voucher" system, known as Section 8, became popular. Section 8 would provide tenants with a voucher they could take to help pay for rent in any approved Section 8 home.

Section 8 came along with a variety of promises, hopes, and expectations. The most basic expectation was that individuals would use Section 8 vouchers to move away from the poverty and problems found in their original neighborhoods. Respondents, the theory went, would use the vouchers to move into suburbs where they would assimilate middle-class values, quit committing crime, have a vested interest in taking care of their homes, and gain employment and lift themselves up from poverty.

The U.S. Department of Housing and Urban Development spends roughly $61 billion per year and employs almost 10,000 people. It monitors and participates in at least 118 subsidy programs (www.downsizinggovernment.org/housing-and-urban-development). About $25 billion taxpayer dollars go to aid low-income renters and another $9 billion per year is spent on pre-existing public housing. HUD also has a long history of politicization, mismanagement, and outright fraud. Nonetheless, HUD pressed full bore with Section 8 and with reinventing public housing.

Moving extremely poor people from public housing projects to suburban residential neighborhoods was a liberal (and liberal criminologist's) dream because it offered the type of radical intervention they believed necessary to reduce inequality and thus a host of other social problems. Moving very poor families out of their awful environmental circumstances, they reasoned, was a win-win situation. The poor families would benefit, the largely white suburbanites would benefit by the injection of "diversity" into their neighborhoods, and the government would benefit by reducing welfare expenditures.

As part of the Section 8 experiment, funding was set aside to evaluate the actual impact of Section 8 on the lives of residents and the neighborhoods they selected. Known as the Moving to Opportunity (MTO) experiment, the study randomized 4,600 tenants into one of three groups: the Section 8 group, a low-poverty voucher group which restricted vouchers to low-poverty areas and included "mobility counseling," and a control group across five cities (Souza Briggs, Popkin, & Goering, 2010).

Recall that one of the promises of Section 8 was that it would encourage tenants— primarily black, female, and with multiple children—to move away from the social networks and areas they were familiar with. This largely did not happen. Only 47 percent of those eligible for the low-poverty/mobility counseling group "leased up," meaning eventually signing a lease and living in the housing unit. About 68 percent of the normal Section 8 tenants leased up. Hence, one of the first findings from the MTO studies was that many tenants didn't leave the neighborhoods and networks supposedly responsible for their problems (Orr et al., 2003; Sanbonmatsu et al., 2011).

Outcomes associated with Section 8 participation were disappointing, to say the least. While tenants reported significant reductions in stress, anxiety, and witnessing crime and violence, Section 8 participation was not associated with gains in employment or income or reductions in welfare use, nor was it associated with increased cognitive performance in Section 8 children. Section 8 was associated with only minor reductions in marijuana smoking and lifetime property crime arrests for females but with significant and meaningful increases in lifetime property crime arrests and behavioral problems for male children (see also Kling, Ludwig & Katz, 2005; Ludwig, Duncan & Hirschfield, 2001; Sciandra et al., 2013).

A complete read of the various statistical analyses and reports produced by the MTO study team, however, reveals that Section 8 participation, and even Section 8 participation limited to low-poverty neighborhoods, had *no* measurable impact on dozens and dozens of measures of behavior and economic standing. A reading of the studies that emerged from the MTO efforts, however, would give an entirely different conclusion. While the vast majority of correlations between receipt of Section 8 and numerous outcomes were statistically insignificant, every significant correlation was published in major scientific journals (Katz, Kling & Liebman, 2001; Leventhal & Brooks-Gunn, 2003; Ludwig et al., 2012). Thus, to read the published research on MTO experiments one could easily walk away with the idea that MTO had a real, meaningful impact on the lives of individuals. However, what readers would not understand is that the vast majority of study outcomes were *not* significant and that there is a reasonable chance that the significant findings so broadly reported were actually the product of chance.

The long and short of the MTO story is that the promises of Section 8 have not materialized, that moving very poor, largely black, single-headed families to "better" neighborhoods had virtually no impact on their life chances or behavior. Despite moving to areas with less crime, better schools, more social resources, and fewer of the "stressors" that accompany living in poverty, MTO families were largely no better off.

The same cannot be said for the neighborhoods they moved to (Galster, Tatian, & Smith, 1999). Across the United States, communities are fighting back against what they rightfully perceive as a threat to the health and welfare of their neighborhoods posed by the expansion of public housing. Communities from Urbana, IL, to Dubuque, IA, to Cincinnati, OH, to Memphis, TN, are now pushing back against a federal juggernaut that has forced, coerced, and litigated its way into local communities to spread public housing into functional communities. Much of the push-back from Section 8 occurs, at least in part, because local residents witness increases in crime and incivility at residences known to be for Section 8 renters. The alleged increases in crime were, according to critics, spreading crime and social pathology to communities traditionally insulated from these problems.

Sometimes unconnected circumstances lead to unforeseen discoveries. The growing use of geographic mapping in policing is one such circumstance. In the city of Memphis, police were using the mapping of crime "hot spots" to direct police resources to solve problems at neighborhood level. The project was known as "Blue Crush" and involved the collection and dissemination of data on arrests made at specific addresses. Working with the Memphis police department was criminologist Richard Janikowski. Janikowski was instrumental in helping make the Memphis police department more data focused. When Janikowski examined the distribution of crime incidents and arrests across Memphis neighborhoods he found that crime had decreased in inner-city Memphis, but he also noticed a new pattern—crime had relocated to other neighborhoods.

Police departments are sometimes selfish regarding their data, but the restrictions they place on it pale in comparison to the paranoia that government housing agencies display in guarding their data. Enter Phyllis Betts, a housing expert with a degree in sociology—and Professor Janikowski's wife. Betts was able to access data on Section 8 addresses across Memphis. When

Betts' data on Section 8 housing addresses were merged with Janikowski's data on crime a clear pattern emerged: many of the crime "hot spots" in Memphis were Section 8 addresses.

Betts and Janikowski, both "liberal," white, academic types presented their findings to the city of Memphis. The resulting coverage in Memphis spurred a lengthy examination of Section 8 in *The Atlantic* by Hanna Rosin (2008). Rosin's conversations with criminologists from Chicago to Louisville to Atlanta documented almost identical patterns (Popkin et al., 2012; Suresh & Vito, 2009; Van Zandt & Mhatre, 2013; conversely, see Ellen, Lens & O'Regan, 2012; Lens, 2014 for conflicting sources). First, crime would be highly concentrated in public housing projects. When those projects were destroyed, crime would disperse across the city and into neighborhoods where crime was a rare event. Crime, moreover, tracked well with Section 8 vouchers.

Apologists, however, remain indignant. They argue, correctly, that many on Section 8 are elderly, disabled, or are unwed women with multiple children. They are, according to the rhetoric, the "truly disadvantaged" and the "marginalized." While it is true that many of the named residents of Section 8 and public housing are elderly, disabled, or women with children, it is also true that many men also occupy those residences, have connections to those residences, and use those residences for a variety of unsavory behaviors.

The idea that public housing generally and Section 8 specifically is only occupied by those too weak or disabled to commit crime denies or overlooks the nature of urban crime. Recall, for example, that the MTO studies found that many potential Section 8 "renters" did not "lease up" in part because they did not want to leave their surroundings and the people in those surroundings. When they did "lease up" they did not break with their social and familial networks. Those networks—the sons, uncles, brothers, friends, drug dealers, and thugs— remained part and parcel of their lives. In other words, Section 8 renters did not extricate themselves from the networks of crime and disrepute despite relocating to sometimes very different neighborhoods. Indeed, they imported those networks into their new settings.

While it would strain credulity to believe that men are simply magically absent from those settings, it would also be empirically false. Reeling from increases in crime, the city of Dubuque, IA, examined the connection between the distribution of Section 8 and crime. The results not only reveal the patterns of crime associated with Section 8 but also point to the intellectual deception engaged in by liberal housing advocates.

Consistent with liberal claims, when looking only at individuals "authorized" to reside in Section 8 properties the Dubuque study found that arrest rates for Section 8 tenants were only slightly higher than non-Section 8 individuals (5.4 percent v. 3.4 percent), that victimization rates were roughly equal, and that complaint rates about property conditions or behavior at the property were only slightly higher (6.2 percent v. 5.7 percent). Interestingly, these are the pattern of findings emphasized by HUD and by housing advocates (Bovard, 2011; Souza Briggs & Dreier, 2008).

Even so, when the authors combined data from police incident databases, new patterns emerged. It would be Janikowski and Betts revisited. Violent crime (murder, rape, robbery, and aggravated assault), they found, was almost two times higher at Section 8 addresses than non-Section 8 addresses, and local ordinance complaints were over five times higher at Section 8 residences. Other types of crime and disorder were at equal or lower levels but the patterns linking serious crime and disorder were evident. However, the authors of the study were also keenly aware that more individuals occupied or were associated with Section 8 addresses than simply those on the lease. With this in mind, the authors examined the addresses given by individuals at the time of their arrest. They then cross-referenced those addresses with Section 8 housing roles. When the researchers added these names to the

Section 8 roles the previous pattern of findings changed: Instead of finding that Section 8 residents experienced parity in criminal victimization, they now found that victimization rates were 1.6 times higher for Section 8 residents. More importantly, they also found that instead of being arrested at roughly equal levels as non-Section 8 residents, the arrest rate for Section 8 "residents" was actually 2.5 times higher. Quoting from the study:

> The above associations involving Section 8 housing units implicate S8 housing in patterns of crime that circumscribe the incident & victim, incident & arrestee, and victim & arrestee locations more than random, independent processes predict. When crimes occur at S8 locations, the victims are more likely to be S8 residents than predicted by chance. When crimes occur at S8 locations, the arrestees for those crimes are more likely to be S8 residents than predicted by chance. And when victims live at S8 locations, the arrestees are more likely to live at S8 locations than predicted by chance. In sum, the pattern of interactions involving S8 address locations among incidents, victims, and arrestees is consistent with the interpretation that crime in Dubuque is probabilistically circumscribed by S8 address involvement rather than diffused across address locations.
>
> *(NIU Center for Governmental Studies, 2010: 49)*

Cabrini Green became a symbol for the failure of the public housing experiment. The failure was more than a failure to understand how environmental design could affect living patterns, however. The larger failure was twofold: First, liberal housing advocates and most sociologists/criminologists have simply not confronted the powerful forces of culture—especially underclass culture. In avoiding the issue of culture they have ignored how the receipt of welfare benefits is socially understood by the underclass. Instead of being viewed as a temporary band-aid to immediate and dire economic circumstances and as an opportunity to rearrange and better one's life, far too many who receive these benefits view them as a right or an entitlement. They arrange their lives and lifestyles around the receipt of government handouts, trade them for favors, sex, drugs, guns and cars, and they have intimate knowledge of how the welfare system works, its policies, laws, even the names of individual bureaucrats and case workers. Indeed, they speak of welfare in highly personal and possessive terms: It is not uncommon, for instance, to hear of "my welfare," or of "my Section 8" when the issue is discussed.

The second failure was in identifying neighborhood "structural" variables as responsible for individual criminal behavior and the concomitant assumption that if the cause of crime is environmental then it is amenable to change. This is where criminologists, with their almost fanatical focus on poverty, residential mobility, and the newly packaged and more politically correct term "collective efficacy," come into play (Sampson, Raudenbush, & Earls, 1997). Much of the assumption about the possible crime reducing influence of decentralizing crime and poverty emerged out of research into neighborhood factors associated with crime. There is a long history of sociological criminology searching for "structural" variables that can account for differences in crime rates across neighborhoods or places. But to be clear: Almost every sociological/structural theory of crime would have predicted success with the MTO intervention. Indeed, MTO interventionists used and included in their reports almost all of the major structural theories of crime as justifications for the MTO intervention (Sanbonmatsu et al., 2011). Hence, the failure of the MTO experiments reflects a failure not only of the intervention but also of the ideas and theories that justified the intervention.

The receipt of a Section 8 housing voucher is highly valuable amongst members of the underclass, in part because it can substantially increase their standard of living and reduce their overall financial expenditures without any effort on their part. Unfortunately, Section 8 is viewed as the new golden goose of welfare. One needs only to look at the behaviors of the large crowds that frequently line up for a voucher to see the degree to which Section 8 is valued and decent behavior is not. In August 2010, over 30,000 people turned out in the Tri-Cities Plaza Shopping Complex at East Point (Atlanta) in the hopes of receiving a Section 8 voucher. Over 62 people were injured in what was described by the *Atlanta Constitutional Journal* as a "mob scene." Fights broke out as people cut in line. Police, dressed in riot gear, had to call in backup from surrounding counties, while ambulances ushered infants, children, mothers, and the elderly to local hospitals. The same pattern was on display in Dallas, TX, where hundreds of people broke off from a crowd of at least 5,000 and rushed the stadium doors. The same thing has happened in Memphis, TN, and even Galveston, TX, where individuals traveled hundreds of miles for the chance to gain a voucher.

For men in these areas, Section 8 simply represents yet another opportunity to live parasitically off of the benefits of grandmothers, their disabled friends, and any number of girlfriends. Such an understanding necessarily means that the promises and hopes of Section 8 and other housing programs will not be met with any degree of success. Moreover, it also means that underclass culture, with its emphasis on "getting over" and all its deeply embedded social pathologies (teen pregnancy, crime, incivility, slothfulness), will be imported into neighborhoods and into the social institutions in those neighborhoods. This breaks down social order and trust, and it can send neighborhoods on the economic tipping point over the edge, creating new ghettos.

The "Family" Court: The Last Vestige of Blatant Discrimination

Imagine a court where the outcome of a case could be predicted with 95 percent accuracy simply by knowing the sex of the respondent. Would that qualify as institutional discrimination? Assuming it would, what would be the political ramifications if the discrimination harmed women as opposed to men? Would liberal reformers and criminologists sound the hue and cry? Would they mount a social movement against institutional sexism? Would they cite due process concerns and call for equal treatment under the law? We suspect so.

But that court system actually exists in the United States. Daily, and without much reflection, the court strips fathers of ownership of all or most of their possessions, it strips them of their ability to make enough money to live on, much less to start another family, it socially stigmatizes all fathers as "deadbeats," and it places in jail fathers who, sometimes through no fault of their own, cannot pay the sometimes draconian levels of child support. As if that were not enough, family courts routinely rescind the rights of fathers to have a say in the upbringing of their children. At best, fathers get to "visit" their children periodically, often only when approved by the "custodial parent," a euphemism for the mother, and at worse, they see their children turned against them. By no great stretch of the imagination, if this were happening to mothers, liberals would take to the streets. But men in general, and fathers specifically, are not victims that excite sympathy. Men do not fall into the protected classes that women and children do, nor do they raise much fuss about the fact.

The narrative underpinning the operation of the family court, still widely taught in sociology and criminology programs across the United States, goes something like this:

> When parents divorce, the woman falls into poverty and the husband abandons his children. Because of patriarchy, women are not as educated as men, don't have as many opportunities for good paying jobs, and thus cannot make enough to support her

children. Thus, it is not fair that women and children suffer and that fathers get to live the high life, free of their commitment to the family.

Like any myth, there are sometimes elements of truth woven through the fabric of the narrative. But myths are usually only glimpses into the complexity of a social problem, telling a story that is only somewhat true some of the time under some situations. Myths emphasize some information and overlook or ignore others; they provide for quick understanding without any real intellectual effort. Jim Crow laws, for example, were supported by the myth that blacks could not be trusted to vote and could not become full and participating citizens. Problems emerge, however, when myths serve as the basis for law, especially when the application of law systematically rewards one party at the expense of the other. But this is the system we have currently, and like any institutionalized system of sexism or racism, it claims moral legitimacy by appealing to the myth.

This myth has threads to which there are actual answers. For example, liberal reformers of the family court, especially feminists, based much of their argument on three interrelated "facts." First, that divorce crippled women economically and threw them and their children into poverty. Second, that most fathers were deadbeats and did not want to support their children, emotionally or financially, and third, that men were unfazed by divorce and ultimately benefited from it. We address these arguments below, but we urge the reader to keep in mind that the point is not to demonize mothers or arbitrarily elevate fathers but to show how specific liberal reforms have created harm, invited totalitarian thinking, and erected and sustained a system of abject discrimination. Moreover, we encourage the reader to recognize the role of social science research in the crafting of family court policies and how this research was accepted as "true" by scholars who simply failed to critically analyze the claims made by liberal scholars.

The feminist movement of the 1970s and 1980s enjoyed an unmitigated success in framing the debate about the consequences of divorce in the United States. The debate reached a tipping point when a book by Harvard sociology professor Lenore Weitzman was published. In her book, *The Divorce Revolution: The Unexpected Social and Economic Consequences for Women and Children in America*, Weitzman (1985) argued that after divorce, women suffered a 74 percent reduction in their standard of living while men enjoyed a 42 percent increase. To put that in perspective, if the mother's income was $10,000 prior to divorce, after divorce, with a 74 percent reduction, the woman would have only $2,600, while the father would see his income increase from $10,000 to $14,200. Even by contemporary standards, these differences would be difficult to overlook. Weitzman also argued that because divorced women suffer from several disadvantages, that they should have a right to a large chunk of her ex-husband's salary in order to forever maintain their standard of living.

Some studies hit at the right time and are swept instantly into the vernacular of public policy. This was one of those studies. It is difficult to express the influence that Weitzman's book exerted on feminists and liberal reformers, but it still stands as one of the most cited books in the area. Indeed, a past president of the American Sociological Association referred to it as "social science at its best," and Weitzman was invited to testify to Congress; her work was even cited by the Supreme Court (Braver & O'Connell, 1998: 56). Her research also invigorated feminist scholars to pour over census data looking for evidence of economic fatalities. They quickly found it, and launched an assault on what they saw as a system that discriminated against women and children. Women, the narrative went, were being thrown into poverty by the greedy self-interest of men, were not capable of negotiating within the patriarchal structures of the family court, and thus required the protection of the state.

History, however, is littered with examples of the results of a single study being used to justify the creation of laws, only for it to be found later that the study was flawed, biased, or so severely compromised methodologically that the results were called into question or were outright rejected. Later examinations of these studies, however, usually have little impact as the laws have already been passed, leaving little political momentum to admit much less rectify a mistake. Years after the release of Weitzman's book, a psychologist at Arizona State University, Sandford Braver, began to interview divorced men and women. In trying to reconcile the census data feminists pointed to as showing that women fell off an economic cliff after divorce he found that the 74 percent decline in the standard of living allegedly experienced by divorced women was the result of an arithmetic error. Women did see a decline in their income, but the decline was 26 percent, not 74 percent. Again, in practical terms, this meant that an income of $10,000 would decrease to $7,400, which is substantively different from the $2,600 noted by Weitzman. Follow-on work confirmed Braver's analysis. Peterson's (1996) publication in the *American Sociological Review* drew on Weitzman's own data and found *exactly* the error noted by Braver. In that same issue, Weitzman acknowledged the mistake.

If women didn't suffer the massive economic setback Weitzman claimed, was it still true that most fathers sought to abandon their children emotionally and financially? After all, the image of most divorced fathers is that they are "deadbeats," a term of derision used to justify sometimes incredible state encroachments. Alleged "deadbeats" have become the fodder for prosecutors seeking a name for themselves, for conservatives who wish to emphasize the moral responsibility of fathers, and for liberals who see men as uniquely flawed (Baskerville, 2002). The idea that divorced men are largely "deadbeats" came out of feminist efforts to draw attention to what they perceived as an inequity in the system. Following Weitzman's lead, feminists used data from the United States Census to argue that men were not living up to their responsibilities—census data revealing that between 50 to 60 percent of women did not receive all of their child support. Consistent with the myth, feminists immediately jumped to the conclusion that divorced men simply walked out on their responsibilities.

This is a powerful element of the overall myth. It conforms to liberal and feminist ideology, supports harsh and repressive efforts to sanction divorced fathers, and it reduces what is undoubtedly a complex problem into a simple phenomenon that can be easily understood: men are bad (Baumeister, 2010). Each year, for example, calls for men to return to the lives of their children are echoed by politicians. Presidents Clinton and Obama, for example, joined the chorus of anti-father rhetoric; each Father's Day, a day set out to recognize the contributions of fathers, both have pled for fathers to live up to their responsibilities. Again, we can hardly imagine the political and social fallout if a president of the United States took it upon himself to castigate mothers on Mother's Day.

The problem with the image of the divorced father as a "deadbeat" is that it is almost wholly countered by data. Braver and O'Connell (1998) point out that the census data used by feminists to justify the creation of harsh, punitive, redistributive laws were seriously flawed. Virtually all analyses of how much child support was received by mothers and how compliant the father was in meeting his obligations to his children were reported solely by mothers. It doesn't take much in the way of understanding human behavior to understand that divorced parents, men and women alike, may have a serious bias in their reports about the behavior of their ex-spouse. Braver and O'Connell's analysis of over 1,000 divorcing couples makes this obvious: in virtually every measure assessed, mother and father reports significantly differed. Mothers reported significantly less father involvement in their children's lives, while fathers reported significantly more. For example, compared to mother reports, fathers reported spending 33 percent more total time with their children, 22.1 percent more hours per week, 37 percent more distinct visitation day, and 22.3 percent more days visiting over the month. Measured three years later, the pattern remained the same, with fathers reporting spending 40 percent more time with their children than mothers reported. Mothers also reported significantly less financial aid given by fathers. Custodial mothers reported receiving 66 to 75 percent of child support owed. Fathers, on the other hand, reported paying more than 90 percent.

Why do some mothers not receive child support? Is it because a majority of men simply do not pay it? The answer is simply no. When fathers are employed, Braver and O'Connell found, almost all of them pay their child support in full. The few that don't constitute about 3 to 7 percent of all divorced fathers—hardly enough to label all divorced fathers as "deadbeats" (see also U.S. Census Bureau, 2012). Problems occur, however, when a man loses his job. Unable to pay, his child support bill continues to mount month after month, leaving the father with a non-dischargeable debt he did not intentionally create and cannot ever pay off. In many ways it is a form of legal indentured servitude. This problem largely affects lower-class, largely uneducated men who are always on the periphery of the economy (Kaufman, 2005). Follow-on studies have also found the same pattern: when men are employed, they pay, when they are not employed, they don't (Bartfeld & Meyer, 1993).

Another aspect to this myth is that women are powerless in a system managed largely by men. Again, the data show a very different picture. Women initiate the majority of divorce proceedings, and they usually cite "mundane factors" such as not being emotionally satisfied as the primary reasons for seeking divorce. The decision to seek divorce is clearly influenced by a balance between the varied costs and rewards of staying in a marriage. Women clearly see the rewards of divorce to be greater than the rewards of staying in a marriage, and they know that the system will go to great lengths to protect their interests. Indeed, many financial incentives make it profitable for women to leave marriage. They are guaranteed alimony, child support, most of the property, and more importantly, possession of the children. Consider too Braver and O'Connell's finding (1998: 103) that "not a single father thought that the system favored them in the slightest, and three-quarters thought that it favored mothers. And mothers tended to *agree* that the system was slanted in their favor." In every area measured, custodial mothers reported increased satisfaction with custody and visitation, with child support and the division of property, and with the child's financial status (Lin, 2000). Far from being unwitting pawns in a patriarchal system, the data show that maternal interests trump paternal desires, and they do so systematically (Mincy, Jethwani, & Klempin, 2015). Even the majority of divorced women agree (Gardner, 1993)!

Finally, it is remarkable that so many believe that fathers, who disproportionately have their children taken from them or lose their day-to-day involvement with their children, lose sometimes 50 percent or more of their income, lose their status and authority as a parent, are viewed with suspicion and even disdain, and believe they have little chance of a fair hearing in the family court, do not suffer. Alcoholism and abuse, bankruptcy, depression and anxiety, or even suicide are experienced by an overwhelming proportion of divorcing fathers. These problems are exacerbated when mothers interfere with, or outright deny, the father's legitimate access to their children. Data from Wallerstein and Kelly (2008) found that a majority of divorced women, women who by and large initiated the divorce, express extreme anger, bitterness, and a desire to punish their ex-husband. Moreover, they frequently share their anger with their children, and many openly admitted that they throw up obstacles to prevent fathers from enjoying a relationship with their children. The courts, moreover, rarely sanction women for interfering with a father's visitation right. It is small wonder then that time and again divorced fathers report being alienated from their children. According to Braver and O'Connell (1998: 156):

> Fathers felt that everything about the divorce, especially anything concerning the way the children were raised, was completely out of their control. They felt as if the child was in no real sense *theirs* anymore. The child, in effect, belonged now to someone else, someone who, not uncommonly, despised and disparaged them.

Braver goes on to note that every single study since his landmark study has reported the same pattern. "Divorced fathers," more than one father in Braver's study commented, "have no rights." Far from being "deadbeats," most divorced fathers are pushed away from their children by mothers who actively work against them and by a system that views them as a mere paycheck.

Liberal Harm through Expansive Government

The family court holds little legitimacy with divorced men, largely because they uniformly believe, and with good cause, that the deck is stacked against them. In most jurisdictions across America, women are *automatically* awarded custody of the children. The reasons for this may be cultural, a belief that women are better parents; structural, the fact that traditionally men have been responsible for working full-time and thus could not spend as much time with their children; or simply traditional, the courts have always awarded women custody of children. Whatever the reason, it is fair to say that unless a woman is a drug addict or incarcerated she will be awarded custody. Even today, "shared custody" or "joint custody" occurs in about 10 to 15 percent of all divorces. Overlooking this for a moment, the broader story here is how progressive ideology contributed to expanding the federal government into the lives of men, how they have used the instruments of government to force the redistribution of wealth to a politically protected class, and how in the process they have destroyed the relationships of millions of children and fathers. Only the brute power of government unleashed could accomplish this, and only an appeal to "doing good" could justify it.

Prior to 1975, federal entanglement in child support efforts extended only to children on welfare. Until then, the issue was considered the province of state and local courts. This changed in 1975, when President Ford, bowing to the pressure of the American Bar Association and a variety of feminist groups, signed legislation that created the Office of Child Support Enforcement (OCSE). At the time, Ford argued that the creation of the OCSE literally invited the tentacles of the federal government into the homes of America's families. His words of caution could not have been more prescient. From 1978 to 1998, the program grew tenfold in size. By 2000, OCSE employed directly or indirectly over 58,000 agents, many of whom have the authority to issue arrest warrants and seize property. By 2007, the OCSE collected almost $25 dollars from non-custodial parents, accessed the private employment information of almost five million NCPs, and accessed information on the financial accounts of 2.6 million NCPs, almost all men. The OCSE provides approximately $35 billion to states to implement and enforce child support guidelines, and works with states to provide the information infrastructure necessary to keep millions of NCPs under constant surveillance (Baskerville, 2002, 2007).

Child support is also big business. In 1984, legislation supported by OCSE created federal child support guidelines. The "guidelines" were at first aimed only at individuals on welfare, as a way, the reasoning went, to reduce welfare expenditures by increasing the amounts paid by NCPs. The guidelines were hastily constructed by a paid consultant to the Department of Health and Human Services, and were based on a set of highly questionable assumptions. No major studies on the validity or impact of the guidelines were conducted. They were simply approved with little forethought. However, suddenly and largely without warning, the guidelines were extended to all divorce cases in 1988. To be clear, the guidelines were originally designed to make sure women did not qualify for welfare benefits. Their application to the millions of parents for whom there was no possibility of this happening has produced a full range of odd, harmful, and entirely inexplicable support awards. There are documented examples of men being forced to pay more than they actually make in a month, or having so little left over after their support payment that they have no funds for basic living necessities.

Along with these guidelines came the governmental machinery to enforce payment by NCPs. Estimates now indicate that child support collection is a $500 billion a year enterprise. Because it can be lucrative, companies such as Lockhead Martin IMS began to contract with OCSE. States, moreover, were incentivized by the federal government to accept federal enforcement practices or lose federal money. They responded rapidly by hiring thousands of agents whose sole purpose was to collect money from divorced fathers. Even local prosecutors got into the game as they saw a new funding stream.

Federal expansion into the very minutiae of families, however, is minimal compared to the power wielded by the family court. The family court is one of the most secretive courts in America, and one that has almost unlimited power over the lives of individuals under its jurisdiction. It regularly issues orders of protection against men for various alleged behaviors. To be certain, many of these orders are for purpose but all too often orders of protection are used as weapons in divorce proceedings. The family court can also require "supervised parenting" in cases where abuse, neglect or some other offense has been merely alleged. This is not a free service by the court, with the cost of "supervision" breaking $200 per hour in some jurisdictions. And in contested divorce cases, the court can require psychological evaluations, social work evaluations, and a host of other information gathering adventures … all at a cost to the petitioning parties. Again, a common criticism amongst divorced fathers is that the instruments of the court are decidedly used against them. In part due to the costs involved, many divorcing fathers may simply be unable to incur the financial expenses imposed by the court. And many simply do not wish to suffer the indignities associated with an investigation of allegations of domestic violence so often made in divorce cases.

Given its importance, we might assume that the family court would generate interest amongst criminologists. That assumption would be incorrect. Virtually nothing has been written by criminologists and very little data are available about the practices of the court. That said, critics have been growing in number. Indeed, national organizations for men's rights now exist. These groups are active and have been successful, sometimes, in petitioning the government for redress. Here, however, criminologists do have something to say. In the pages of *Feminist Criminology* one can readily find articles that reduce the obvious problems associated with the family court to a mere backlash against feminism.

In the typical impenetrable language employed by most feminist scholars, Mann (2008) "deconstructs" the men's rights movement when she writes that:

> men's advocates deploy a rhetoric of hatred and victimization that they have honed through internationally linked Web site diatribes against feminism, ex-wives, child support, shelters, and the family law and criminal justice systems. Inflamed by the stories they tell each other and themselves, men's advocates demand entrance into policy deliberations. They refuse, however, to abide by norms of "mutually respectful" policy

dialogue, and thus project not consonance but dissonance with governmental goals. Again and again they conclude and proclaim that the system is biased and that feminism is behind a pervasive and persistent assault on men and "cover-up" of men's victimization.

Contrary to a large body of evidence showing that men are systematically disenfranchised by the family courts, Mann seemingly attributes men's perception of victimization to some form of mental delusion (sort of like calling a woman crazy, we add). They are merely hate-filled at having lost their esteemed status as vanguards of patriarchy and have used the internet to solidify their sexist views. Adding insult to injury, she then argues that men's rights groups should subjugate themselves to "government goals."

She then goes on to lay out what men's rights groups have to do in order to be heard:

> participants must demonstrate willingness and ability to participate in the new demo-cratized gender order … . They must demonstrate that they recognize the scope and seriousness of the domestic violence problem, that they eschew violence and bullying absolutely, that they respect difference, that they recognize each other as equals, and that they are willing to prioritize children. Finally, they must demonstrate commitment to collective efforts to eradicate social harm through partnership and dialogue. They must show that they are willing and able to play the community civility game mandated for our advanced liberal moment.

Stated differently, Mann is essentially saying that men's rights groups have to buy in to the very system they find so oppressive, accept, without reason, the arguments of feminists, and follow the scriptures of established liberal political correctness. Personally, we find the idea of a "gendered democracy" frightening, and anathema to constitutional jurisprudence. More importantly, Mann's argument strikes us as being at the heart of totalitarian thinking, or the soft despotism noted by de Tocqueville. Amazingly, she then writes that men's rights groups must conform to liberal expectations by playing the "community civility game," whatever that means.

The feminist political agenda and bias is obvious in Mann's work, but if Mann's work is a glaring example of liberal criminological bias, Dragiewicz's paper in the same issue of *Feminist Criminology* exemplifies the thinking of a purely indoctrinated liberal mindset. According to Dragiewicz (2008: 121), any resistance to feminist accounts or claims is equal to "backlash." But "backlash," she writes, "is not simply a sign of resistance to feminism that seeks to slow its progress or temper its impact; it is an effort to reaffirm the patriarchal domination of women." She then goes on to equate the protests of men's rights groups as another form of "abuse," or as the "reassertion of patriarchy." To Dragiewicz and her like-minded colleagues, father's rights groups have taken on many of the characteristics of a terrorist organization; they thus appear to be one step away from calling for criminal oversight of fathers who merely want to be treated with dignity and respect and allowed to be part of the lives of their children. "Rhetoric in the form of calls for "fathers' rights," Dragiewicz (2008: 137) proudly proclaims, "not only fails to challenge feminist research and theorizing on violence, but also points to the centrality of the relationship between patriarchy and men's violence against women." This is the level of criminological reasoning on the topic.

Stepping away from the intellectual strain of reading quasi-scholarly feminist diatribes, we note how feminist ideology explicitly supports blatant discrimination and the use of repressive and invasive methods of governmental control, and how it seeks to "pathologicalize" its critics. Feminist criminologists, who at national criminology conferences pass around pink buttons with the saying "Quiet Women Rarely Make History" stamped on them, have rarely played by the rules of the "community civility game." This is part of the leftist orientation of criminologists that we rail against. They accept, directly or implicitly, tyranny by the state if it conforms to their ideological view, and they "pathologicalize" or discredit those who question their presumed authority

A Conservative Critique

These two examples highlight the ways in which social science has been linked to specific policy recommendations and where those recommendations have had a dramatic and sometimes negative impact on the lives of individuals and communities. We chose these examples because they reveal the important nexus between liberal academic biases, liberal advocacy, and social harm. Nonetheless, our point is not that some of the changes brought about by family courts, child support guidelines, or housing policy have not had a net positive effect but that many of the changes have not. More importantly, the critical, objective analyses that could have reduced the harm done by these policies have been almost entirely absent. We suggest one reason for this is what is called "confirmation bias." Confirmation bias occurs when results of scientific analyses supportive of one's political or personal biases emerge and are not then subject to critical examination. Studies, for example, showing alleged racism against blacks are given much greater methodological latitude by reviewers than are studies that show no racism. Studies that show sex discrimination, the failings of the death penalty, or the benefits of "diversity" or affirmative action, or studies that support other liberal views are often simply given a pass because they confirm the worldview of the author's and reviewers. Confirmation bias then produces a body of studies that allegedly show a pattern of results allowing liberal scholars to argue that "science is on their side." In reality, however, what is on their side is a bias that applies different standards to different studies based in part on their political leanings.

Confirmation bias is alive and well (Ceci, Peters, & Plotkin, 1985; Fanelli, 2010; Franco, Malhotra, & Simonovits, 2014; Goodstein & Brazis, 1970; Koehler, 1993; Peters & Ceci, 1982). It was alive and well with the studies on child support and it was alive and well in the MTO studies where scholars largely highlighted the supposed beneficial correlations and severely downplayed the null findings. Confirmation bias is also alive and well in a host of other areas where some studies are given elevated priority and others are entirely ignored, severely scrutinized, or simply rebuked on political grounds. This is the warning we issue, the problem we see, and the point of our book: the biases that infuse liberalism through social science produce an inaccurate portrait of individuals, communities, our society and the rules and policies we create. It strangles critical inquiry and can result in objectively measured harm. We believe the story told by the injection of feministic views on divorce prove this point, as does the story told about the deleterious effects of Section 8.

Aside from the problems that emerge when scholars work from within a single, dominant paradigm, we note that conservatism would also offer a balanced critique of these policies. From a conservative viewpoint, for example, Section 8, in its current form is unacceptable for at least three reasons: First, the federal government, through HUD, exercises tremendous power and economic clout when it seeks to expand Section 8 into new areas. Some communities have fought back against HUD but have, in turn, been sued by HUD in federal court. Small communities and counties are no match against the power of the federal government, so HUD can act as a bully and litigate its way into functional neighborhoods. HUD can also bribe local jurisdictions through the use of grants and infrastructure monies—monies that go, at least temporarily, to create local jobs. Many communities, in need of cash, simply take the money despite knowing the problems that are attached to it. From a conservative point of view, this is a gross abuse of federal power.

Second, conservatism emphasizes a basic morality that should follow or guide the receipt of social welfare benefits. The reasoning is simple: If you live off of the work of others, you should act responsibly. Of course, acting responsibly translates into not committing crime, into taking care of your children, into sacrificing certain desires, and into transitioning as quickly as possible from dependency to self-sufficiency. Hence, receiving social welfare benefits, benefits that are paid for by others, should also bring with it basic social obligations. Various studies now show that far too many of those who receive Section 8 do not engage in a moral exchange. Instead, they take Section 8 and still refuse to lead a non-criminal, largely responsible lifestyle.

This is tied in to our third reason why Section 8, as currently implemented, is unacceptable. For many adults, purchasing a house is their single largest investment. It takes a large percentage of their income and it requires constant maintenance and upkeep. More importantly, their choice of the home they purchased and the neighborhood they purchased it in comes on the heels of years, if not decades, of hard work, schooling, and sacrifice. To many homeowners, their home thus represents not only their financial status but also their hopes and aspirations for their future and the future of their children, it represents the reward of their sacrifices, and it represents their investment in their community and in the institutions within their community. So it takes little imagination to understand why homeowners are suspicious, cautious, or even outright hostile to Section 8 being installed in their neighborhood. Section 8 not only threatens their property values, it threatens the vitality, safety, functioning, and institution of their community. When Section 8 arrives in neighborhoods, those who can leave do and they take with them the taxes and social capital that made the community functional.

But this is only part of the problem. For homeowners who have worked all their lives to be able to choose where they live, Section 8 is simply viewed as unfair. It unfairly rewards individuals who have behaved irresponsibly, those who have not worked all their life, who have not sacrificed for their future, and who largely continue to behave without regards for their long-term interests. Section 8, in the eyes of many, not only threatens the financial investment they have in their homes, the social investments they have in their communities, but is also viewed as a form of "cheating" that some individuals engage in to gain entrance into a neighborhood that everyone else has had to work to gain entrance into. This is a primary reason why conservatives oppose the expansion of Section 8—because it rewards behavior that should not be rewarded and because it equates outcomes (housing) when the inputs (work and self-sacrifice) are radically different.

Similarly, conservatives should be very concerned about the institutional operations of the family court. While conservatives have fought any number of cultural battles to keep the family as the cornerstone of American society, conservatives have lost sight of the fact that an American institution functions in ways that brings harm to children and parents. We suggest that conservatives have chosen to ignore the problems endemic in the family court because they want to appear to support family functioning and do not want to appear unsupportive of women and children. Yet a reasonable conservative argument in favor of eliminating or reining in the family court can be made without appearing patriarchal or callous.

First, the family court is an institution of law and is thus required to act impartially and without bias. There is simply no justification for the way the court systematically awards custody of children to women, for the hostility extended to fathers, or for the economic incentivizing of divorce for women. In many cases men are better parents than some mothers, and in most cases they are at least equal. In other cases, obviously, children are better off with their mothers. Yet it takes almost a miracle in many jurisdictions for a reasonable, caring father to be awarded custody—even in situations where the mother may be addicted to drugs, may abuse the children, and may subject the kids to every form of hostile parenting imaginable.

Second, the discrimination argument aside, conservatives should be concerned that the current situation creates financial incentives for women to divorce men and to act with impunity in ways that damage their children's relationships with their fathers. There are no serious laws against mothers or fathers intentionally damaging their children's relationships with their other parent. Indeed, we find it odd and perplexing that, on the one hand, states have uniformly adopted the principles of "family reunification" where serious abuse and neglect have occurred, while on the other hand have created the conditions that sponsor or incentivize divorce amongs couples with children. Conservatives should recognize, first, the harm done by the current operation of the family court, and second, the various ways that the state has inadvertently incentivized divorce. Indeed, our suggestion would be to treat divorce through mediation, to make joint custody a reality where possible, and to revamp the draconian, invasive, and harmful child support system now in place.

We also believe the time is ripe for reconciliation. For decades fathers have been systematically discriminated against: their children taken from them, their financial resources decimated, their reputations sullied. They have not found the courts a place where fair treatment could be expected; instead have found they have no voice and no rights. Because of this, men have suffered in ways that would simply be considered unacceptable and immoral if imposed on women. Divorced men are twice as likely to commit suicide compared to married men and almost five times more likely to commit suicide than divorced women (Kposowa, 2003). Other data show that divorce can also trigger alcoholism and a range of other mental health problems in men and that part of the reaction is related to the all-encompassing sense of loss, anger, and helplessness fathers feel because the courts have taken from them everything that matters to them. Indeed, we believe it a gross injustice that violent criminals receive more legal protection from state abuses than do divorcing fathers. Because fathers have been systematically discriminated against for decades, because the discrimination has been institutionalized by the state, and because the harm done has been widespread, measurable, and unnecessary, we argue that it is time not only for major reforms in the family court but also for a public apology and acceptance of wrongdoing, complete with compensation accorded any other group that has been victimized by discriminatory treatment.

References

Bartfeld, J., & Meyer, D. R. (1993) Are there really deadbeat dads? The relationship between ability to pay, enforcement, and compliance in nonmarital child support cases (DP 994–93). University of Wisconsin-Madison Institute for Research on Poverty Discussion Papers. Retrieved from www.irp.wisc.edu/publications/dps/pdfs/dp99493.pdf.

Baskerville, S. (2002) The myth of deadbeat dads. *Liberty*, June, 27–32. Retrieved from www.canadiancrc.com/Fatherlessness/deadbeats.pdf.

Baskerville, S. (2007) *Taken into custody: The war against fathers, marriage, and the family.* Nashville, TN: Cumberland House Publishing.

Baumeister, R. F. (2010) *Is there anything good about men? How cultures flourish by exploiting men.* New York: Oxford University Press.

Bovard, J. (2011) Raising hell in subsidized housing: Section 8 subsidies have long helped ruin neighborhoods. Obama administration policies are making things worse. *The Wall Street Journal*, August 17. Retrieved from www.wsj.com/articles/SB10001424053111903520204576480542593887906.

Braver, S., & O'Connell, D. (1998) *Divorced dads: Shattering the myths. The surprising truth about fathers, children, and divorce.* New York: Tarcher/Putnam.

CATO Institute (2015) Department of Housing and Urban Development. *Downsizing the Federal Government.* Retrieved from www.downsizinggovernment.org/housing-and-urban-development.

Ceci, S. J., Peters, D., & Plotkin, J. (1985) Human subjects review, personal values, and the regulation of social science research. *American Psychologist*, 40(9), 994–1002.

Dragiewicz, M. (2008) Patriarchy reasserted: Fathers' rights and anti-VAWA activism. *Feminist Criminology*, 3(2), 121–144.

Ellen, I. G., M. C. Lens, & O'Regan, K. M. (2012) American murder mystery revisited: Do housing voucher households cause crime? *Housing Policy Debate*, 22(4), 551–572.

Fanelli, D. (2010) "Positive" results increase down the hierarchy of the sciences. *PLoS ONE*, 5(4).

Franco, A., Malhotra, N., & Simonovits, G. (2014) Publication bias in the social sciences: Unlocking the file drawer. *Science*, 345(6203), 1502–1505.

Galster, G. C., Tatian, P., & Smith, R. (1999) The impact of neighbors who use section 8 certificates on property values. *Housing Policy Debate*, 10(4), 879–917.

Gardner, M. (1993) Finding fairness in family court. *The Christian Science Monitor*, October 12. Retrieved from www.csmonitor.com/1993/1012/12121.html.

Goetz, E. G. (2013) *New Deal ruins: Race, economic justice, & public housing policy.* Ithaca, NY: Cornell University Press.

Goodstein, L. D., & Brazis, K. L. (1970) Psychology of scientists: XXX. Credibility of psychologists: An empirical study. *Psychological Reports*, 27(3), 835–838.

Hunt, D. B. (2009) *Blueprint for disaster: The unraveling of Chicago Public Housing.* Chicago, IL: University of Chicago Press.

Katz, L. F., Kling, J. R., & Liebman, J. B. (2001) Moving to Opportunity in Boston: Early results of a randomized mobility experiment. *Quarterly Journal of Economics*, 116(2), 607–654.

Kaufman, L. (2005) When child support is due, even the poor find little mercy. *The New York Times*, February 19. Retrieved from www.nytimes.com/2005/02/19/nyregion/when-child-support-is-due-even-the-poor-find-little-mercy.html.

Kirk, R. (2001) *The conservative mind: From Burke to Eliot.* Washington, DC: Regnery Publishing.

Kling, J. R., Ludwig, J., & Katz, L. F. (2005) Neighborhood effects on crime for female and male youth: Evidence from a randomized housing voucher experiment. *Quarterly Journal of Economics*, 120(1), 87–130.

Koehler, J. J. (1993) The influence of prior beliefs on scientific judgments of evidence quality. *Organizational Behavior and Human Decision Processes*, 56(1), 28–55.

Kposowa, A. J. (2003) Divorce and suicide risk. *Journal of Epidemiology and Community Health*, 57, 993–995.

Lens, M. C. (2014) The impact of housing vouchers on crime in US cities and suburbs. *Urban Studies*, 51(6), 1274–1289.

Leventhal, T., & Brooks-Gunn, J. (2003) The early impacts of Moving to Opportunity on children and youth in New York City. In *Choosing a better life: Evaluating the Moving to Opportunity social experiment*, ed. J. Goering and J. Feins. Washington, DC: Urban Institute Press.

Lin, I. F. (2000) Perceived fairness and compliance with child support obligations. *Journal of Marriage and Family*, 62(2), 388–398.

Ludwig, J., Duncan, G. J., Gennetia, L. A., Katz, L. F., Kessler, R. C., Kling, J. R., & Sanbonmatsu, L. (2012) Neighborhood effects on the long-term well-being of low-income adults. *Science*, 337(6101), 1505–1510.

Ludwig, J., Duncan, G. J., & Hirschfield, P. (2001) Urban poverty and juvenile crime: Evidence from a randomized housing-mobility experiment. *Quarterly Journal of Economics*, 116(2), 655–680.

Mann, M. (2008) The autonomous power of the state: Its origins, mechanisms, and results. In N. Brenner, B. Jessop, M. Jones, & G. Macleod (eds), *State/Space: A Reader.* Malden, MA: Blackwell Publishing, pp. 53–64.

Mincy, R. B., Jethwani, M., & Klempin, S. (2015) *Failing our fathers: Confronting the crisis of economically vulnerable nonresident fathers.* New York: Oxford University Press.

Minogue, K. (2010) *The servile mind: How democracy erodes the moral life.* New York: Encounter Books.

Northern Illinois University Center for Governmental Studies (2010) *Dubuque 2010 crime & poverty study summary report,* 1–71. Retrieved from www.cityofdubuque.org/1446/Study-on-Crime-Poverty -Report.

Orr, L., Feins, J. D., Jacob, R., Beecroft, E., Sanbonmatsu, L., Katz, L. F., Liebman, J. B., & Kling, J. R. (2003) *Moving to Opportunity for Fair Housing Demonstration Program: Interim impacts evaluation.* Washington: U.S. Department of Housing and Urban Development, Office of Policy Development and Research.

Peters, D. P., & Ceci, S. J. (1982) Peer-reviewed practices of psychological journals: The fate of published articles, submitted again. *Behavioral and Brain Sciences,* 5(2), 187–195.

Peterson, R. R. (1996) A re-evaluation of the economic consequences of divorce. *American Sociological Review,* 61(3), 528–536.

Popkin, S. J., Gwiasda, V. E., Olson, L. M., Rosenbaum, D. P., & Buron, L. (2000) *The hidden war: Crime and the tragedy of public housing in Chicago.* Piscataway, NJ: Rutgers University Press.

Popkin, S. J., Rich, M. J., Hendey, L., Hayes, C., Parilla, J., & Galster, G. (2012) Public housing transformation and crime: Making the case for responsible relocation. *Cityscape: A Journal of Policy Development and Research,* 14(3), 137–160.

Rosin, H. (2008) American murder mystery. *Atlantic Monthly,* July/August. Retrieved from www. theatlantic.com/magazine/archive/2008/07/american-murder-mystery/306872/.

Sampson, R. J., Raudenbush, S. W., & Earls, F. (1997) Neighborhoods and violent crime: A multilevel study of collective efficacy. *Science,* 277(5328), 918–924.

Sanbonmatsu, L., Ludwig, J., Katz, L. F., Gennetian, L. A., Duncan, G. J., Kessler, R. C., Adam, E., McDade, T. W., & Lindau, S. T. (2011) *Moving to Opportunity for Fair Housing Demonstration Program: Final impacts evaluation.* Washington, DC: U.S. Department of Housing and Urban Development, Office of Policy Development and Research.

Sciandra, M., Sanbonmatsu, L., Duncan, G. J., Gennetian, L. A., Katz, L. F., Kessler, R. C., Kling, J. R., & Ludwig, J. (2013) Long-term effects of the Moving to Opportunity residential mobility experiment on crime and delinquency. *Journal of Experimental Criminology,* 9(4), 451–489.

Souza Briggs, X., & Dreier, P. (2008) Memphis murder mystery? No, just mistaken identity. *Shelter Force,* July 22. Retrieved from www.shelterforce.org/article/special/1043/.

Souza Briggs, X., Popkin, S. J., & Goering, J. (2010) *Moving to Opportunity: The story of an American experiment to fight ghetto poverty.* New York: Oxford University Press.

Sowell, T. (2010) *Intellectuals and society.* Philadelphia, PA: Basic Books.

Suresh, G., & Vito, G. (2009) Homicide patterns and public housing: The case of Louisville, KY (1989–2007), *Homicide Studies,* 13(4), 411–433.

U.S. Census Bureau (2012) *Current population survey: Custodial mothers and fathers and their child support: 2011* (Series P60–246). Retrieved from www.census.gov/people/childsupport/data/files/ chldsu11.pdf.

Van Zandt, S. S., & Mhatre, P. C. (2013) The effect of housing choice voucher households on neighborhood crime: Longitudinal evidence from Dallas. *Poverty & Public Policy,* 5(3), 229–249.

Wallerstein, J. S., & Kelly, J. B. (2008) *Surviving the break-up: How children and parents cope with divorce.* Philadelphia, PA: Basic Books.

Weitzman, L. J. (1985) *The divorce revolution: The unexpected social and economic consequences for women and children in America.* New York: Free Press.

Whitaker, D. T. (2000) *Cabrini-Green: In words and pictures.* London: LPC Group.

6

A CRITIQUE OF LIBERALISM

Above this race of men stands an immense and tutelary power, which takes upon itself alone to secure their gratifications and to watch over their fate. That power is absolute, minute, regular, provident, and mild. It would be like the authority of a parent if, like that authority, its object was to prepare men for manhood; but it seeks, on the contrary, to keep them in perpetual childhood: it is well content that the people should rejoice, provided they think of nothing but rejoicing. For their happiness such a government willingly labors, but it chooses to be the sole agent and the only arbiter of that happiness; it provides for their security, foresees and supplies their necessities, facilitates their pleasures, manages their principal concerns, directs their industry, regulates the descent of property, and subdivides their inheritances: what remains, but to spare them all the care of thinking and all the trouble of living?

Thus it every day renders the exercise of the free agency of man less useful and less frequent; it circumscribes the will within a narrower range and gradually robs a man of all the uses of himself. The principle of equality has prepared men for these things; it has predisposed men to endure them and often to look on them as benefits. After having thus successively taken each member of the community in its powerful grasp and fashioned him at will, the supreme power then extends its arm over the whole community. It covers the surface of society with a network of small complicated rules, minute and uniform, through which the most original minds and the most energetic characters cannot penetrate, to rise above the crowd. The will of man is not shattered, but softened, bent, and guided; men are seldom forced by it to act, but they are constantly restrained from acting. Such a power does not destroy, but it prevents existence; it does not tyrannize, but it compresses, enervates, extinguishes, and stupefies a people, till each nation is reduced to nothing better than a flock of timid and industrious animals, of which the government is the shepherd.

Alexis de Tocqueville, Volume II, Book 4, Chapter 6 of Democracy in America

We open this chapter with an extensive quote from Alexis de Tocqueville, the French political thinker who toured America at the start of the nineteenth century. His classic book, *Democracy in America* (1835) contains penetrating insights into American democracy, culture, and religion, and how America had created a unique system that effectively balanced individual rights against community needs and religious freedom against state-imposed religious dogma. Tocqueville is required reading for all political science students and students of American history, but he has received scant criminological attention.

Tocqueville was a classical liberal much like contemporary conservatives. Classical liberalism sought to "liberate" people from institutions and political power structures, freeing them to pursue their own talents and desires. Liberalism, as a general political framework, emerged as a response to the despotic rule of kings and to the omnipotent power of the church. At the time, especially prior to the Age of Enlightenment, men were subjugated by a feudal system that insured the absolute right and heredity of kings. Rights, as understood at the time, were "given" by the king, and thus could just as easily be taken away by the king. Land belonged only to the monarch or to individuals approved by the monarch. Moreover, the church wielded almost absolute power, and often formed the intellectual and moral backbone of the monarchy.

Life in feudal Europe was hard. Child mortality rates were high, diseases wiped out large swaths of the population, systems of justice were arbitrary and the punishments they dispensed were brutal. Kings leveled taxes as they saw fit and countries engaged in wars with each other almost out of habit. Tens of thousands of souls were lost, often for no better a reason than to honor the name of a monarch or to satisfy the ego of church authorities. Moreover, history has documented well the excesses of evils passed off as punishments for crimes, especially crimes against the state and the church. Individuals were routinely tortured on the whims of noblemen and church elders, often in ways that can only be described as barbaric.

Standing against these excesses were classical liberals, such as Montesquieu and especially Thomas Hobbes, John Locke, and Thomas Paine. They challenged the core assumptions that kept the monarchy and church in power in at least three ways: First, and most importantly, they challenged the assumption that "rights" were to be provided by the government or church. Rights, according to Kant, Hobbes and Locke, did not originate in government but were, instead, *natural*—that is, that men were born with inalienable rights that could not, without just cause, be restricted by government. Some philosophers, such as Immanuel Kant argued that human reason dictated the existence of natural rights, but others located the origin of rights in Divine Providence, or God. This was a powerful argument because it had the effect of empowering the individual at the same time as it reduced the moral of authority government and established religion (Hall, 1987).

What were these inalienable, God-given rights? Locke identified three, the right to life, liberty, and estate. By this he meant that an individual has a right to live his life in the way that suits him best, to pursue his own interests, his own free will, and to enjoy a life of self-determination. Moreover, the enjoyment of private property gained usually through self-determination was considered an important, fundamental right. (Recall that property in feudal Europe fell under the purview of the monarch and noblemen and that common individuals and peasants enjoyed no right to the accumulation of wealth they generated on the property to which they were granted access). Because of this, individuals were kept poor, paid high taxes on their economic exchanges, and could, if the landowner chose, be removed from the land they worked. The right to estate, as Locke called it, sought to empower individuals to improve their life through the accumulation of assets that emerged from their labors. Locke's ideas about natural rights were clearly articulated by Thomas Jefferson, author of the Declaration of Independence: "We hold these truths to be self-evident, that all men are created equal, that they are endowed by their Creator with certain unalienable rights that among these are Life, Liberty, and the Pursuit of Happiness."

If rights were to be protected, liberals at the time argued, government had to have only limited powers—powers that were to be kept in check by a constitution that separated the powers of government. This is the second element of classical liberalism—limited government. There is no greater threat to inalienable rights than an all-powerful, all-knowing centralized government. Thomas Paine famously echoed this liberal sentiment precisely when he said, "Government, even in its best state, is but a necessary evil; in its worst state, an intolerable one." The point is, classical liberals saw the necessity of government, but at the same time they viewed government as a threat to the lives, rights, and happiness of individuals. After all, much of their ideology was about "freeing" or "liberating" individuals from the clutches of institutions that substituted their views, their perceptions, and their priorities for those of the individual. That classical liberals wanted constitutionally limited government, government that existed only to protect the rights of individuals, may come as a surprise to contemporary readers, but it was this strain of liberal thought that influenced the crafting of the United States Constitution and the creation of coequal branches of government. Moreover, classical liberalism assumed that inequality would exist, if for no other reason than individuals varied in their talents and motivations to capitalize on their talents (Hall, 1987). Some individuals may want to pursue wealth, others may want to pursue education, and still others may want to pursue neither. By stepping in to reduce inequality, government would inevitably have to trample on the rights of citizens. In some ways classical liberalism saw the existence of inequality as a social positive because it signified restrained government and, more importantly, it signified individual freedom of choice.

Third, classical liberalism argued for the rule of law (Sandel, 1998). The rule of law as a philosophy contrasted sharply with the rule of man. In essence, the rule of law takes away power from the government and other institutions and places that power in a codified set of legal prohibitions that apply to all men. No longer, according to classical theorists, would those in power be able to use the justice system to enforce their views, arbitrarily strip individuals of their rights, or punish their political enemies. Laws, however, had to have the consent of the governed for them to be viewed as legitimate. Classical liberals realized that government often operated by using law as a repressive instrument, and laws not derived for the benefit of the governed threatened individual rights to life, liberty, and property. In part because of their mistrust of government and their concomitant desire to limit the power of government, colonial liberals elevated the power of the courts to equal that of the legislative and executive branches. The theory was that if the other two branches passed and/or enforced laws that violated the rights of individual citizens, the courts could invalidate those laws. Rule of law also helped take the passion out of the administration of justice, and it replaced it with process and deliberate decision making. Many innocent men and women, and many guilty ones, owe their lives to the processes that slow down the administration of justice.

Finally, classical liberalism with its emphasis on individual liberty and the pursuit of private property was easily aligned with capitalism. Capitalism, with its emphasis of the free exchange of goods and services, its unique ability to reward success and efficiency, its remarkable ability to allow for the private accumulation of fortunes, and its ability to raise the standard of living for people *en masse*, fits precisely into the ideology of classical liberals. According to the theory, freedom extended into the economic decisions that people make in their best interest. For people to be free and exercise liberty, they had to be masters of their own fortunes, they had to be able to acquire wealth and fortune, and they had to be able to lose it all as well. Government encroachment into private economic activity was anathema to classical liberals because it invited the government to substitute its preferences and its desires for those of individual actors. Classical liberals were believers in *laissez-faire* economics, argued for free and open markets, and argued against state and federal meddling in economic activity (for an overview, see Dryzek & Dunleavy, 2009).

Classical liberals understood that a benevolent government was as much a threat to the individual rights of citizens as was a monarch or dictatorship. As Tocqueville noted, benevolence can produce a soft form of tyranny where the motivations of government slowly but assuredly supplant the motivation of individuals. Indeed, the Founding Fathers had more fear that the United States would eventually morph into a centralized government—or welfare state—than that democracy would be replaced by a monarchy. They understood that, as President Ford would later state in an address to Congress, "a government big enough to give you everything you want, is big enough to take away everything you have." A government big enough to give you everything you want is just a pen stroke away from doing anything it wants to you.

Strains of classical liberalism can still be seen in liberal and conservative thought, and it informs the core ideology of the modern Tea Party movement. The emphasis on individual rights over government authority remains a philosophical cornerstone of American political thought and is in constant tension with efforts to control crime. Indeed, it is not always clear where to draw the line in the creation of law, as law serves to prohibit individual behavior. Liberals and conservatives alike are often inconsistent in their application of this principle, wanting laws that favor government in some situations and laws that protect individual rights in others.

The classical liberal beliefs in the rule of law, due process, and legal restraints on the power of government remain powerful American ideals (Sandel, 1998). Liberals and conservatives advocate for due process restraints in the application of criminal justice, for instance, but conservatives also try to be cognizant that too much "process" can interfere with the administration of justice. For example, debates rage about "handcuffing the police" with legal restraints that interfere with their ability to apprehend suspects, but nowhere is this debate more apparent than in death penalty cases. Liberals have been successful in infinitely delaying the administration of the penalty by building in lengthy, costly appeals (and then lamenting the costs of a death penalty case). They then argue that it costs more to administer the death penalty than to incarcerate someone for life. Nonetheless, it is important to note the shared belief in the rule of law and in due process. When debate emerges, it usually has little to do with questioning the validity of the rule of law and due process and more to do with the appropriateness of extending further due process protections.

That threads of classical liberalism are shared by some liberals and conservatives denotes the power of shared American ideals. The vast majority of Americans, liberal or conservative, extend legitimacy to the ideas of individual rights, the rule of law, and due process. Some would argue that this makes the political parties too similar, but we see this as support for the basic conservative principle of the power of shared norms, ideals, and vision. These shared values have helped to create social changes when necessary and have been largely responsible for the tremendous political stability the United States has experienced since the Civil War.

Yet the fact remains that classical liberalism in contemporary America is aligned with a conservative worldview more than a contemporary "liberal" worldview (for instance, see Himmelfarb, 1995). This is because classical liberalism was challenged by a new political orthodoxy, a political orthodoxy that turned classical liberalism on its head. The new orthodoxy advocated for a strong centralized government, a government of almost unlimited power, and a government that would take an active role in nudging, shaping, creating, and limiting individuality. This new orthodoxy viewed the government as a benevolent dictator, capable of exercising pure political power, even violence, in the name of doing good. Alexis de Tocqueville's warnings about the corrupting influence of benevolent power escaped these new reformers as they sought to create a system of government that infused itself through virtually every domain of life.

The Progressives

The Progressive Era occurred at the start of the twentieth century, and left a permanent mark on United States politics. Much of this change occurred within the context of the industrial revolution. The industrial revolution transformed America from an agrarian economy to an economy of mass production and mass consumption. It ushered in rapid changes in the methods of production, in modes of transportation, in the availability and dissemination of information, and in the recognition that science could be used to help solve social and economic problems. These seismic changes to Western society formed the basis of the sociological canon in the works of Durkheim, Marx, and to a lesser extent, Weber.

Progressivism emerged out of several historical factors. First, while the industrial revolution brought with it the rapid expansion of economic activity, employment, and the accumulation of wealth, it did so at a large social cost. Because it happened with such rapidity, laws and rules for the protection of employees were, at best, antiquated, and at worse, non-existent. Factories housing new, dangerous, machines were sometimes placed in pre-existing wooden structures, structures that could and did easily catch fire. The history of the industrial revolution is replete with examples where hot machinery sparked a fire that spread rapidly through an old wooden structure and killed all employed. Moreover, America was transitioning from an agrarian economy in which families produced a relatively large number of children to work on the farm to an industrial economy. Child labor—common on the farms at the time—was imported into new factories. Children worked on and around dangerous machines, often in conditions that were far more risky and dangerous than could be found on any farm. The Library of Congress contains numerous photos of children with only one arm, the other having been mangled or ripped off by the machines they worked. They also worked long hours, sometimes 12 to 14 hours daily.

As much as the industrial revolution spurred increased manufacture of goods and services, increased the employment opportunities for a broad section of individuals, and created unprecedented wealth, it also created a host of social problems. Many people left the relative confines of rural life and moved to emerging cities, cities that did not have the capacity to adequately house them. In due course, crime and gangs, political graft and corruption, and slum housing developed. Adding to the problems associated with mass migration was the mass of immigrants from Western European countries, many of whom could not speak English. Immigration caused social and economic conflict and it also further strained available resources. The immediate strains placed on industrial cities shocked the conscience of progressive reformers who argued that the preservation of liberty was no longer a core, limiting function of government and that *laissez-faire* economic policies brought with them too many social harms.

Second, progressive political thought was strongly influenced by the rapid accumulation of wealth and power of newly formed corporations. Corporations or legal entities that exist for the sole purpose of commerce had existed since Roman times. Yet during the industrial revolution the wealth and political power obtained by corporations reached stratospheric heights. Magnates of industry, including now famous names as Ford, Carnegie, Morgan, Frick, Hill, Rockefeller, and Stanford accumulated wealth and exercised political power that easily rivaled the power of states and even the federal government. They created, through ingenuity, by taking risks, and by exercising sheer economic power, trusts that consolidated the production and distribution of goods and services—also known as monopolies. In response, progressive reformers saw these men and the businesses they created as self-centered, amoral, and egotistical, as threats to the common good, and as enemies of labor.

Instead of being seen as "captains of industry," these men became known in progressive circles as "Robber Barons" who cared little for their employees, sought profit beyond what progressives thought reasonable, polluted the environment, and acted without charity towards the poor.

Third, the advent of the social sciences gave reformers the intellectual foundation to advance government control and regulation over virtually every aspect of democratic life. The social sciences promised to use data and the scientific method to make government work better. No longer would policy be left to the political whims of politicians who were seen as irrational, ignorant, and corrupt, nor would policy be left to the uneducated masses that could not be trusted. The new science of society promised to make policy formulation an objective, rational, and analytical task. To accomplish this, part of the power to influence policy would be transferred to individuals trained in the social sciences. In short order, a new intellectual class developed in universities across the United States. Trained primarily in psychology, social psychology, economics, sociology, and political science, the new experts were to dissect policy proposals, conduct cost/benefit analyses, and formulate the multitude of regulations that would guide social, military, and economic activity. They were precisely the group that Adam Smith described as the fashionable ones.

Progressive reformers transformed American society. In due course, laws were passed regulating virtually every aspect of American life and economic activity. Anti-trust laws were passed that allowed the federal government to dissolve monopolies, child labor was banned, a compulsory system of public education was created, labor safety laws were instituted, and America saw the creation of regulatory agencies charged with protecting food supplies, the environment, and workers. Applied to crime, progressive reformers developed the first juvenile justice system in 1899, ushered in the idea of rehabilitation as the dominant goal of corrections, and intellectually linked social and economic deprivation as the cause of crime.

A Conservative Critique of Progressivism

There can be little doubt that the Progressive Era ushered in a new view of the role of government and that some of the changes created a net positive social good. As a society, we are likely better off with some of the changes brought about by "progressives." However, like any other social movement, progressive politics also came with excesses, with drawbacks, and with policies and intellectual ideologies that brought harm to people. Liberal academics tend to view the Progressive Era with approval, even admiration, and many not only yearn for a return of the social activism that swept progressives into power but identify themselves as progressive. Yet rarely have they critically examined the dark side of progressive ideology, and in a strange abandonment of historical fact, some have gone so far as to link progressive abuses to conservative doctrine!

Progressives, writes Goldberg (2009: 15) "were also imperialists, at home and abroad. They were the authors of Prohibition, the Palmer Raids, eugenics, loyalty oaths, and, in its modern incarnation, what many call "state capitalism." We discuss each of these progressive ideas below, borrowing heavily from Goldberg (2009) but also adding important distinctions. First, recall that progressive ideology viewed government as an ultimate source of power to be used for the creation or imposition of good. Progressives—unlike liberals of the past—did not see government as a threat to individual liberty in part because they did not value the idea of individualism and individual liberty. Indeed, progressive ideology largely ridiculed the idea of inalienable individual rights, for no other reason than "rights-based" approaches limited the power of government and hence their ability to "do good." Deriding the concept of individual rights, President Wilson wrote: "No doubt a lot of nonsense has been talked about the inalienable rights of the individual and a great deal that was mere sentiment and pleasing speculation has been put forward as fundamental principle." Without the pesky inalienable rights in place to restraint the power of government, "[g]overnment," according to Wilson, could do "whatever experience permits or the times demand … ." With this sentiment rooted firmly in mind, progressives unleashed government on people.

Prohibition

Liberals forget that progressives were often deeply religious people. Indeed, references to Christianity were frequently made in imposing progressive doctrine and justifying governmental intrusion into the lives of individuals. After all, what better way to justify a benevolent government, a government obsessed with "doing good" than to root its motivations in New Testament beliefs? Out of this union between church and state came Prohibition, the Eighteenth Amendment to the United States Constitution, which banned the creation, sale, distribution, and consumption of alcohol. This was followed by the Volstead Act later that year that gave the states and the federal government the authority to regulate the sale and manufacturing of alcohol.

The history of Prohibition is well known but wrongly understood. For example, most believe that Prohibition was an utter failure but Moore (1989) notes that the policy resulted in dramatic declines in alcohol use; death rates attributed to cirrhosis dropped from 29.5/100,000 to 10.7/100,000 by 1929; hospitalization rates for alcoholism dropped over 60 percent; arrests for public disorder dropped a remarkable 50 percent; and alcohol consumption, Moore estimates, declined between 30 and 50 percent overall. Moore also notes that violent crime did not substantively increase during Prohibition.

There were, of course, costs to Prohibition. One of the most obvious was the rapid expansion of the criminal justice system into the personal lives of citizens. Prohibition forced the criminal justice system to be the arbiters of vice among the citizenry. No longer free to buy liquor or beer, many turned to making their own and selling what they made to others. Due to Prohibition, armed officers were then legally allowed to raid premises, including people's homes, where they thought alcohol was being made and to arrest offenders. This had the effect of making alcohol a highly sought-after commodity, but also one that brought with it risk of arrest and incarceration. In short order, criminal syndicates emerged that organized alcohol production, distribution, and sale. Moreover, the money made from the sale of alcohol found its way into the coffers of local politicians and the pockets of police officers. Corruption due to Prohibition was rampant. By 1933, in the midst of the Great Depression, the progressive experiment in temperance was over as the Amendment was finally repealed.

We can learn many lessons from Prohibition. First, people, even honest people, will resist overt government intrusion. Some will seek to exploit that intrusion for profit and status while others will simply find ways to subvert the law. Second, people will rebel when government attempts to severely limit or ban behaviors and traditions—especially those traditions that have been around for hundreds and even thousands of years. Third, government will sometimes use coercion and violence against its citizens to enforce laws—even very unpopular laws. People were killed and incarcerated for making and distributing liquor. Finally, regardless of the efficacy of the law, some individuals will go to great lengths to prosecute and to persecute those who violate the law. We would do well to keep these lessons in mind.

Palmer Raids and the quieting of dissent

Amazing abuses can occur when people are afraid, and history has taught us that liberal and conservative ideology can be used to suppress dissent. While many progressives strongly believed in the free exchange of ideas, others did not, especially when those ideas were believed to be dangerous to the state. In 1917, communist revolution gripped Russia as the Bolsheviks took power. Eventually, power would be taken by Lenin who would go on to impose a highly repressive totalitarian government. The "revolution" would eventually land on American shores under the name of "anarchism" (Preston, 1963).

Three years prior to the Palmer Raids, President Wilson had warned about "hyphenated Americans," arguing that they were disloyal to national life. Anarchists would eventually detonate a series of bombs, and would send some thirty letter bombs to various government authorities. Against this backdrop, President Wilson appointed Alexander Palmer as attorney general, leading the Unites States Department of Justice. Palmer had been the target of an anarchist letter bomb, a bomb that detonated and damaged his home.

Palmer would eventually put a young J. Edgar Hoover in charge of the General Intelligence Division of the Justice Department. Hoover and Palmer, acting on behalf of Congress, would eventually conduct a series of raids that they argued were necessary to root out radicals bent on undermining the United States. Anarchists were not the only group targeted by Palmer: union leaders, Russian emigrants, and even innocent American citizens were arrested, often without warrants, and detained for months. In the end, the Palmer Raids were responsible for the arrest of thousands of Americans, often for nothing more than holding different political views.

Fear is a remarkable emotion. It keeps us safe and helps to guide us in our daily lives. Unfortunately, politicians have learned how to manipulate our fears. During World War II, for example, Japanese citizens were moved to camps in western states—stripped of their rights, their property, and their dignity. This was done by Franklin D. Roosevelt—the great progressive leader of the time. More recently, we find politicians of all stripes supporting the now infamous Patriot Act and supporting widespread spying on American citizens by the National Security Administration. Fear is to be feared when it is mobilized for political purposes.

Eugenics

If ever a policy existed that captured the combined forces that propelled progressive thought to the forefront of American politics it was eugenics. The eugenics movement was born in Europe but was fully endorsed and executed in the United States during the Progressive Era. Advocates argued that to build a better society some individuals would have to be sterilized and that a form of "social Darwinism" should be practiced. Of course, the decision of who should, or should not be, sterilized would fall to the new class of social engineers—professional scientists, sociologists, and psychologists. Emboldened by the principles of Darwinian evolution, progressive sociologists traveled the world promoting eugenics, arguing that the forced sterilization of "defects" was a necessary social good. Indeed, academic eugenic conferences were held in New York and in England, American sociologists went on record praising Nazi eugenic efforts, scientific journals on eugenics emerged, and states created offices of eugenics. In the end, over 60,000 people were forcibly sterilized—the practice not ending until 1975 (cf. Allen, 1997; Hart, 2012; Kevles, 2009).

In true progressive fashion, the aim to make a better society prioritized the power of the state over the rights of individuals. In this sense, the idea was to have trained professionals, scientists, sociologists, medical doctors, and psychologists, determine the fitness of some people to have children. At first the eugenics movement was aimed at reducing the social costs associated with mentally retarded people having children, but in due course the idea was expanded to include the poor, criminals, homosexuals, and religious and racial groups who were thought to impose a financial burden on the state. Eugenics was a pragmatic social policy aimed, according to advocates, at improving society through improving the gene pool. It was implemented and practiced in the United States during the Progressive Era, and it was also practiced in various other countries.

What makes American eugenics unique, however, is that it infused "science" into social policy, a policy that was eventually challenged in the Supreme Court. Consistent with progressive thinking at the time, Oliver Wendell Holmes, chief justice of the Supreme Court, wrote in *Buck v. Bell* (1927) that states have the right to forcibly sterilize citizens:

> We have seen more than once that the public welfare may call upon the best citizens for their lives. It would be strange if it could not call upon those who already sap the strength of the State for these lesser sacrifices, often not felt to be such by those concerned, to prevent our being swamped with incompetence. It is better for all the world, if instead of waiting to execute degenerate offspring for crime, or to let them starve for their imbecility, society can prevent those who are manifestly unfit from continuing their kind. The principle that sustains compulsory vaccination is broad enough to cover cutting the Fallopian tubes.

He finished by stating: "three generations of imbeciles is enough."

At the Nuremburg trials, held after World War II, Nazi officials were asked where the idea to create extermination camps had come from. Their answer: from American eugenics efforts. While this is an obvious simplification of the causes of the "Final Solution," we find no small degree of totalitarian states that contributed to the murder of millions of innocent people. In many ways, and we do not wish to paint too broad or careless a stroke here, Nazism was consistent with progressive ideology. Both elevated the state above the rights of the individual, both prioritized state efforts at defining and creating "social good," both advocated efficiency and pragmatism as social virtues, both used the military to expand their sphere of influence, and both used the social sciences to provide the necessary intellectual justification for their endeavors. We note, too, that Hitler obtained a copy of *The Case for Sterilization* by writing directly to the president of the American Eugenics Association. Moreover, Hitler referred to Madison Grant's book *Passing of the Great Race* as his "bible." Grant was an advisor to President Teddy Roosevelt, a progressive (Goldberg, 2009).

Progressives, as the historical record shows, advocated for eugenics because they thought they could improve society through tinkering with the machinery of sexual reproduction. They were the scientists who measured "fitness" and developed the tests to assess IQ and other individual traits, they were the lawmakers who pushed through the laws, the judges who found them constitutional, they were managers of the institutions that held society's social defects, and they were the governors and the presidents that provided political and legal support to eugenic efforts. Even so, the myth that eugenics emerged out of a conservative effort to repress the poor and minorities or exalt their superior ethnic or social status is widespread and often repeated. It is taught as a matter of fact to criminology students and to students in the social sciences, yet it remains to some degree political mythology.

The lessons of the eugenics movement are similar to the lessons we can garner from the horrible Nazi government. First, intelligent people can do irreparable harm and they can convince others to support their causes. Ideas do have consequences and intelligent people are capable of generating a range of ideas that appear logical, pragmatic, and even moral. Second, unchecked governmental power can lead to horrible abuses, including war, genocide, and the unadulterated abridgment of individual and human rights. Indeed, the greater the power of government the greater the ability of that government to bring harm to its citizens and to the rest of the world. Third, democracy and constitutional protections are not always enough to protect Americans from an over-reaching government. Remember, even the Supreme Court of the United States approved eugenic laws. Finally, as was the case in the example of Prohibition and the Palmer Raids, government frequently uses the criminal justice system to enforce its mandates.

Social Causes for Everything

Progressive ideology ushered in a "new" understanding of social behavior, one that removed individual differences in motivation, talent, and intellect from any understanding of social outcomes (see Sowell, 1995, 1999). Pointing to rapid industrialization, immigration, and widespread social and economic problems, progressives offered a view of man that gained widespread acceptance and still resonates in the halls of academia today. That view holds that all human behavior is the product of "social" processes, processes that are largely beyond the control of the individual. Progressives believed, essentially, that man was "born good" and that exposure to social conditions forced him to engage in bad behavior. This is the intellectual fiber of criminological theoretical traditions ranging from differential association to social disorganization. Bad places: yes. Bad people: no.

Much of this view was predicated on a "blank slate" understanding of human nature. According to Pinker (2002), blank slate notions of human nature reduce all human differences to differences in exposure to culture or social conditions. Blank slate views deny that humans have any inborn traits or instincts, and they deny any role for biological and genetic factors to influence human behavior. Nobody captured the essence of blank slate theorizing better than the "behaviorists," a group of scholars who argued that all human behavior was the product of conditioning and social learning. Echoing the behaviorist emphasis of the blank slate, John B. Watson (1930: 82) famously stated:

> Give me a dozen healthy infants, well-formed, and my own specified world to bring them up in and I'll guarantee to take any one at random and train him to become any type of specialist I might select—doctor, lawyer, artist, merchant-chief and, yes, even beggar-man and thief, regardless of his talents, penchants, tendencies, abilities, vocations, and race of his ancestors.

To the progressive mindset, humans were simple repositories of culture and experience. If they were corrupted, it was only because they had been exposed to corrupting influences or social conditions that compelled them to act violently or aggressively. Hence, if mankind was to be perfected, which was the goal of the progressive movement, all that was necessary was to change the environment. Of course, who better to analyze which parts of the environment to change than the new experts in the social sciences, and who better to force these changes than the progressives in government?

Blank slate notions were widely popular, remain so today, and are closely linked with contemporary liberalism (Sowell, 1995). At the core of the idea is a denial of human beings as biological agents, as agents subject to many of the same evolutionary and genetic forces that influence other animals. It is, as Pinker (2002) argues, "The modern denial of human nature." Indeed, contrary to a staggering volume of empirical evidence that all human traits and characteristics are influenced by biological and genetic forces, blank slate thinking remains pervasive in criminology and most other social sciences.

We offer some reasons. The first has to do with the undisciplined use of the terms "social" and its cousin "environmental." As the famed Nobel economist F. A. Hayek once argued, "the adjective 'social' was capable of reducing any expression to vacuity." What he meant by this was that virtually any behavior or exchange between human beings could be covered under the social or environmental definitional umbrella. The absence of any precise definition of what constitutes an "environment" or what is or is not "social" virtually invites broad definitional abuse. As this applies to understanding crime, it is a deeply held conviction among most criminologists that crime is caused by "environmental" forces or "social conditions." Yet a quick examination of most criminological theories will readily reveal that what constitutes an "environment" can be anything from the nation one lives in to the economy one interacts with, from the census track a home or business resides in to the school attended. An environment can also reflect a child's home life, his or her peer group, their geographic region, the time period in which they were born, their culture, or virtually any other characteristic the theorist wishes to emphasize. Because the terms are used with so little definitional regard, they frequently evolve into meaninglessness.

This influences our second reason for the retention of blank slate theorizing in criminology, what we call the "seduction of grandiose social theorizing." The denial of human differences leads to a certain type of theorizing about crime and other social problems; at the same time it leads away from other types of theorizing. If all human differences are discounted, or are believed to be the product of differential social or environmental processes, then virtually any causal relationship linking some aspect of "environment" can be posited. That human beings vary, sometimes tremendously, within the same "environment" is simply overlooked in favor of making broad claims that usually push an ideological agenda. As Seymour Martin Lipset (1994a) noted in his presidential address to the American Sociological Association, theories advanced by Cloward and Ohlin and other sociological giants were advanced not only to explain crime and other social problems but also to infuse socialistic ideas into the conversation of the American mainstream (see also Lipset, 1994b).

They have succeeded. The fact that most traditional criminological theories were inspired by socialists and other leftist radicals who sought to criticize capitalism and other uniquely American traditions has been forgotten, overlooked, or simply relegated to the dustbin of history. Nonetheless, grand social theorizing is made possible only because great intellectual liberties can be taken when everything is defined as "social" or "environmental" and when, correspondingly, innate human differences are reduced to triviality.

Third, the connection between blank slate theorizing, environmental or social theorizing, and politics should be obvious. By locating the "causes" of crime and other social pathologies in the "environment," progressives justified an ever more expansive role for government. If crime, for example, was the result of blocked opportunities, disorganized communities, institutional or de facto racism, or any other politically favored cause, then governmental intervention and programming would be justified. All evidence suggests that this is exactly what has transpired. Cloward and Ohlin's (1960) work, for example, set the stage for President Johnson's 1965 Commission on Law Enforcement and Administration of Justice. The "blueprint" drawn up by the commission promised to "banish crime" by creating and funding a host of "anti-poverty" and other redistributive programs and by increasing the powers of the federal government to criminalize and police crime. Billions, if not trillions, of dollars have been spent on social programs to address crime—with little to no evidence that such expenditures in fact reduce criminal behavior. But there is better evidence that these programs have undermined family formation to such an extent that they have produced a caste system in American society (Hymowitz, 2006).

It was not by accident that progressivism and blank slate notions of human nature were coupled, nor was it by accident that these ideas were so readily embraced by social scientists. It is not by accident that these broad-based viewpoints have so permeated universities. Intellectuals are subject to the same human frailties as anyone else; ego, the desire for power, the desire for external recognition, and the desire for political influence. Progressive ideology empowered social scientists, it gave them new-found legitimacy, it elevated their status, and it gave them unprecedented political influence. Blank slate theorizing, moreover, gave them license to make sweeping generalizations about the causes of crime, poverty, unemployment, capitalism and various other "social problems." It was the perfect storm. Progressive ideology expanded the state, elevated the newly found professional class that would administer the state, and it provided the intellectual justification for a continuing symbiotic relationship between intellectuals and the state that still exists in most social science disciplines today. In the end, progressivism co-opted the intellectual independence of many scholars in the social sciences by seamlessly infusing progressive politics with scholarly activity. That the bias exists today is a testament to the power of ideas; that so many social scientists remain blind to these connections is a testament to the power of self-deception.

Creeping Totalitarianism

Progressive ideology is often advanced as a way to improve the lives of individuals through the exertion of governmental power (Sowell, 1999). Indeed, advocates constantly link their desire to influence political decisions with the aim of doing good (this forms the basis for the light-hearted label that conservatives have for liberals: do-gooder). Yet doing good can easily be turned into an ever-expanding desire to address even the slightest perception of injustice, inequality, or unfairness. Once set into motion, doing good takes on an almost endless, even cultish quality to it. Social commentator Charles Krauthammer (1993) has described this phenomenon as "defining deviancy up," where antisocial behavior is normalized to such an extent that previously virtuous behavior (often the behaviors and views of conservatives) is portrayed as deviant.

This can be seen in social movements relating to traffic behavior. In the mid-1980s, a social movement swept the country to reduce the often tragic consequences of drunk driving. Prior to the 1980s, tragedies caused by drunk driving were viewed as "accidents," and people were generally unwilling to use the criminal law as a sanction against the behavior. This changed when Mothers Against Drunk Driving began to persuasively argue that the deaths and injuries from drunk driving were preventable, and that the criminal law should be employed to combat the behavior. MADD has been very successful and many more people are alive today because of their efforts (Fell & Voas, 2006).

Unfortunately, a range of scientists have continually sought to expand the use of the criminal law to include driving under any condition that may affect one's ability to operate a motor vehicle. Take cough medicine and drive? You may be under the influence and charged with a crime. Text, eat, or engage in any other "distracting" behaviour … and yes, you too may now, in some jurisdictions, be charged with a crime. Similarly, seat belt use is now mandated across the United States. In many states, driving without a seat belt on is grounds for being pulled over and cited. There are even police roadblocks to enforce seat belt use and other "safety" laws. In most states, however, seat belt laws were initially passed so that a motorist could not be stopped by the police and ticketed solely because of a seat belt infraction. If a motorist was pulled over for speeding or some other primary offense, he could then be ticketed if he was found to be not wearing a seat belt. Critics of seat belt laws warned at the time that it would be only a matter of time before police would be allowed to pull over and cite motorists for not wearing a seat belt. Their concerns have been wholly realized. Again, the point is not that seat belt use saves lives but that reformer ideology constantly pushes for an expansive use of government power. Who would have thought that in modern America we would have "roadblocks" or "police checkpoints"? These are the actions of communist and totalitarian countries, not of a country that prides itself on individual rights and liberty (see Minogue, 2010).

In their unending desire to keep people safe from themselves, we now see "experts" advancing ideas to regulate everything from the food we are "allowed" to eat, to when and where we can talk on cell phones, to how many firearms we can purchase in a 24-hour period. More importantly, there is simply no countervailing force in the academy to address the left's continued assault on liberty and individual freedom, especially when benevolent "experts" tell us that the only way to "save lives" is to infringe the rights of others. Indeed, we are often struck by the ability of respected scholars to completely suspend disbelief and forsake critical inquiry when policies are advanced that toe the progressive line, when causes to complex issues are reduced to politically acceptable definitions, or when calls are made to infringe or eliminate the rights of individuals in return for advancement of their political agenda.

The Nanny State and Culture of Entitlement

We opened this chapter with a lengthy quote from de Tocqueville about the danger of soft despotism. Soft and hard tyranny are two sides of the same coin, they are simply different forms or degrees of despotism. For example, where brutal rulers and dictatorial regimes use the power of the state to enforce, sometimes by violence, state priorities, soft despotism uses the legitimacy of government institutions to supersede, nudge, or cajole the thoughts and behaviors of citizens. Soft despotism, as Goldberg (2009) points out, is about using the power of the state to sway individual preferences and to subvert individuality. It changes the role of the state to that of "benevolent nanny."

A culture of entitlement reflects a belief, shared by some citizens and groups, that they have some intrinsic claim to government services, to a set of undefined "rights," or to materials and services which they have not exerted effort to earn. Entitlement thinking can be seen in college students who believe that merely showing up for a class should qualify them for an "A" grade. It can be seen in college faculty who believe their advanced degree should guarantee them a job for life. It can be seen among underclass denizens who believe their mere existence confers on them the right to lifetime welfare benefits. And it can be seen in the constant progressive desire to define the acquisition of goods and services as "rights" instead of privileges.

Entitlement thinking stands in sharp contrast to conservative belief in individual merit and individual responsibility. From a conservative point of view, able-bodied individuals should work, sacrifice, and delay gratification to be able to earn what they consume. Working, sacrificing, and delaying gratification are time-tested ways of achieving long-term stability and status and are thus elevated to a moral priority under conservatism. As Edmund Burke (1791) noted, "Men are qualified for civil liberty in exact proportion to their disposition to put moral chains on their own appetites." An entitlement perspective, however, uncouples individual responsibility from individual outcomes and it short-circuits the pathway to adult responsibility. It does so because a culture of entitlement removes individual motivation and individual responsibility to self, family, and community and instead grants enormous power to government which becomes the provider of goods and services. In turn, entitlement culture fails to recognize the merits of work and personal sacrifice, and instead rewards slothfulness, outright laziness, and cheating.

Criminologists have long known that criminals have a unique worldview. This worldview emphasizes uncontrolled hedonism, the unconstrained antisocial pursuit of wealth, status, and power, and a remarkable degree of self-aggrandizement. Persistent criminals are perhaps the best example of entitlement culture, largely because they almost uniformly believe that they are "owed" all the material possessions and social advantages earned by prosocial individuals. They desire "credibility," or "street cred," and will fight on a dime if they perceive they are being "dissed" or "disrespected." Yet they frequently refuse, if not outright reject, prosocial means to gain respect and credibility. They refuse to work because the jobs they are qualified to work at are beneath them. They refuse to participate in their own education because they view it as unnecessary. They refuse to settle down into monogamous relationships because to do so would cramp their lifestyle. And they live in the moment, making impulsive, sometimes dangerous, decisions that can only sacrifice their already tenuous future. Even so, criminals have a strong sense that their failings are society's failings, and because they can offload their individual failings onto society, they believe with conviction that society owes them a certain standard of living. Needless to say, the antisocial and the slothful know more about the ins and outs of the criminal justice system, the social welfare system, and the disability system than do most practitioners. They should—they have made taking from those systems their livelihood (Mead, 2004).

Progressives constantly wish to expand the range of social services and goods available to a broader and broader base of people, and they wish to disconnect individual conduct from the receipt of services provided by taxpayers. They also advocate constantly for more tax money to be spent so that those receiving it can live a more lavish lifestyle. Housing, rent, schooling, babysitting, food, medicine, medical care, access to the internet, and transportation: all become indelible "rights" under progressive dogma—rights that must be paid for by individuals who have to play by a different set of rules.

Conservatives decry entitlement thinking not because they are heartless and want to see people suffer but because to submit to entitlement thinking is a guaranteed pathway towards self-destruction. A belief that you are entitled to a specific standard of living, a monthly paycheck, the receipt of goods and services without effort or responsibility in action destroys human potential, it destroys the human spirit, and it makes individuals subservient to governmental power. Most conservatives accept a social safety net that is temporary and provides for the maintenance of a minimalist lifestyle while requiring conformity to basic social rules and expectations. What they reject is the idea that government should do for individuals what they refuse to do for themselves. Helping the needy is a belief held widely by many liberals and conservatives, but there is a short distance between "helping" and "enabling." Unfortunately, too many Americans fail to recognize their human potential, fail to live a life of discovery and achievement, and fail to develop a spirit of connectedness in large part because progressive ideology has made it so they don't have to.

Political philosophy shapes how we see the world. It shapes how we think about relationships, how we see economic exchanges, and how we view the role of government in our lives. Yet political philosophy can also "blind and bind" us to bad ideas, to ways of thinking that are imprudent, and to support for policies that are damaging to the social fabric. Worst yet, political philosophies can encourage us to create and reinforce social myths—myths that stigmatize some groups while elevating the moral superiority of other groups. And taken to the extreme, strict adherence to a political philosophy can lead us to unjustly condemn some others and thus to justify harm against those we view as different.

We believe the evidence shows that these factors have gelled, to varying degrees, on college campuses across the United States (see Bloom, 1987; D'Souza, 1991). When one political ideology controls dialogue, campus priorities, and faculty research agendas (out of fear or through incentive), it can easily be used to bring harm to others. Indeed, there is even a name for this: academic mobbing. Academic mobbing occurs when a faculty member, a student group, or an administrator violates liberal dogma. When this happens, those most "offended" charge the ramparts demanding their grievance result in the punishment of the culprit. It occurred, for example, to Linda Gottfredson because of her work on intelligence. It occurred to James Watson (who co-discovered the double helix) because of an off-handed comment he made to a reporter linking race to intelligence. It occurred to the president of Harvard for opening comments he made at the start of a conference on why so few women can be found in the ranks of top science programs. It has occurred to several student Republican groups due to their opposition to affirmative action (and just because they are Republicans). While the names and faces may vary from one campus to another, the common thread does not. Offend the established liberal dogma and liberals—those who so often speak of tolerance, compassion, and academic freedom—will circle the wagons and demand that a career be ended, an idea be silenced, or a group be dismissed from campus. And try as we have, we have not been able to find a single occurrence where conservative faculty "mobbed" a liberal professor on a public campus.

The blinding nature of political ideology is especially potent on university campuses (D'Souza, 1991). Research findings are viewed through the lens of political, not scientific, ideology. Courses are created and taught out of political ideology. Guest speakers are brought in because of their political ideology. Administrators are appointed and promoted in part because of their adherence to political ideology, and relationships between faculty are governed by political concerns. Unfortunately, this has translated into the creation of social myths that are presented as "facts" to students and that form the bedrock of understanding between faculty and administrators. These myths, like any other myths, overlook the complexity of reality and they make heroes out of some and villains out of others. The academic treatment of progressive ideology, and conversely, conservative ideology, serves as an example of one of the myths. According to this myth, political progressives rescued society from the clutches of evil conservatives and even more evil corporations. Progressives brought forth equal rights, they gave us food safety, and worked to make the world fair. And they did all of this despite the best efforts of conservatives to stop them. The drama of the struggle is apparent and the motifs of good v. evil are obvious. But as we have shown, despite some good brought about by progressive ideology, progressive ideology was also associated with a lot of bad ideas and in the end caused at least as much harm as good.

Conservative ideology is hardly without problems, but conservative ideology does not exist on university campuses. Not only does it not exist, it is typically excoriated by those who work to twist it into something of a caricature. However, conservatism offers a different view of the proper role of government in the lives of individuals, a different way of understanding an individual's relationship with government, and unique insights into how people live meaningful, productive, and responsible lives. The stabilizing force provided by tradition, by shared cultural beliefs, by uplifting religious and spiritual work, by individual charity, and by the rule of law and by restrictions placed on government also deserve to be highlighted, presented to students, and to be treated with the same degree of respect that other political traditions receive.

References

Allen, G. E. (1997) The social and economic origins of genetic determinism: A case history of the American Eugenics Movement, 1900–1940 and its lessons for today. *Genetica*, 99(2/3), 77–88.

Bloom, A. (1987) *The closing of the American mind*. New York: Simon and Schuster.

Buck v. Bell, 274 U.S. 200 (1927).

Burke, E. (1791) A letter to a member of the National Assembly. In *The Works of Edmund Burke*. Cited in G. Himmelfarb (2001) *One nation, two cultures*. New York: Vintage, p. 555.

Cloward, R. A., & Ohlin, L. E. (1960) *Delinquency and opportunity: A theory of delinquent gangs*. New York: The Free Press of Glencoe.

Dryzek, J., & Dunleavy, P. (2009) *Theories of the democratic state*. Basingstoke: Palgrave Macmillan.

D'Souza, D. (1991) *Illiberal education: The politics of race and sex on campus*. New York: The Free Press.

Fell, J. C., & Voas, R. B. (2006) Mothers Against Drunk Driving (MADD): The first 25 years. *Traffic Injury Prevention*, 7(3), 195–212.

Goldberg, J. (2009) *Liberal fascism: The secret history of the American left from Mussolini to the politics of meaning*. New York: Doubleday Books

Hall, J. A. (1987) Classical liberalism and the modern state. *Daedalus*, 116(3), 95–118.

Hart, B. W. (2012) Watching the "eugenic experiment" unfold: The mixed views of British eugenicists toward Nazi Germany in the early 1930s. *Journal of the History of Biology*, 45(1), 33–45.

Himmelfarb, G. (1995) *The demoralization of society: From Victorian virtues to modern values*. New York: Vintage.

Himmelfarb, G. (2001) *One nation, two cultures*. New York: Vintage.

Hymowitz, K. S. (2006) *Marriage and caste in America: Separate and unequal families in a post-marital age*. Chicago, IL: Ivan R. Dee.

Kevles, D. J. (2009) Eugenics, the genome, and human rights. *Medicine Studies*, 1(2), 85–93.

Krauthammer, C. (1993) Defining deviancy up. *The New Republic*, November 22, 20–25.

Lipset, S. M. (1994a). The social requisites of democracy revisited: 1993 Presidential Address. *American Sociological Review*, 59(1), 1–22.

Lipset, S. M. (1994b). The state of American sociology. *Sociological Forum*, 9(2), 199–220.

Mead, L. M. (2004) The culture of welfare reform. *The Public Interest*, 154(3), 99–111.

Minogue, K. (2010) *The servile mind: How democracy erodes the moral life*. New York: Encounter Books.

Moore, M. H. (1989) Actually, Prohibition was a success. *The New York Times*, October 16. Retrieved from www.nytimes.com/1989/10/16/opinion/actually-prohibition-was-a-success.html.

Pinker, S. (2002) *The blank slate: The modern denial of human nature*. New York: Viking.

Preston, W. (1963) *Aliens and dissenters: Federal suppression of radicals, 1903–1933*. Cambridge, MA: Harvard University Press.

Sandel, M. J. (1998) *Liberalism and the limits of justice*. Cambridge: Cambridge University Press.

Sowell, T. (1995) *The vision of the anointed: Self-congratulation as a basis for social policy*. New York: Basic Books.

Sowell, T. (1999) *The quest for cosmic justice*. New York: The Free Press.

Tocqueville, A. de (1835/2003) *Democracy in America*, Vols 1 and 2. New York: Penguin.

Watson, J. B. (1930) *Behaviorism*. Chicago, IL: University of Chicago Press.

7

A CONSERVATIVE CRITIQUE OF CRIMINOLOGY

The intellectual's struggle to deny the obvious is never more desperate than when reality is unpleasant and at variance with his preconceptions and when full acknowledgement of it would undermine the foundations of his intellectual worldview.

Theodore Dalrymple, Life at the Bottom *(2000)*

The Innocent Man: Criminology's Account of the Criminal

Imagine a patient with a specific injury to the chest, stomach, hand, or eye. The patient would present with symptoms that are indicative of some type of injury. It could be chest pains, a stomach ache, a swollen hand, or a reddened eye with blurred vision. The symptoms would persist for some time, impair the functioning of the affected area, and reduce the patient's health overall. In time, the patient would see a physician to explore the causes and treatment of the injury. The doctor would examine the affected area and other areas directly connected to the injury. Some remedy would be provided. It might be a diet and exercise regimen to improve cardiovascular health, antacids to reduce stomach irritation, a cast to immobilize a bruised bone in the hand, or the removal of an embedded piece of dirt to heal the eye. In all these scenarios, the problem and the solution are interrelated and localized to a specific area. It is obvious to connect the causes of the problem to the problem. And causes that are the plainest to see are often true.

Criminology should operate in a similar fashion. Historically it has not. Unlike the generic medical examples described earlier, criminology has sought to avoid theories that show a clear and straightforward explanation for antisocial behavior. Usually these theories suggest that specific individual-level personality factors are the best explanation of crime. Conservative criminology, with its interest in evidence-based, commonsense explanations at the simplest unit of analysis, prefers individual-level approaches to explaining crime. Instead, a cardinal feature of traditional criminology has been to move outside the individual altogether. Rather than attribute crime to variance in personality features, or behavioral disorders, or decision making, or neuropsychological functioning, criminology has cited statuses, social conditions, and social structure as the mechanisms that push, coerce, or influence the likelihood that someone will commit crime. Examples of these approaches include anomie theory, social disorganization theory, differential association theory, labeling theory, social learning theory, and multiple iterations of conflict theory.

Criminology has favored this indirect approach for at least three reasons. First, criminology is an academic discipline that developed under the parent discipline of sociology. Since its founding, sociology has attempted to develop social explanations that cite superindividual factors as the causes of individual behavior. From this vantage point, simpler explanations that utilized constructs from psychology or biology committed a sin of sorts: reductionism. To sociology, and by extension to criminology, reducing the scientific explanation for crime to a simpler explanation is misguided. As Durkheim asserted (cited in Giddens, 1972: 66; italics added), "the sociologist undertakes the investigation of a given order of social facts, *he must endeavor to consider them from an aspect that is isolated from their individual manifestations.*" From this view, Occam's razor is wrong. Instead, convoluted explanations, analytical sophistication, and clever obfuscation are used to counter straightforward explanations. As such, criminologists have used a double dose of venom to respond to attempts to explain criminal behavior with more parsimonious explanations. First, criminologists have historically expressed sheer hostility to individual-level approaches and only have tempered that hostility when the evidence was so overwhelming that to deny individual-level factors became professionally embarrassing (this can be seen in the response to self-control theory).

Second, notwithstanding the supremacy of individual-level constructs, criminologists still believed that a macro approach to explaining crime was necessary because it would locate theorizing to its rightful super-individual context. In other words, individual-level constructs that lead to crime are okay, but they must be seen in their larger context to be understood. There is condescension inherent in this preference for macro-explanations that are presumed to be more sophisticated and, thus, accurate. For instance, in a comment about self-control theory, Geis (2008: 203) stated, "I found *A General Theory of Crime* often dogmatic and categorically dismissive of matters that deserved much more nuanced treatment … as an old-fashioned out-of-style liberal I also found irritating Gottfredson and Hirschi's dismissal of social injustice."

The second and third reasons are interrelated. By eschewing individual-level factors as the likely causes of crime in favor of external social forces, criminology has relocated the moral blameworthiness of crime from the delinquent to the clique, from the offender to the context, from the criminal to the circumstance. When moral blameworthiness is shifted from the individual to society, it also involves the shifting of blame, the shifting of stigma, and the shifting of fault. Thus, criminals are not morally blameworthy, bad society is. Social conditions are. Social structure is. Environments are. This segues to the third reason that relates to policy. If criminals are more Rousseauian than Hobbesian, then the natural targets for crime reduction are the environmental conditions that putatively mold human behavior.

Preferred and Non-preferred Explanations

Before delving into explanations of crime, consider this digression into basketball history. Which Hall of Famer is the only person to be the all-time statistical leader in two major categories? For most people, the following names will come to mind: Wilt Chamberlain, Michael Jordan, Kareem Abdul-Jabbar, Julius Erving, Magic Johnson, Oscar Robertson, Jerry West, Bill Russell, or Larry Bird. None of these are correct. The correct answer is John Stockton, the all-time NBA leader in assists and steals. A private man who avoided publicity and played his entire career in the relatively obscure market of Utah, Stockton never fitted the public image of an NBA superstar. In this way, his actual or empirical value was outshone by the flamboyance, media focus, and assorted talents of the other NBA greats.

A similar thing occurs in criminological thinking where the most empirically strong explanations are not necessarily given the most credit. Instead, various criminology theories are anointed as preferred explanations for crime because they accord with a pre-existing ideological worldview or an explanatory framework that is compatible with the domain assumptions of a particular academic discipline. An easy way to tell what a discipline prefers and what it dislikes is to monitor works that it immediately accepts as gospel and those it repeatedly criticizes. Three examples immediately come to mind. James Q. Wilson and Richard Herrnstein's *Crime and Human Nature* (1985) was a direct attack on the notion that a sociological worldview somehow had sovereignty rights over criminological theories. Less of a theory than an overview of research areas from the social and biological sciences, Wilson and Herrnstein's work demonstrated the strength of individual-level constructs to understanding crime. For many reasons, their work was criticized in the criminological literature as being both wrong and wrong-headed (for an overview of this history, see DeLisi, 2003). Wilson and Herrnstein became shorthand for research that focused on individual-level traits as the ultimate causes of crime, often in discussing concepts such as criminal propensity, criminality, or population heterogeneity. Even if their work was pejoratively cited, it is important to acknowledge that it was cited often—more than 2,928 times according to Google Scholar on June 9, 2015.

Academic criminologists are not, like conservatives, comfortable with evidence-based explanations that also happen to align with common sense, populist notions of crime. In criminology, straightforward theories of crime that suggest that individual-level factors are the best explanation are derided as simplistic, crude, lacking nuance. Consider this passage from Steffensmeier and Ulmer (2005: 364):

> In effect, scholars, journalists, and the conventional public sometimes create negative imagery of criminals by highlighting their shortcomings, and suggesting that they really are incapable of, and do not manifest, any valued traits ... however, we suspect that writers like Gottfredson and Hirschi or James Q. Wilson (see also Delisi [sic] 2003) exaggerate the lack of these behaviors among criminals, and overgeneralize the image of the impulsive, dissolute criminal.

Fortunately, not all in criminology responded to Wilson and Herrnstein's thesis that people differ at birth in their risk for criminal behavior in such a negative and obscurantist way. In his review of *Crime and Human Nature* in a sociology journal, Cohen (1987) not only reviewed and critiqued Wilson and Herrnstein for their work and their approach but also took mainstream criminologists to task for responding to Wilson and Herrnstein in such an ideological way. Some of Cohen's assessment of criminology is chilling as he shows how it has willfully discounted perspectives that fall outside of its preferences. According to Cohen (1987: 204), "We are the only branch of social science that has, for the most part, failed to recognize openly the possible influence of nature on human behavior, and nowhere is this more evident than in our studies of crime." Cohen also lamented that criminologists, most of them trained in sociology, have simply refused to take the time to read conceptually related work from other fields that bears on crime. Instead, it was as if criminology refused to broaden its intellectual horizons, and gleefully ignored the evidence presented by Wilson and Herrnstein.

Another example is the self-control theory developed by Michael Gottfredson and Travis Hirschi in *A General Theory of Crime* (1990). Briefly, Gottfredson and Hirschi suggested that a single individual-level construct called self-control was not only the indispensible cause of crime but also the best likely explanation for conceptually similar behaviors such as imprudence and vice. True to form with the sociological orthodoxy, self-control was also said to be the outcome of parental socialization that occurred in the first decade of life. Parents who closely monitored their children's behavior and provided appropriate reinforcements for positive behavior and sanctions for negative behavior taught children to appreciate the effects of their behavior on themselves and on others. Parenting with the appropriate investment produced children who could recognize that others existed, who could regulate and control their thoughts and actions, and who could generally comply with the program of life. Parents who loosely monitored their children's behavior and inconsistently responded to it produced children characterized as self-centered, who had a short time horizon, and who lacked the wherewithal to comply with the demands of life.

Although Gottfredson and Hirschi endured their share of conceptual, methodological, and theoretical critiques (e.g. Akers, 1991; Barlow, 1991; Geis, 2000) similar to those incurred by Wilson and Herrnstein, most evaluation of their theory was data-driven. And this makes critiques of their theory even more specious since the empirical status of the theory is so strong. Criminologists have busily tested propositions derived from self-control theory and almost always supported it empirically (the book has been cited more than 7,600 times between 1990 and 2015). Yet, even while scholars were conducting studies to test self-control theory and confirming it, there was an undercurrent of skepticism about whether the theory was truly as accurate as advertised, whether self-control could withstand confounding effects from a lengthy list of control variables, whether the theory could explain demographic variation in crime, whether the theory was applicable to females, whether the theory was specified only to street crime and not white-collar crime, whether the theory was ethnocentric to the United States, and others. Another interesting issue was that Gottfredson and Hirschi were taken to task for not specifying the role of opportunity, even though, as they have repeatedly claimed, opportunity to commit crime is ubiquitous. Other theories in criminology were not denigrated for specifying the role of opportunity along with the particular ideas inherent to the theory. That criticism was only reserved for self-control. And despite it all, meta-analyses, summary reviews, and edited anthologies resoundingly show that the theory is correct: a single construct relating to self-control predicts crime and homologous behaviors.

Unlike Wilson and Herrnstein, and Gottfredson and Hirschi, the third example, Robert Sampson and John Laub's (1993; Laub & Sampson, 2003) age-graded theory of informal social control was instantaneously accepted and anointed as a leading theory of crime. There are many reasons for this. The authors are successful criminologists (especially Sampson), whose work attracts attention, and both are accomplished empirical researchers whose work demonstrates the validity of their theoretical ideas. Briefly, the theory indicates structural context is mediated by informal social controls in family and school relationships. When there are strong bonds to institutions and relationships within those institutions, there is less crime. When bonds are attenuated, risk for crime is higher. Importantly, these effects develop and change over time. Although Sampson and Laub consistently acknowledge the variance in underlying criminal propensity, they suggest that the continuity in antisocial conduct is affected by the life circumstances of the actor, such as getting married or being employed. Over and over again (their work has been cited more than 2,000 times), Sampson and Laub's theoretical stance of criminal lives marked by plasticity and change (and thus the hope for redemption) stands in contrast to the darker views of Wilson and Herrnstein, and Gottfredson and Hirschi, which suggest that criminal behavior is relatively intractable. Indeed, as noted in a leading criminological theory text, "Sampson and Laub's perspective may well be locked in a continuing competition with Gottfredson and Hirschi's self-control theory and, more generally, with life-course theories attributing continuity in offending to underlying individual differences" (Lilly, Cullen, & Ball, 2007: 329).

Theoretically speaking, an interesting "us versus them" was established in the scholarly journals and articulated at professional conferences. On one hand was an audacious, person-specific, cynical view of the criminal offender that, although influential in terms of citations and professional chatter, was not the preferred way to conceptualize crime or criminals. It was too brutish, too antithetical to the "nuance" of scholarly analysis, and too interested in the most severe offenders as a way of demonstrating empirical points. The preferred approach, exemplified by Sampson and Laub's work, quietly nodded to the sheer individual differences in criminality that are apparent in childhood but contested that the pathways and turning points through life wear that propensity down. These more proximal situations are ultimately the causes of crime and, importantly, deal more with the situations that actors find themselves in as opposed to the actors themselves. This debate about the intrinsic character of the criminal is explored next.

The Innocent Man

The differential response to the works described earlier could be attributed to a variety of factors, including the tone in which they were written, the specificity with which the theories offered ways to be tested, and even the professional reputations of the authors. But a more meaningful explanation for the differential responses to these works relates to perceptions about the moral blameworthiness of the offender. To theorists who locate the causes of crime within the individual, the blameworthiness squarely rests on the offender, and in an indirect way, the mistakes made by the offender's parents. To theorists who are uncomfortable with the idea of an innate criminal propensity, the blame must be located elsewhere, and if pathways push people into crime, then pathways are primarily to blame.

An indirect way that this issue has been raised relates to the types of samples that are used to evaluate theories and the potential sample selection biases that might occur. This point has been raised by a handful of scholars who have quibbled with the merits of Sampson and Laub's work (see Blumstein, 2005; Gottfredson, 2005; Osgood, 2005; Robins, 2005; Sampson & Laub, 2005; Thornberry, 2005). For instance, in his review of *Shared Beginnings, Divergent Lives: Delinquent Boys to Age 70*, Toby (2005) articulated that a weakness in their theory is the likely dearth of truly pathological offenders, the type who do not reform their behavior and remain antisocial indefinitely. Indeed, living to an advanced age of 70 is highly unlikely for those who lead antisocial lifestyles characterized by substance abuse, woeful health problems, and immersion in a dangerous street culture. It is kill-or-be-killed for serious, violent criminals, and mellowing to age 70 is not part of that trajectory.

In other words, several commentators have noticed that sociological theories that favor context and statuses are well represented by community samples; theories that focus on psychopathology are better represented by clinical or correctional samples. Dark and cynical theories seemingly require severe offenders; and theories that view the human condition in more Pollyanna terms require low-risk samples. Previously, we (DeLisi et al., 2011) have attempted to demonstrate these issues empirically using two samples of very different offenders selected from the same place. One was a random sample of 500 adult arrestees and the other was a purposive sample of 500 career offenders with a minimum criterion of 30 career arrests. Their criminal activity was measured across seven age ranges spanning adolescence through age 59. The results demonstrate evidence of a declining, "not too bad" group and a relentlessly antisocial group. Even in middle age and beyond, the latter group is demonstrably more violent and criminal than "normal" criminals are during their most crime-prone years

These data provide compelling evidence for two main offender prototypes, what Moffitt (1993) calls adolescence-limited and life-course-persistent offenders. They can be used to tell competing stories, one of a flawed but ultimately redeemable offender who despite a serious involvement in crime will mature and desist. By the fifth decade of life or so, these offenders are doing okay, a far different prognosis than if we plotted their early-life pathology and extrapolated it until death. This story supports the notion of change, and the changeability of criminals. But another story can also be told: one of a pathologically antisocial offender who is always—during childhood, during adolescence, and throughout adulthood—more anti-social than his peers. In terms of the severity of his conduct and psychopathology, it is as if the life-long criminal is qualitatively distinct from others. Such extremity seemingly requires an explanation that invokes constructs related to extremity.

In a way, the unwillingness of academic criminology to tell the truth about the negative features of criminals is defensible in two ways. First, it could be that criminologists have simply been behaving as good scientists and attempting to remain value-free when conduct-ing their research. Thus, even though they were studying people who committed the most antisocial and depraved forms of conduct, criminologists were able to rise above the morally repugnant nature of this conduct and simply collect and analyze data in a phlegmatic, Joe Friday manner. They were nonjudgmental and unbiased. But if that were the case, crimin-ology would be objective across the board. Instead, the discipline is replete with platitudes about the appropriate way to respond to certain problems, whether it is the war on drugs, the use of prison, the use of boot camps, the community supervision of sex offenders, or the disproportionate minority contact (cf. Beckett & Herbert, 2009; Clear, 2007; Pratt, 2009; Simon, 2009; Western, 2006). On these, as on so many issues, criminologists were not shy about having values and expressing them.

A second way to defend the criminological solicitude for offenders centers on the diversity of the criminal population. The empirical research clearly shows that most offenders are relatively unimpressive in terms of their offending careers. They accrue few arrests over a short period of time, and the criminal conduct is unexceptional and generally unserious. Indeed, the bulk of crime is committed by a cadre of offenders, usually about 5–10 percent of the criminal population. This is useful information. Criminology has overwhelmingly focused on adolescent delinquents and community samples of adults, the type of people who are not violent career offenders. Even the most widely used datasets in the field, including the National Youth Survey, the 1945 Philadelphia birth cohort, and the National Longitudinal Study of Adolescent Health, contain a paucity of truly severe offenders. Still another way that criminology has kept the focus on benign offenders is to give short shrift to the severe offenders in textbooks. Richard Wright (1993, 1994) found that most criminology textbooks significantly limit their discussion of career criminals, especially vis-à-vis the extent to which the topic is covered in refereed journals. Wright (1994) provided further evidence that textbook authors with the most stridently left-wing political ideologies, such as William Chambliss and Raymond Michalowski, devoted zero discussion of career criminals in their texts.

Who knows the ultimate reason why scholars do or do not focus on severe offenders and the assorted psychopathology that those offenders present. It is not likely an oversight, however. Pathological offenders and their pathologies do not fit the narrative of a discipline whose preferences are that pathology be found in the environment. If criminals are more or less like normal people then attention can be focused on the conditions and processes that turned them into criminals. It is proverbially "society's fault," and we explore that orientation next.

The Guilty Society

The thrust of sociological criminology is to demonstrate the importance of structure and other environmental conditions that seemingly push individuals—innocent individuals as the prior section suggests—into antisocial conduct. Central to this worldview is the idea that the stratification of American society, and the differential values and behaviors that develop therein, is largely responsible for the creation of delinquency and related problem behaviors. In this way, crime is the outgrowth of groups, roles, and processes inherent in social structure and social dynamics. This sentiment permeates much criminological scholarship of the past several decades (see Cloward & Ohlin, 1960; Cohen, 1955; Short & Strodtbeck, 1965) and continues to the present day (see, e.g., Bursik, 2009; Short, 2009; Thornberry, 2009). Indeed, a focus on structure is viewed as the rightful tradition, and the right way, to think about crime.

Criminology has pointed to the primacy of social structure in understanding the etiology of crime by conducting two avenues of research. At the individual level, a consistent body of research has cast considerable doubt on the notion that basic personality differences exist between offenders and non-offenders and thus that personality features are related to criminality. If criminals and non-criminals are similar in terms of their decision-making processes, their impulse control, their neuroticism, their activity level, their agreeableness, their sociability, their extraversion, their temper, their conscientiousness, their morality, and other dispositional traits, then how can these traits by used to explain crime? And if criminal offenders display an array of personality features, which they do, then how does personality differentiate offenders from non-offenders? Indeed, this is the very logic of labeling theory.

An overview of criminological research on personality and crime demonstrates the skepticism with which scholars viewed the construct. In their study of 113 comparisons of criminals and non-criminals on personality features, Schuessler and Cressey (1950) found that 42 percent of studies found significant differences whereas 58 percent did not. However, in the abstract of their study, Schuessler and Cressey doubted the validity of those 42 percent of studies for several reasons. They suggested that interest in personality differences is a popular issue (read: not scientific), that it is practically impossible to predict delinquency from personality scores, that personality is at best a correlate of crime, that affirmative research was overly reliant on prisoner samples (recall the discussion about sample selection in the beginning of this chapter), that the research is not generalizable, and that there are methodological problems with the research. Years later, Waldo and Dinitz (1967) reviewed 94 studies and found that 81 percent produced significant personality differences between criminals and non-criminals, whereas 19 percent of studies did not. Despite the promising evidence that personality does in fact differentiate between the two, Waldo and Dinitz (1967: 185) wrote a similarly pessimistic abstract: "Although the results are an improvement over those reported in Schuessler-Cressey study, the same types of problems and criticisms generally prevailed." The authors also noted that their findings were "far from conclusive," and that the "conflict over the role of personality in criminality has not been resolved" (1967: 202).

A decade later it was more of the same. Tennenbaum (1977) examined studies conducted from 1966 to 1975 and found that approximately 80 percent of them demonstrated significant personality differences between criminals and non-criminals. Evidence of a personality–crime link was again met with a disbelief that belied the findings of his own study. Tennenbaum's (1977: 228) conclusion was that, "Essentially, the data do not reveal any significant differences between criminal and noncriminal psychology because most results are based on tautological argument. The conclusion remains that cursory personality testing has not differentiated criminals from noncriminals." Of course, another way to look at it is to conclude that 80 percent of studies differentiate criminals from non-criminals on the basis of personality features. Years later, Andrews and Wormith (1989a) explicated the personality–crime story for what it is: knowledge destruction and construction in criminology. Their article precipitated an interesting comment (Gibbons, 1989) and rejoinder (Andrews & Wormith, 1989b), and we'll let readers decide which is more convincing.

At another level, criminology has simply gone macro. The apotheosis of this perspective is social disorganization theory. Using the City of Chicago as a natural experiment of sorts, Clifford Shaw and Henry McKay, criminologists at the University of Chicago, advanced that neighborhoods characterized by specific environmental features were conducive to crime irrespective of the demographic characteristics of the persons living there. Thus, neighborhoods with high rates of residential mobility, family disruption, ethnic heterogeneity, and poverty were unstable and had weak community control. Over time, and across generations of immigrants moving through the stratification system, conventional people would flee socially disorganized neighborhoods toward the suburbs. And only the most socio-economically vulnerable people would reside in socially disorganized neighborhoods, but they too would flee after climbing the ladder of American society. The theory was not limited to an American context; similar neighborhood dynamics were seen using data from England and Wales (Sampson & Groves, 1989; see also Lowenkamp, Cullen, & Pratt, 2003), and social disorganization is viewed as a macro-theory of crime *par excellence*.

The unfolding of immigration and crime patterns in Chicago seemed to follow the social disorganization playbook. As immigrant groups from Western, Southern, and Eastern Europe arrived in the United States, they were met with considerable public distrust and dislike, and their involvement in crime, vice, and poverty seemed part and parcel of their status as newcomers to the American Dream. Over time, as these groups raised their socioeconomic status and decreased their use of violence, they were absorbed into the mainstream. Assimilation brought behavioral as well as economic prosperity—and neighborhoods and communities were considered the engines that drove all of these behaviors.

Yet even when the evidence did not align with the theory, there was a strident effort to interpret the findings for the reader. For instance, Bursik and Webb (1982) found that it was the African American population that was associated with delinquency in Chicago since 1950, and the neighborhood-centric approach of social disorganization theory was pertinent for crime trends prior to 1950. Yet they advised that it would be "naïve and racist" to interpret the association between minority status and delinquency (p. 39). However, the empirical evidence suggests it is indeed prudent to associate race/ethnicity with crime. For instance, exhaustive reviews of the criminological literature (Ellis, Beaver, & Wright, 2009) indicate that macro-criminological research on the association between percent African American population and violent crime produced affirmative evidence that outweighed negative evidence by a ratio of 39 to 3 or 13 to 1. For property crime, the relationship was much smaller at 7 to 5. For delinquency, the evidence was 4 to 1, and for general adult offending, the ratio was 11 to 1. Thus, what guardians of social disorganization theory would call naïve and racist, empiricists would call something else.

It is also possible that social disorganization theorists were off target about the inter-relationships between poverty, neighborhood structure, and crime. To the criminological orthodoxy, poverty meant socioeconomic poverty. To conservatives, poverty means behavioral poverty. It was not the percentage of renters versus homeowners that drove residential mobility and weakened social bonds: it was crime and other underclass trappings. To extend this logic further, it was crime, not various structural features of neighborhoods, that drove citizens away from the dangerous cities and to the safe suburbs. There is ample evidence for this. Julie Berry Cullen and Steven Levitt (1999) analyzed crime rates in U.S. cities and urban flight and found that each additional reported crime occurring in a city contributed to a one-person decline in the city population. This effect remained regardless of the time scale of the observations (annual, five-year, or ten-year), level of aggregation, or control variables included in their equations. Boggess and Hipp (2010) found that the effect of crime on changes in residential instability is twice as strong as the reverse effect, and a 1 percent increase in violent crime rate was associated with a 1.5 percent increase in the number of homes sold—reflecting conventional citizens leaving the behavioral poverty behind. The idea that crime and related bad behaviors drive neighborhood composition and structure—not the other way—is also seen with international data. Surveys of nearly 50,000 respondents from 17 nations in Latin America indicated that families that were victimized by crime were 30 percent more likely than families not personally affected by crime to emigrate to the United States (Wood, Gibson, Ribeiro, & Hamsho-Diaz, 2010).

Another problem with the theory is that research has also found that neighborhoods have little to no effect on crime (to which can be added the enormous anecdotal power of the tens of millions of Americans who were raised in impoverished, disorganized neighborhoods yet never became criminals). Levitt and Venkatesh (2001) explored the lives of a cohort of young men who grew up in crime-ridden Chicago public housing. The big difference in their lives was not their neighbourhood—a bad neighborhood was a constant—but the decision to join gangs. Compared to their peers who joined gangs, prosocial young men had higher levels of employment, higher incomes, less involvement in drug sales, higher educational attainment, and higher likelihood of graduating from high school. This rationale is also shown when neighborhood and individual level factors are considered simultaneously in multilevel statistical models. For instance, a recent study of over 7,000 male juvenile delinquents in Philadelphia (85 percent of whom were black or Hispanic) found that neighborhood characteristics had no effect on violent crime, property crime, and an aggregated measure of recidivism, and were only significantly related to drug offenses (Grunwald et al., 2010). Using data from the Project on Human Development in Chicago Neighborhoods (the data that largely promulgated the idea of collective efficacy), Gibson and colleagues (2010) found that neighborhood structural factors had no effect on the development of self-control of adolescents once individual-level characteristics were considered. Interestingly, research utilizing the same data but steeped in the macro tradition of criminology suggests that neighborhood effects are a prime explanatory factor on a construct that is clearly better explained by psychological and biological perspectives: the sex gap in violence. For instance, Zimmerman and Messner (2010) also used data from the Project on Human Development in Chicago Neighborhoods, but found that neighborhood disadvantage and peer networks were important determinants of sex differences (in sociology, referred to as gender differences) in the perpetration of violence. Thus, even today, the neighborhood can be called upon by criminologists to report more likely and believable individual-level answers.

Even to its proponents, social disorganization theory is a bit outmoded, and it has since been replaced by theory and research that documents the importance of social networks, social capital, and collective efficacy to understanding crime. Generally speaking, neighborhoods where residents know one another, have a shared investment in their street and neighborhood conditions, and are willing to look out for their fellow residents (e.g. watch their house when they're out of town, keep an eye on children to make sure they are safe, respond to problems or concerns that affect the neighborhood, etc.) are viewed positively. Neighborhoods where residents are strangers who retreat into their own lives and are uninterested in the greater good are viewed negatively. Although the research is not unequivocal, the former neighborhoods generally have less crime, whereas the latter neighborhoods have more crime (cf. Browning, Feinberg, & Dietz, 2004; Sampson & Raudenbush, 1999; Sampson, Raudenbush & Earls, 1997). Ideologically speaking, of course, nothing has changed. The Chicago School advances that crime and assorted vices, such as rampant drug selling and drug use, prostitution, loitering, graffiti, blighted lots, houses, and neighborhoods, and the like are cultural problems. Interestingly, although the Chicago School of criminology was comfortable talking about the issue of culture, or more accurately, oppositional subculture, subsequent generations were not and over time the neighborhood literature largely dropped discussions of culture in favor of purely socioeconomic structural factors. Cultural or economic, these features are viewed as the result of emergent social dynamics over and above the traits and behaviors of the individuals living there. The more diffuse and collective the level of explanation for crime, the better. This has been criminology's past, and is unfortunately its present.

In his presidential address to the American Society of Criminology in 2010, Richard Rosenfeld (2011) illustrated the general preference for macro-perspectives, what Rosenfeld called the big picture, as opposed to individual-level perspectives. Interestingly, this proclivity exists even though the scientific importance of individual-level approaches is acknowledged, and in many respects viewed favorably. According to Rosenfeld (2011: 1–2, italics added):

> The current period, with its breakthrough studies of gene-environment interactions and individual development, epitomizes the dominance of microcriminology. In this address, I nudge the pendulum back the other way by highlighting the value for theory, research, and public policy of macrocriminology. I do not claim that knowledge of the cultural and social conditions that influence crime rates is to advocate for (or argue against) multilevel research or integrated theories. *I maintain simply that criminology would be better off* with more systematic and sustained attention to the big picture.

What a curious desire. If "breakthrough" studies using statistical models that include both measured genes and measured environmental conditions working in tandem are shedding light on the causes of crime, why go in the opposite direction? What is to be gained from it? Hypothetically, scientists could discover the cause of crime and yet many in criminology would not want to know about it (let alone publish such research in their journals).

It is one thing for a theory to accumulate thousands of citations and serve as an impetus for hundreds of studies. It is another thing for everyone to believe it. And the unfortunate news is that the criminological tradition of doubting the pathology of the criminal offender, and even doubting the more innocuous notion that offenders might evince personality differences from non-offenders, in favor of neighborhood effects is conventional wisdom. What Shaw and McKay called social disorganization, millions of Americans today call the "hood." In prior eras, socially disorganized neighborhoods were characterized by poverty, ethnic heterogeneity, high turnover, renters not homeowners, and weak informal controls. Today's hoods are characterized by poverty, usually ethnic homogeneity, and social indicators that resemble those of third-world nations. The weak social controls that once enabled crime have been replaced by strong social controls in the name of a snitch culture and pervasive animosity toward the criminal justice system that also enable crime. These features also enable victimization. To be sure, the near-religious focus on neighborhood and community effects on crime has produced benefits, namely articulating the environmental conditions that moderate individual-level traits to explain crime. But it has come at a cost. To explain individual-level acts such as assault and burglary at an ecological level is troubling on logical grounds. That was never the point to criminology, however.

But the hood is more than a modern-day incarnation of Shaw and McKay. The true legacy of the neighborhood, and it is a pyrrhic theoretical victory, is that the hood is short-hand for the removal of responsibility. It is shorthand for the removal of stigma. The hood means "not my fault," and for many years it has been socially acceptable for young people to claim to be from the hood, as if such a place confers a set of benefits. Indeed, to stake a claim on the hood means to "keep it real." The problem is that using a macro-phenomenon to explain individual-level behaviors is incorrect and obfuscates the moral and personality defi-cits of criminals. Bad neighborhoods don't just happen. They are the outgrowth of the commensurate bad habits of their residents.

The Tangle of Pathology

If the theoretical impulses of mainstream criminology and its presumably liberal scholars are wrong or misguided, what is the alternative? Before exploring the advantages of conservative theorizing about crime, some important caveats should be considered. First, there is not an explicitly conservative theory of crime that exists in the same way that conflict or Marxian theory in the social sciences can be associated with the political left. In this way, the per-spectives we explore are more conservative in their implications. It is likely, indeed probable, that most of the scholars whose work we review would never claim to be conservatives (exceptions might include James Q. Wilson, John Dilulio, Jackson Toby, and the current authors. That is a very brief list).

Second, a conservative theoretical perspective on crime is evidence-based in its approach and unafraid to comport with populist, common sense understanding about criminals. The greatest example of this commonality centers on the relation of personality to behavior gen-erally and antisocial behavior specifically. As examined earlier in this chapter, whereas main-stream criminologists were unwilling to acknowledge the empirical relation of personality to crime (even when their own studies demonstrated such an association), conservative crimin-ologists embrace the tremendous individual-level differences that exist in the population. This connects to the third caveat, which is a preference for parsimonious individual-level explanations for behavior. To the conservative criminologist, wringing one's hands about the "root causes" of crime is an intellectually dishonest way of avoiding the truth. And the truth is the pathology that permeates the lives, behaviors (and even neighborhoods) of serious criminal offenders.

Similar to the broad approach of Wilson and Herrnstein, and Gottfredson and Hirschi, a straightforward way to demonstrate pathology is to examine variation among individuals on a set of traits, values, and, most importantly, behaviors. These subtle incremental differ-ences that define human diversity in terms of executive functioning, egocentricity, impul-sivity, self-regulation, negative emotions, use of aggression, and the like have a way of adding up over time. Those who have a preponderance of prosocial traits are susceptible to prosocial behaviors. Those who have a preponderance of antisocial traits are susceptible to antisocial behaviors. Our traits do not steadfastly determine our life's course, but they have an important place in the driver's seat. When the constellation of traits clusters at the extreme tails of the trait distribution—positively or negatively—there are, not surprisingly, extremes in behavior.

Historically, social scientists have utilized personality as a way to capture the essential characteristics of individuals in a systematic manner. A major structural model of personality is the Five Factor Model, which is comprised of five dimensions conveniently encapsulated by the acronym OCEAN. O is for openness to experience and relates to a person's openness to new experiences, emotions, values, and beliefs. C is for conscientiousness and relates to the ability to persevere in the face of difficulty, gratification delay, and consideration of the consequences of one's behavior. E is for extraversion and relates to an approach-based behavioral style characterized by social interaction and the experiencing of positive emotions. A is for agreeableness and relates to interpersonal strategies and reactions to other. N is for neuroticism and relates to the frequency of experiencing negative emotions.

Within each domain are six facets. Within O are fantasy, aesthetics, feelings, actions, ideas, and values. Within C are competence, order, dutifulness, achievement striving, self-discipline, and deliberation. Within E are warmth, gregariousness, assertiveness, activity, excitement seeking, and positive emotions. Within A are trust, straightforwardness, altruism, compliance, modesty, and tender-mindedness. Within N are anxiety, angry hostility, depression, self-consciousness, impulsiveness, and vulnerability.

Readers can easily imagine these constructs and evaluate how well they map onto the personality of criminals, and non-criminals. Common sense would suggest that criminals have high levels of anger and hostility and are prone to impulsive reactions. Indeed, the instantaneous blend of short-sighted, angry reaction goes a long way to describe many forms of crime against person (e.g., a bar fight involving two intoxicated young men) and property (e.g., vandalism involving intoxicated young men). (These examples also show that age and sex are important correlates of crime.) Common sense is one thing; science is another. But regarding the role of personality and crime, they largely converge. Jones, Miller, and Lynam (2011) conducted a meta-analysis of 53 studies to explore the associations between personality and antisocial behavior and personality and aggression. As shown in Table 7.1, the bolded mean effect sizes show significant associations between several personality facets and both antisocial behavior and aggression.

It is important to note that these are normal personality traits that in combination and at concentrated levels contribute to antisocial conduct and related forms of problematic conduct. From these normal traits, one can draw conclusions about the pathology of criminal behavior that have clear moral overtones. Consider the Conscientious domain and its facets (all of which are significantly associated with antisocial conduct and aggression according to meta-analyses). Criminal offenders are likely to be low scorers on every facet. They are incompetent (which contributes to school and work problems), disorderly (which contributes to a wanton lifestyle), lack a sense of duty (which contributes to school and work problems), are not achievement striving (which contributes to school and work problems), are lacking in self-discipline (which some have argued is the indispensible cause of crime (Gottfredson & Hirschi, 1990), and are lacking in deliberation (which contributes to an improvident lifestyle). Conversely, high scores on each facet read like a recipe for an anti-criminal offender: competent, orderly, dutiful, disciplined, achievement-oriented, accomplished, self-composed, thoughtful, deliberative, planning, and the like.

History buffs will likely notice the subheading that marks this section. The phrase "tangle of pathology" appeared in Daniel Patrick Moynihan's 1965 treatise *The Negro Family: The Case for National Action*. The Moynihan Report, as it has since been known, warned of the negative social consequences that would stem from the issue of single-parent families and

TABLE 7.1 The Five Factor Model and its relation to antisocial behavior and aggression

Facet scale		Antisocial behavior	Aggression
		Mean effect size	Mean effect size
N1	Anxiety	−.047	−.038
N2	Angry hostility	**.197**	**.213**
N3	Depression	**.081**	**.105**
N4	Self-consciousness	−.005	.014
N5	Impulsiveness	**.179**	**.084**
N6	Vulnerability	.021	**.099**
E1	Warmth	**−.195**	**−.231**
E2	Gregariousness	−.034	−.022
E3	Assertiveness	.031	**.063**
E4	Activity	−.016	−.017
E5	Excitement seeking	**.140**	−.022
E6	Positive emotions	−.113	**−.166**
O1	Fantasy	.023	−.035
O2	Aesthetics	.020	−.032
O3	Feelings	−.041	**−.117**
O4	Actions	**.060**	.021
O5	Ideas	**.065**	.005
O6	Values	−.012	−.095
A1	Trust	**−.174**	**−.181**
A2	Straightforwardness	**−.297**	**−.246**
A3	Altruism	**−.210**	**−.256**
A4	Compliance	**−.268**	**−.264**
A5	Modesty	**−.170**	**−.162**
A6	Tender-mindedness	**−.113**	**−.171**
C1	Competence	**−.159**	**−.170**
C2	Order	**−.092**	**−.065**
C3	Dutifulness	**−.217**	**−.170**
C4	Achievement striving	**−.106**	**−.054**
C5	Self-discipline	**−.125**	**−.060**
C6	Deliberation	**−.252**	**−.181**

Source: Adapted from Jones et al. (2011).

illegitimacy generally and in the African American community specifically. Like criminologists who have been keen to deny the relevance of personality features to understand crime, social scientists and media commentators *writ large* have similarly denied the destructive effects of the dissolution of the traditional family and its implications for the socio-behavioral development of children. This family background continues to be a striking feature of the antisocial population. Nearly 50 years after the Moynihan Report, a lack of parental investment is seen in the lives of youth in detention facilities in the United States. According to the most recent data, less than half of confined youth had two parents as caretakers (at any point during their lives). In terms of their living arrangement when taken into custody, 70 percent of confined youth did not live with two parents. Fully 25 percent lived with neither of their biological parents upon admission to custody (Sedlak & Bruce, 2010).

In her thought-provoking work on the importance of marriage, Hymowitz (2006) provides an explanatory framework linking family structure, its differential effects by race, and the inculcation of prosocial characteristics:

> [W]hat happens when marriage disappears, for that is what has happened in the black community. Daniel Patrick Moynihan warned of this impending disaster in 1965, but the nation, on the verge of a cultural revolution that insisted things be otherwise, was in no mood to listen. Instead elites built an elaborate edifice of denial and rationalization whose ruins spoil the political landscape to this day and whose consequences continue to roil the inner city.
>
> *(Hymowitz, 2006: 49)*

Notwithstanding the other forms of pathology that accompany the breakdown in family structure, there is a larger importance missing from single-parent families compared to the traditional family. According to Hymowitz's thesis, the larger importance is what is known as the "Mission," and it is geared first and foremost to the social, behavioral, emotional, and cognitive development of the child. It goes something like this:

> The Mission aims at far more than promoting children's self-reliance or ensuring that they make the soccer team or get into an impressive college. The Mission's deepest ideal is the pursuit of happiness. In their minivan runs to swim meets and choir practices, middle-class parents give their children a chance to discover their talents as well as learn the self-discipline that makes those talents shine. In the best scenario the project leads not only to satisfying work lives but to full self-development and self-cultivation.
>
> *(Hymowitz, 2006: 83)*

Criminologists will recognize this for what it is: the basic logic of the parental socialization processes inherent in self-control theory. But the mission also aligns with the stock of criminological theories that point to the importance of parenting, parent–child dynamics, and a healthy and stable family life.

Pathology exists in normal personality traits that in certain combinations are abnormal in their manifestations. Pathology exists in family structures that are demonstrably known to facilitate crime. And pathology also works in tandem where individual deficits and family dynamics interact to produce still more pathology. The product of this interaction results in blighted neighborhoods characterized by broken windows. Here we are in agreement with the criminological mainstream that neighborhoods matter, with one important difference. Whereas sociological criminology elevated the neighborhood into a social force that molded individual lives, we view neighborhoods as simply the aggregation of concentrations of people with pathological forms of behavior. Neighborhoods with concentrations of people engaged in pathology are as plain as day, characterized by litter, vacant lots, abandoned vehicles, and buildings in disrepair (generally known as physical incivilities) and rampant drug sales, drug use, prostitution, vagrancy, and loitering (generally known as social incivilities). As noted by Wilson and Kelling (1982) in their influential broken windows theory, places characterized by disorder engender continued crime and disorder, and by having zero tolerance of this vice and disorder, the police can dramatically reduce crime rates. Police behavior in large cities since 1993 or so generally supports this logic.

To close, Wilson and Kelling's thesis has achieved the trifecta by gaining prominence in popular, policy, and scholarly audiences. But it should not be considered a preferred explanation of crime. Indeed, unlike other ecological explanations of crime (e.g. social disorganization theory, collective efficacy, and the like) that blamed a negative environment enveloping innocent individuals, broken windows blamed both. Which is correct? We are confident that prosocial, functioning individuals could be experimentally placed in bad neighborhoods and in relatively short order, they would clean up the place. A corollary experiment would involve placing pathological individuals in gorgeous new homes in a clean, tidy neighborhood. In short order, they would mess up the place.

References

Akers, R. L. (1991) Self-control as a general theory of crime. *Journal of Quantitative Criminology*, 7(2), 201–211.

Andrews, D. A., & Wormith, J. S. (1989a). Personality and crime: Knowledge destruction and construction in criminology. *Justice Quarterly*, 6, 289–310.

Andrews, D. A., & Wormith, J. S. (1989b). Rejoinder—personality and crime: Toward knowledge construction. *Justice Quarterly*, 6(3), 325–332.

Barlow, H. D. (1991) Explaining crime and analogous acts, or the unrestrained will grab at pleasure whenever they can. *Journal of Criminal Law and Criminology*, 82, 229–242.

Beckett, K., & Herbert, S. (2009) *Banished: the new social control in urban America*. New York: Oxford University Press.

Blumstein, A. (2005) An overview of the symposium and some next steps. *Annals of the American Academy of Political and Social Science*, 602(1), 242–258.

Boggess, L. N., & Hipp, J. R. (2010) Violent crime, residential instability and mobility: Does the relationship differ in minority neighborhoods? *Journal of Quantitative Criminology*, 26(3), 351–370.

Browning, C. R., Feinberg, S. L., & Dietz, R. D. (2004) The paradox of social organization: Networks, collective efficacy, and violent crime in urban neighborhoods. *Social Forces*, 83(2), 503–534.

Bursik, R. J. (2009) The Dead Sea scrolls and criminological knowledge: 2008 Presidential Address to the American Society of Criminology. *Criminology*, 47(1), 5–16.

Bursik, R. J., & Webb, J. (1982) Community change and patterns of delinquency. *American Journal of Sociology*, 88(1), 24–42.

Clear, T. R. (2007) *Imprisoning communities: How mass incarceration makes disadvantaged neighborhoods worse*. New York: Oxford University Press.

Cloward, R. A., & Ohlin, L. E. (1960) *Delinquency and opportunity: A theory of delinquent gangs*. New York: The Free Press of Glencoe.

Cohen, A. K. (1955) *Delinquent boys: The culture of the gang*. New York: The Free Press.

Cohen, L. E. (1987) Throwing down the gauntlet: A challenge to the relevance of sociology for the etiology of criminal behavior. *Contemporary Sociology: A Journal of Reviews*, 16(2), 202–205.

Cullen, J. B., & Levitt, S. D. (1999) Crime, urban flight, and the consequences for cities. *The Review of Economics and Statistics*, 81(2), 159–169.

Dalrymple, T. (2003) *Life at the bottom: The worldview that makes the underclass*. Chicago, IL: Ivan R. Dee.

DeLisi, M. (2003) Conservatism and common sense: The criminological career of James Q. Wilson. *Justice Quarterly*, 20(3), 661–674.

DeLisi, M., Kosloski, A. E., Drury, A. J., Vaughn, M. G., Beaver, K. M., Trulson, C. R., & Wright, J. P. (2011) Never-desisters: A descriptive study of the life-course-persistent offender. In M. DeLisi & K. M. Beaver (eds), *Criminological theory: A life-course approach*. Sudbury, MA: Jones & Bartlett, pp. 241–256.

Ellis, L., Beaver, K., & Wright, J. (2009) *Handbook of crime correlates*. New York: Elsevier/Academic Press.

Geis, G. (2000) On the absence of self-control as the basis for a general theory of crime: A critique. *Theoretical Criminology*, 4(1), 35–54.

Geis, G. (2008) Self-control: A hypercritical assessment. In E. Goode (ed.), *Out of control: Assessing the general theory of crime*. Stanford, CA: Stanford Social Sciences, pp. 203–216.

Gibbons, D. C. (1989) Comment—personality and crime: Non-issues, real issues, and a theory and research agenda. *Justice Quarterly*, 6, 311–324.

Gibson, C. L., Sullivan, C. J., Jones, S., & Piquero, A. R. (2010) Does it take a village? Assessing neighborhood influences on children's self-control. *Journal of Research in Crime and Delinquency*, 47(1), 31–62.

Giddens, A. (1972) *Emile Durkheim: Selected writings*. New York: Cambridge University Press.

Gottfredson, M. R. (2005) Offender classifications and treatment effects in developmental criminology: A propensity/event consideration. *Annals of the American Academy of Political and Social Science*, 602(1), 46–56.

Gottfredson, M. R., & Hirschi, T. (1990) *A general theory of crime*. Stanford, CA: Stanford University Press.

Grunwald, H. E., Lockwood, B., Harris, P. W., & Mennis, J. (2010) Influences of neighborhood context, individual history and parenting behavior on recidivism among juvenile offenders. *Journal of Youth and Adolescence*, 39(9), 1067–1079.

Hymowitz, K. S. (2006) *Marriage and caste in America: Separate and unequal families in a post-marital age*. Chicago, IL: Ivan R. Dee.

Jones, S. E., Miller, J. D., & Lynam, D. R. (2011) Personality, antisocial behavior, and aggression: A meta-analytic review. *Journal of Criminal Justice*, 39(4), 329–337.

Laub, J. H., & Sampson, R. J. (2003) *Shared beginnings, divergent lives: Delinquent boys to age 70*. Cambridge, MA: Harvard University Press.

Levitt, S. D., & Venkatesh, S. A. (2001) Growing up in the projects: The economic lives of a cohort of men who came of age in Chicago public housing. *American Economic Review*, 91(2), 79–84.

Lilly, J. R., Cullen, F. T., & Ball, R. A. (2007) *Criminological theory: Context and consequences*, 4th edition. Thousand Oaks, CA: SAGE.

Lowenkamp, C. T., Cullen, F. T., & Pratt, T. C. (2003) Replicating Sampson and Grove's test of social disorganization theory: Revisiting a criminological classic. *Journal of Research in Crime and Delinquency*, 40(4), 351–373.

McWhorter, J. (2000) *Losing the race: Self-sabotage in black America*. New York: The Free Press.

McWhorter, J. (2005) *Winning the race: Beyond the crisis in black America*. New York: Gotham Books.

Moffitt, T. E. (1993). Adolescence-limited and life-course-persistent antisocial behavior: A developmental taxonomy. *Psychological Review*, 100(4), 674–701.

Osgood, D. W. (2005) Making sense of crime and the life course. *Annals of the American Academy of Political and Social Science*, 602(1), 196–211.

Pratt, T. C. (2009) *Addicted to incarceration: Corrections policy and the politics of misinformation in the United States*. Thousand Oaks, CA: SAGE.

Robins, L. N. (2005) Explaining when arrests end for serious juvenile offenders: Comments on the Sampson and Laub study. *Annals of the American Academy of Political and Social Science*, 602, 57–72.

Rosenfeld, R. (2011) The big picture: 2010 Presidential Address to the American Society of Criminology. *Criminology*, 49(1), 1–26.

Sampson, R. J., & Groves, W. B. (1989) Community structure and crime: Testing social disorganization theory. *American Journal of Sociology*, 94(4), 774–802.

Sampson, R. J., & Laub, J. H. (1993) *Crime in the making: Pathways and turning points through life*. Cambridge, MA: Harvard University Press.

Sampson, R. J., & Laub, J. H. (2005) When prediction fails: From crime-prone boys to heterogeneity in adulthood. *Annals of the American Academy of Political and Social Science*, 602(1), 73–79.

Sampson, R. J., & Raudenbush, S. W. (1999) Systematic social observation of public spaces: A new look at disorder in urban neighborhoods. *American Journal of Sociology*, 105(3), 603–651.

Sampson, R. J., Raudenbush, S. W., & Earls, F. (1997) Neighborhoods and violent crime: A multilevel study of collective efficacy. *Science*, 277(5328), 918–924.

Schuessler, K. F., & Cressey, D. R. (1950) Personality characteristics of criminals. *American Journal of Sociology*, 55 (March), 476–484.

Sedlak, A. J., & Bruce, C. (2010) *Youth's characteristics and backgrounds: Findings from the survey of youth in residential placement*. Washington, DC: Office of Juvenile Justice and Delinquency Prevention.

Short, J. F. (2009) Bursik introduction: "Criminology like it oughta be!" *Criminology*, 47(1), 1–4.

Short, J. F., & Strodtbeck, F. L. (1965) *Group process and gang delinquency*. Chicago, IL: University of Chicago Press.

Simon, J. (2009) *Governing through crime: How the war on crime transformed American democracy and created a culture of fear*. New York: Oxford University Press.

Steffensmeier, D. J., & Ulmer, J. T. (2005). *Confessions of a dying thief: Understanding criminal careers and illegal enterprise*. New Brunswick, NJ: Aldine/Transaction.

Tennenbaum, D. J. (1977) Personality and criminality: A summary and implications of the literature. *Journal of Criminal Justice*, 5, 225–235.

Thornberry, T. P. (2005) Explaining multiple patterns of offending across the life course and across generations. *Annals of the American Academy of Political and Social Science*, 602(1), 156–195.

Thornberry, T. P. (2009) The apple doesn't fall far from the tree (or does it?): Intergenerational patterns of antisocial behavior—the American Society of Criminology 2008 Sutherland Address. *Criminology*, 47, 297–326.

Toby, J. (2005) Shared beginnings, divergent lives: Delinquent boys to age 70. *Contemporary Sociology: A Journal of Reviews*, 34(1), 65.

Waldo, G. P., & Dinitz, S. (1967) Personality attributes of the criminal: An analysis of research studies, 1950–1965. *Journal of Research in Crime and Delinquency*, 4, 185–202.

Western, B. (2006) *Punishment and inequality in America*. New York: Russell Sage Foundation.

Wilson, J. Q., & Herrnstein, R. J. (1985) *Crime and human nature: The definitive study of the causes of crime*. New York: Simon and Schuster.

Wilson, J. Q., & Kelling, G. L. (1982) The police and neighborhood safety: Broken windows. *Atlantic Monthly*, March, 29–38.

Wood, C. H., Gibson, C. L., Ribeiro, L., & Hamsho-Diaz, P. (2010) Crime victimization in Latin America and intentions to migrate to the United States. *International Migration Review*, 44(1), 3–24.

Wright, R. A. (1993) The two criminologies: The divergent worldviews of textbooks and journals. *The Criminologist*, 18, 1, 8, 10.

Wright, R. A. (1994) Stopped for questioning, but not booked: The coverage of career criminals in criminology journal and textbooks, 1982 to 1992. *Journal of Criminal Justice Education*, 5, 251–256.

Zimmerman, G. M., & Messner, S. F. (2010) Neighborhood context and the gender gap in adolescent violent crime. *American Sociological Review*, 75(6), 958–980.

8

CONSERVATIVE CRIMINOLOGY

Throughout this book we have endeavored to highlight the ways that liberal thought influences criminology and the social sciences. We have tried to show some of the limits of liberal ideology, as well as where liberal dogma has caused harm. In the following pages we advance specific principles of what we term "conservative criminology." Given the broad swathe of our critique, we offer principles that cut across several areas, including science, society, and the criminal justice system. As principles, these statements merely advance positions rooted in conservative beliefs of restraint in relation to government, tradition, social order and public safety, and redemption.

We begin with principles regarding the nature of science. We argue that:

- All aspects of human social behavior should be open to unfettered empirical investigation without fear of reprisal or career harm.
- All scientific findings should be viewed with caution if not skepticism, especially those not subject to experimental conditions.
- In the social sciences, professional bodies should agree on minimal scientific standards and what constitutes meaningful effect sizes.
- Potentially controversial studies should be published, as should studies that show a null effect or that fail to replicate the findings from other studies.
- Constructive scholarly exchanges should take a higher priority in scientific journals.
- All data collected with taxpayer funds should be open to legitimate investigators and should be as useful to scholars as possible.
- Institutional Review Boards (IRBs) should be reformulated and definitions of what constitutes "harm" should be narrowed considerably.
- Conflict of interests statements should include language requiring authors to specify any political or ideological conflict of interest that may affect their work. This would include political donations made to political parties or interest groups and it would include working for or being a member of those groups. Conflict of interest statements should also outline any ideological sentiments that may affect the published research. The point is to make political-moral biases transparent so others can better scrutinize the study.

Our core belief is that science should be open, honest, and as unbiased as possible (it should not be based on activism, as exhorted by the outgoing president of the American Society of Criminology, Joanne Belknap). Science should welcome competing, even inconsistent findings because that is how science progresses. Unfortunately, a variety of gates exist that sometimes limit science or that produce a body of science that is highly circumspect. Some of these gates are ideological, but others are structural. For example, recent changes in the way that data, bought and paid for by federal taxpayers, are collected and disseminated have reduced access to legitimate scientists and imposed heavy administrative and legal burdens on those who wish to analyze the data. Institutional Review Boards, especially in the social and behavioral sciences, also frequently work to thwart legitimate research. By imposing often ridiculous requirements on social scientist, IRBs have become nothing more than an administrative mechanism to reduce university liability. In doing so, they squash much necessary research and overly burden those who receive their blessing.

Science should not only be as open as possible, scientists should be able to publish their findings and to argue their points without fear of academic mobbing (Twale & DeLuca 2008). Academic mobbing occurs when scientists publish or present research that some groups, almost always liberal groups, find offensive. In turn, the offending scholar is subject not only to criticism but to pointed efforts to undermine her career and reputation. Academic mobbing has injured the livelihoods and reputations of many and resulted in scholars making conscious decisions to abandon certain types of research in favor of safer topics (Kempner, 2008). Self-censorship has no place in science and threatens the integrity of science. Likewise, intellectual bullying, harassment, rumor-mongering, libel, and the filing of politically motivated ethics complaints has no place in science—regardless of how "good" the motivation. Such activities, moreover, should be roundly condemned.

Lastly, we believe it time for journals and professional organizations to address the issue of political-moral bias more directly. This can be done in a variety of ways, including viewing political-moral biases as a potential conflict of interest. While the details would have to be worked out, it seems reasonable to suggest that a major source of bias in social science research findings emanates from the political-moral views of professors. We suggest that it is best simply to make these potential biases as visible and transparent as possible. Scholars have a right to engage in political activities of their choosing, but readers and reviewers also have a right to know how these activities may influence reported findings.

We next turn our attention to universities:

- The purpose of a university is rigorous education—not political indoctrination. Obviously partisan classes should not be approved. Similarly, all students should be required to take a full battery of liberal arts courses, including courses in philosophy, economics, and the humanities.
- Efforts to increase optimal diversity should be reduced or entirely eliminated. Merit, instead, should be the guiding principle in all university endeavors, including student admission, the award of scholarships, and faculty hiring.
- Tenure should be reformed, not eliminated. Instead of junior scholars having a few years to prove themselves able before applying for tenure, they should be given a ten-year contract. The contract would guarantee their academic freedom. At the end of their contract they can then be evaluated and, if approved, moved into the full professor ranks if deemed meritorious.

- Universities should take no position on controversial topics or on controversies caused by professors. Doing so necessarily translates into the university becoming an arbitrator of truth and supporting one view of reality over another.
- Universities should scrap all speech codes and rescind any policy or mechanism that places restrictions on speech. All groups should be welcome on campus, especially those with minority, different, and even unscientific views.
- University administrators should rebel against and refuse to allow the expansion of Title IX efforts that reduce fundamental fairness and due process of those accused of harassment or discrimination.
- University judicial affairs offices should be stripped of their powers to hear and to adjudicate matters that involve the violation of criminal law. The police are the proper authorities to investigate allegations of crime.
- Administrative bloat and federal regulations should be reduced. Growth in college administration has been nothing short of staggering and has been economically expensive.
- Universities should understand and appreciate the problems that occur when they view students as "customers" instead of students in need of an education. Education is not a product to be sold.

We call for a return to classical liberal principles that once guided our great universities. Universities should be places where art, culture, debate, and science flourish. Anything that infringes on these principles should be eliminated and roundly condemned. We believe the university is a great institution and that it reaches its true potential when it shelters no idea from criticism, serves as the springboard for openness and unfettered debate, and creates an environment where scholars are free to be honest with students and their colleagues. Free speech is the only way to achieve this goal. All speech, no matter how seemingly ludicrous, should be protected on campus. All of it.

Along these lines, it is (well past) time that universities stand up to the continued expansion of the federal government in their operations. This includes taking principled stands against federal efforts to make it easier to convict individuals alleged of harassment or discrimination or worse. The "star chamber" inquiries that now populate our campuses are dangerous and erode public confidence in the institution. Accommodate no more. Similarly, the rather ludicrous and unfounded efforts of IRBs should be reviewed and their jurisdiction limited. IRBs are a perfect example of an institutional response to a perceived problem metastasizing into an uncontrollable mess of subjectively enforced guidelines.

Our belief is that by universities doing less they will achieve more. There is no need to have legions of administrators and deans who neither conduct research nor teach students. It is the nature of administration and bureaucracy to expand in ever broader and more invasive ways. Today, faculty-hiring committees have to include administrators to make sure they are taking diversity seriously enough. We have administrators in student life who involve themselves in decisions about which student clubs can exist on campus and which cannot. We have administrators who lead inquisitions into alleged Title IX complaints. We have administrators who … the list is endless and expensive.

Lastly, we believe that only the best should be welcomed into the professor ranks and that universities should not lose their ability to regulate departments. These points may seem incongruent but that is only at first blush. To be blunt, the typical five-year tenure evaluation cycle is insufficient and invites awarding tenure to people who have not shown prolonged and serious effort at crafting their skills. It takes time to learn the art of being a professor and it takes time to learn the science behind science. This cannot be learned in a few short years. Instead, we believe it is time to adjust tenure, not eliminate it. Extending contracts to ten years will give individuals time to learn the art and science of their discipline and it will better weed out those who are not dedicated to the profession. The rewards of tenure are too important to give away. Similarly, we believe that it is entirely too difficult for universities to close or otherwise alter non-productive and dysfunctional academic departments. Some departments have been dysfunctional for decades and have, we suggest, harmed the students who have entered into those programs. The criteria to close or reshape these departments are ludicrous—often involving a declaration of financial exigency. A more reasonable guideline could be developed and implemented. One that is fair to faculty, to students, and to taxpayers.

Our next set of principles involves the criminal justice system. We argue that:

- We need to be tough on some crimes but also need to be smart about how we manage criminal offenders.
- The criminal justice system should prioritize public safety by focusing on individuals who represent a serious threat to society.
- The criminal justice system not only punishes offenders, it saves lives. It saves lives of potential victims but it also saves the lives of offenders, drug addicts, and alcoholics. Used appropriately, the criminal justice system is also a source of good.
- Science, tradition, and cultural values should be used to guide criminal justice policy, this includes retribution.
- Criminal justice should remain local and decentralized.
- Federal criminal justice should remain restricted in scope and influence.
- Intervention efforts with families, with drug addicts and alcoholics, and with juveniles should be based in science and should be externally validated.
- Efforts to increase the electronic surveillance of citizens, through data mining, drones, police-controlled cameras, or red light cameras, should be better regulated by the courts.
- Mandatory arrest policies should be overturned.
- Efforts to increase the certainty and immediacy of state intervention should be made. Programs, such as the HOPE program in Hawaii, should be implemented more broadly.
- Redemption, once achieved, should be recognized by the criminal justice system.

Despite much criticism, the criminal justice system largely works as advertised. Decisions made by criminal justice professionals are usually, but not always, predictable and justifiable. That said, thousands and thousands of laws and ordinances govern our behavior and give police more cause to investigate our lives. Advances in technology are now promising increased public safety but also threatening our privacy. The new surveillance state includes satellites, drones, massive databases, social networking sites, license plate readers, smart phones, and red-light cameras that now document in intimate detail our lives, our beliefs, and our behaviors. The threats to liberty, it appears, have simply changed form. We believe the ability of the state to utilize these sources of information must be better regulated and controlled and that, in some instances, their use should be prohibited. That said, the widespread use of surveillance provides evidence to counter anecdotal, and at times patently false, claims that criminal justice practitioners abuse the rights of citizens and suspects. Already, dashboard cameras record police interaction with traffic suspects, and in most jurisdictions, police interrogations and booking procedures are videotaped. These data could be utilized to demonstrate the professionalism of the criminal justice system.

Conservatives are strong supporters of law and order. Unfortunately, support for law and order has sometimes resulted in support for practices and procedures that are neither smart nor effective. Recognizing the need to balance public safety, public freedom, and a responsibility to taxpayers, some states, such as Texas, have recently "reinvented" their criminal justice systems. Backed by conservative action groups such as the Texas Public Policy Foundation's "Right on Crime," conservative legislators are using science and conservative values to address overcriminalization, juvenile justice, substance abuse, probation and parole, law enforcement and prisons, and victims (www.rightoncrime.com). Conservatives are now advocating for the use of drug courts, the abolition of mandatory minimums, and evidence-based programs that have been shown to reduce recidivism. Punishment philosophies are not a zero-sum game, and most conservatives understand a balanced need for rehabilitation, deterrence, incapacitation, and retribution.

We also note that conservatives are now questioning a range of criminal justice policies—especially those policies that are costly to taxpayers and do not produce results. The use of prison, for example, is incredibly expensive and its effectiveness is dependent on the type of person incarcerated. Incarcerate a high-rate offender and we reduce crime. Incarcerate a low-level offender and we do not. What Texas taught us, and a range of studies have found, is that some offenders must be locked up for long periods of time but that others can be kept in the community with little risk. Many offenders can be placed on probation with little to no oversight, while others may be best handled with a simple fine. In this sense, we should be smart about who we send to prison and why we send people to prison. Yet we should also be smart about how we punish people who violate one of the thousands of laws and ordinances we have on the books. Conservatives would be entirely happy to make better use of fines, mediation, and reparative efforts in many cases, while in other cases the severity of the crime or the length of the offender's prior record may dictate prolonged periods of confinement.

Less often considered, however, are the multitudes of interventions offered to criminal offenders by the state and by local social welfare groups. Unfortunately, many of the interventions used by the state or offered by social welfare groups do not work. Some have even been shown to increase reoffending. A large body of research now details the conditions that must be met for interventions to work. They must focus on high-risk offenders, they must address a range of criminogenic needs, and they must deliver the intervention in a way that is meaningful and deliberate. Programs that do not work, or that make offenders worse, should be abandoned in favor of programs that have proven effective.

From a conservative point of view, the criminal justice system should be about public safety but it should also be about reformation and redemption. Support for rehabilitative efforts aimed at families and juveniles are widely supported by conservatives, as are some programs aimed at bringing reformed offenders back into society. Remember, conservatives donate more of their time and money to charity efforts than do liberals—efforts that include helping those in the criminal justice system and those in prison (Brooks, 2006). Implicit in this discussion is the notion that the offender actually has an interest or ability to desist from crime. The criminal justice system needs to stop pretending that all offenders are worthy of redemption and lawfully punish those who are not. The use of capital punishment should also be expanded according to already specified procedural guidelines and stop kowtowing to patently specious claims that attempt to undermine the death penalty. By embracing our instinctual capacity for retribution, the criminal justice system can condemn offenders whose crimes are monstrous and pathological.

This set of principles deals squarely with the law and with law-making. We argue that:

- The size and scope of criminal law, especially federal criminal law, should be reduced.
- A moratorium on law-making should be introduced in all states until old, useless, non-enforced laws and laws that unfairly restrict liberty are eliminated.
- Mandatory and structured sentencing schemes should be abolished. These schemes promised that similar offenders would be treated similarly but they have failed to effectively deal with individual circumstances. Reducing or eliminating these schemes will give some discretion back to judges and take some away from prosecutors.
- "Hate crimes" and various other criminal enhancements should be abolished.
- Family courts should be restructured to prioritize mediation and studies of their operation should be immediately undertaken.
- Child protection should take a greater priority. Child protection efforts should be better funded, child protection workers should be better paid, and children from seriously abusive homes should be removed.
- Efforts to use the law to restrict freedom of speech should be eliminated—especially on college campuses.
- Sentences of death should be swiftly and righteously imposed, without fear of this important sanction.

Law is the cornerstone of the criminal justice system. The size and scope of the law dictate the size of the potential criminal population. Each year states pass hundreds to thousands of new criminal laws—laws that always have attached to them a range of criminal sanctions. These laws, moreover, accumulate in number each year thus bringing more and more relatively non-serious and even non-criminal individuals into the criminal justice system. We argue for a legal moratorium until states and the federal government comb through their legal codes and do away with outdated and ridiculous laws.

Efforts to consolidate laws, to make them easier to understand, and to better align the penalties should be a matter of serious concern for legislators. Unfortunately, the monotonous work lacks allure and receives little public or media attention. In contrast, the surge of laws that are passed after a particularly notorious crime occurs almost always receives widespread media attention. For example, after the horrific shooting in New Town, Connecticut, many states rushed—with little deliberation or scrutiny—to implement laws that restricted the rights of citizens to own weapons. New York, Colorado, Connecticut, and other states "toughened" their gun laws without respect for the rights of citizens or costs to the criminal justice system. They simply capitalized on the deaths of children to pass laws they desired. To a conservative, this form of law-making should be unconscionable.

We also note that there are areas in the law that simply need to be overhauled. Two areas come immediately to mind: child protection laws and the family court (sometimes one and the same). Child protective services are often underfunded and the case managers frequently have more cases than they can reasonably handle. That said, the working ideology of "family unification"—where the primary goal is to keep they family intact—is often complicit in the continued physical, emotional, and sexual victimization of children. Unfortunately, laws that guide social services often make it extremely difficult if not impossible to protect children from the people that hurt them. While conservatives support the rights of parents and support efforts to help struggling families, they also have little tolerance for those who harm children.

A recent advancement in criminal law is the idea of "hate crimes" and other types of crime that punish offenders more harshly because of the nature of their victims or because of their intent. If, for example, a white offender beats a black victim because the two got into a bar fight, the white offender will be charged, convicted, and punished for an assault. However, if the same white offender utters a racial epithet during the crime, his sentence can be increased. These types of "enhancements" are now very popular with liberals who see them as a way to address crimes motivated by bias against their favorite groups. From a conservative viewpoint, however, the crime is the assault and the utterance of a word—no matter how ugly—is largely irrelevant. Moreover, carving out criminal enhancements for certain groups or based on certain motivations, such as bias or racism or sexism, plays political favorites with some victims and not others.

In closing, we hope that we have provided the reader with some insight into the academy, into the biases the academy holds against anything thought to be "conservative," and into the sometimes insidious ways that these biases operate to portray conservatism as something it is not. But more importantly, we hope we have given the reader a better understanding of the complexity of conservative political thought. As we said earlier, conservatism is not dogma but rather a dynamic way of seeing the proper role of government in the lives of individuals—especially those individuals who violate our laws or create tremendous harm. Properly understood, conservatism has much to offer to the ongoing conversation about how best to use the criminal justice system to save families and kids, save communities from the ravages of crime, save the lives of offenders and addicts, and save others from the pains of victimization. While there has never been a conservative criminology, and there probably never will be, we encourage academics, especially criminologists, to recognize not only the legitimate role conservative thought has played to keep society stable, predictable, and safe but also the invaluable contributions that conservatives have made to the creation of law, to the criminal justice system, and to society.

We hope that our book helps scholars cast aside their false platitudes about who criminal offenders are, why they commit crime, and what the criminal justice system does to them in response. We also hope our book plays some small role in exposing the bias and liberal dogma that oozes through the academy and distorts research and teaching. When ideology is truly working, it is invisible. In this vein, our book shines a light on that ideology so that others can see.

References

Brooks, A. (2006) *Who really cares: The surprising truth about compassionate conservatism.* New York: Basic Books.

Kempner, J. (2008) The chilling effect: How do researchers react to controversy? *PLoS Medicine,* 5(11), e222.

Twale, D., & DeLuca, B. (2008) *Faculty incivility: The rise of the academic bully culture and what to do about it.* San Francisco, CA: Jossey-Bass Publishers.

INDEX

Page numbers in *italic* refer to tables

Made in United States
Troutdale, OR
08/11/2023

11968674R00084